SAGE was founded in 1965 by Sara Miller McCune to support the dissemination of usable knowledge by publishing innovative and high-quality research and teaching content. Today, we publish over 900 journals, including those of more than 400 learned societies, more than 800 new books per year, and a growing range of library products including archives, data, case studies, reports, and video. SAGE remains majority-owned by our founder, and after Sara's lifetime will become owned by a charitable trust that secures our continued independence.

Los Angeles | London | New Delhi | Singapore | Washington DC | Melbourne

THE INDIA-PAKISTAN SUB-CONVENTIONAL WAR

THE INDIA-PAKISTAN SUB-CONVENTIONAL WAR

Democracy and Peace
in South Asia

SANJEEV KUMAR H.M.

Los Angeles | London | New Delhi
Singapore | Washington DC | Melbourne

First published in 2022 by

SAGE Publications India Pvt Ltd
B1/I-1 Mohan Cooperative Industrial Area
Mathura Road, New Delhi 110 044, India
www.sagepub.in

SAGE Publications Inc
2455 Teller Road
Thousand Oaks, California 91320, USA

SAGE Publications Ltd
1 Oliver's Yard, 55 City Road
London EC1Y 1SP, United Kingdom

SAGE Publications Asia-Pacific Pte Ltd
18 Cross Street #10-10/11/12
China Square Central
Singapore 048423

Published by Vivek Mehra for SAGE Publications India Pvt Ltd. Typeset in 10.5/13 pt Berkeley by Zaza Eunice, Hosur, Tamil Nadu, India.

Library of Congress Cataloging-in-Publication Data

Names: H. M., Sanjeev Kumar, author.
Title: The India-Pakistan sub-conventional war: Democracy and peace in
  South Asia/Sanjeev Kumar H.M.
Other titles: Democracy and peace in South Asia
Description: Los Angeles: SAGE, [2022] | Includes index.
Identifiers: LCCN 2022011854 | ISBN 9789354794209 (hardback) | ISBN
  9789354794216 (epub) | ISBN 9789354794223 (ebook)
Subjects: LCSH: Pakistan—Foreign relations—India. | India--Foreign
  relations—Pakistan. | Pakistan--Politics and government—1988- | Jammu
  and Kashmir (India)—Politics and government—21st century. | National
  security—South Asia.
Classification: LCC DS388 .H57 2022 | DDC
  355.02/17095491—dc23/eng/20220316
LC record available at https://lccn.loc.gov/2022011854

ISBN: 978-93-5479-420-9 (HB)

SAGE Team: Amrita Dutta, Shipra Pant and Rajinder Kaur

To 'Amma',
Late Smt. Renuka Devi,
the eternal source of my inspiration.

Thank you for choosing a SAGE product!
If you have any comment, observation or feedback,
I would like to personally hear from you.

Please write to me at **contactceo@sagepub.in**

Vivek Mehra, Managing Director and CEO, SAGE India.

Bulk Sales

SAGE India offers special discounts
for purchase of books in bulk.
We also make available special imprints
and excerpts from our books on demand.

For orders and enquiries, write to us at

Marketing Department
SAGE Publications India Pvt Ltd
B1/I-1, Mohan Cooperative Industrial Area
Mathura Road, Post Bag 7
New Delhi 110044, India

E-mail us at **marketing@sagepub.in**

Subscribe to our mailing list

Write to **marketing@sagepub.in**

This book is also available as an e-book.

CONTENTS

ACKNOWLEDGEMENTS

This book has been the result of a long journey of academic pursuit, spanning nearly one and a half decades. During this lengthy peregrination, my research initiatives smoothly treaded their course, only because of the help, encouragement and constant support of friends, colleagues and well-wishers, without which my book would not have reached its ultimate destination. Hence, it is my bounden duty to extend heartfelt gratitude to all of them, who have been with me in this academic journey.

First, I would like to thank Ms Amrita Dutta, Associate Commissioning Editor for Academic Books at SAGE India, who has been like my mentor throughout the course of accomplishing this project. Without her constant support and encouragement, this book would not have seen the light of the day. While working with Ms Dutta, I learnt a lot, as she extended her guidance to me with a lot of affection like a loving and caring teacher. Similarly, I would have never succeeded in my academic pursuits, had it not been for the training and mentorship of my teacher, Professor Rajen Harshe. Very tough as a teacher but softest and gentlest as a human being, Professor Harshe's personality has always been a role model which I always aspired to emulate. By monitoring the minutest aspect of my writing, Professor Harshe trained me in the art of doing research in the field of international relations and trained in what he calls the 'method of essay'. I would also like to thank the anonymous reviewer, whose critical comments and suggestions greatly helped me in improving the arguments in the book.

The research for this book was greatly benefited by the generous funding that I received from the Institution of Eminence, University of Delhi, which was granted to me under its scheme of 'faculty research programme'. I would like to thank the institution for the financial support which was extended to me for this project. Further, I will be failing in my duty if I don't thank the team of my dedicated and hardworking students, without whose help this book would not have reached its current form. They not only helped me to collect relevant sources for my research, discussed the project with me and extended their valuable comments, but also rendered great help in the course of the making of the manuscript by copyediting and preparing the document. They have been with me in my tough times and never made me feel alone. Hence, all that is good about this book is because of their efforts and any shortcomings in the book are mine. In this line, my deep sense of gratitude is due to Mr Anubhav Roy, Mr Jatin Kumar, Ms Swathi T., Ms Aakriti Vinayak, Ms Neha Mishra, Ms N. Eshika, Ms Ekta and Dr Vaishali Raghuvanshi.

This project was conceived during June 2009, when I visited the Indian Institute of Advanced Study at Shimla as a UGC IUC Associate. I thank the institute and its then director, Professor Peter Ronald deSouza, for inviting me and granting me a wonderful academic environment. The initial research for the book was carried out in the library of the institute during my three visits in June 2009, June 2010 and June 2013, and I thank the warmth and affection extended to me by the admin and library staff of the institute. Especially, the constant support of the assistant librarian Ms Pushpa during all my three visits was a great source of encouragement. In the institute, I got valuable suggestions and comments on the three lectures that I delivered as part of my work in progress on the book by Professor Peter deSouza, Professor Ghanshyam Shah, Professor Subrata K. Mitra, Dr Bhalchandra Nemade, Professor D. N. Dhanagare, Professor Madhavan K. Palat, Professor Rajkumar Hans, Professor Mangesh Kulkarni, Dr Varsha Bhagat-Ganguly, Dr Vasavi and Dr Sangeetha Menon. I was immensely benefitted by the help and support of my friends Professor Balaganapathi Devarakonda, Professor Sivadasan P. Mankada and Professor Siddharth Singh, during my stay at the Indian

Institute of Advanced Study. I extend my sincere gratefulness to all of them. Further, I thank my friend and colleague at the University of Allahabad, Mr Sandeep Kumar Pankaj, who constantly supported me in all my research activities for this book. Similarly, I also thank my friend and colleague at the South Asian University, Dr Dhananjay Tripathi, for the support that I received from him during the course of writing this book. At the University of Delhi where I am teaching presently, I received valuable suggestions and comments for the book from my colleagues Professor Navnita Chadha Behera and late Professor Veena Kukreja. My colleague Professor Ujjwal Kumar Singh constantly took out time to call me or personally visit my office to ask about the progress of my work. I thank him for all his support and encouragement.

Finally, I thank my wife, Preeti, who has always been my in-house critic.

INTRODUCTION

Postcolonial predicament[1] pertains to the intricate problems which have bedevilled the processes of State-making that the newly decolonized societies of South Asia have been confronted with. These problems have engendered a psyche in the region which has been designated by Akhil Gupta as the postcolonial condition.[2] As regards postcoloniality itself, it is the condition or state of being postcolonial. However, for the decolonized regions like South Asia, there is nothing 'post' about colonialism and the problems and complexities that they have inherited from their colonial histories still persist

[1] The term 'postcolonial predicament' indicates a situation that emerges from an increasing realization among the students regarding the role of their academic disciplines in the reproduction of the forms of domination. As these students think about the erstwhile colonial world, such a realization seems to be strongest when applied to colonial scholarship. On this count, the postcolonial predicament tends to unfold into two dimensions. First, colonial period has handed down to us both the theories and evidence that select and conjoin them. Second, decolonization does not mean that we gain an immediate escape from the chains of colonial discourse. Hence, although there has been a widespread discussion on the agency of the voices from the Global South, this predicament still has the power to define both the ex-colonizer and the ex-colonized. In this sense, postcolonial predicament itself implies that we cannot escape history (Breckenridge & van der Veer, 1993, pp. 1–2).

[2] For Akhil Gupta, 'postcolonial condition' implies towards a sociocultural circumstance, wherein an imaginary of homogeneous identity tends to get nurtured largely among the common people of postcolonial societies. Such a kind of common identity emanates out of the feeling of being part of the structural contours of underdevelopment which largely frames the people's sense of self. This kind of a complex articulation of identity that is framed in the vocabulary of backwardness makes them think as to who they are, why they reached such a situation and as to what the modes to get liberation from the shackles of such a condition are (Gupta, 1998, p. IX).

(Sethi, 2011, pp. 8 & 59). Owing to such a postcolonial predicament, the establishment of lasting peace, a conducive security environment and imparting of permanence to political stability in a democratizing South Asia have been serious challenges. This has been impelled by the fact that the postcolonial history of the region has been heavily loaded with an immensely combustive scenario of violent conflicts. Thus, in this regard, Willem van Schendel raises a pertinent question: 'Is there a special relationship between violence and State in South Asia' (Van Schendel, 2007, p. 36)? Answering this, Van Schendel argues that there exists an idiosyncratic connection between State and violence which has been the product of a specifically regional model of the process of State-making in South Asia. Such an idiosyncrasy seems to have no parallels in the world. The genealogy of such an idiosyncrasy for Van Schendel has been the disintegration of the colonial State of British India and the subsequent creation from its ashes, several new States. It is this very genealogy and the archaeology of the history of State-making which has emerged as a unique phenomenon in the contemporary politics of postcolonial South Asia (Van Schendel, 2007, p. 37). Further for Willem van Schendel, the simultaneous process of the demise of British imperialism in India and State formation in South Asia occurred between 1937 and 1971. In this period, the interplay of these two phenomena witnessed the inception of Burma, Pakistan, India and Bangladesh as liberated postcolonial States. Considering this, 'historians have described the demise of British Empire in India, as an inevitable surgery' which assumed a violent dimension (Van Schendel, 2007, p. 37).

In any case, such a surgery did not prove to be a perfect act which was marked by clinical precision. This is because it did not produce four well-defined national bodies. Rather contrarily, these postcolonial States found that their physical separation which was done through the application of the principle of cartographic fundamentalism emerged to be an incomplete operation. It was unfinished, as they ended up receiving ill-defined nations and fractured formations of the fixity of political territoriality. Owing to this, the notions of sovereignty, fixity of political territoriality and violence tend to get locked up in a kind of negative relationship in South Asia (Van Schendel, 2007, p. 37).

To make sense of such a negative interconnection, this book attempts to understand how the crises associated with the processes of democratization which are rooted in the history of colonialism have largely contributed towards the failure of the liberal model of peace in South Asia. This book attempts at examining the modes by which the crises-prone processes of democratization in South Asia have contested the central thesis of the liberal theory of international relations pertaining to the links between democracy and war. The liberal peace paradigm has hypothesized that 'no two democracies will go to war with each other'. However, the conflict-ridden history of South Asia which manifests in both overt wars and the protracted trail of asymmetric warfare[3] completely negates the democratic peace thesis of the liberal theory of international relations. Hence, the South Asian experience with the relationship between democracy and war becomes a significant empirical case scenario to map heuristic value of the democratic peace thesis.

Taking note of this, *The India–Pakistan Sub-conventional War* aims to understand how the trajectory of the linked histories of South Asia which is suspended between its colonial and postcolonial epochs factors deeply in the moulding of the nature of conflict in the region. Such an endeavour has been undertaken here by mapping the ways in which postcolonial processes of democratization in the region tend to mirror such a kind of linked history. At the bottom of this kind of a trajectory of democratization lie the dilemmas of development that the postcolonial polities have confronted. Sankaran Krishna has designated such dilemmas as 'the cartographic anxiety'.[4] Owing to this,

---

[3] In an asymmetric conflict, the weaker State having revisionist intensions owing to irredentism tries to exploit a particular crisis situation by initiating war (Paul, 1994, p. 19). Owing to this, the status quoist States that are involved in protracted conflicts are more likely to confront crises because of mistrust, anticipation of violence and the resulting perceived value threat (Brecher, 1993, p. 44).

[4] The term 'cartographic anxiety' denotes the acuteness of the anxieties that surround the questions of national identities and survival in postcolonial societies. Such anxieties are part of a larger postcolonial anxiety that is engendered by a country's predicament of being suspended forever in a space between the former colony and not yet nation (Krishna, 1994, p. 508).

the polities of South Asia largely tend to fail in reaching the stage of democratic consolidation.[5] Due to such a lacuna, the countries even though transform into democracies, but they fall short of achieving the fullest realization of the fundamental norms of democratic deepening.

Thus, such a shallow and illiberal nature of democracies turns out to be an affront to the deontological exemplar which has been proposed by the liberal theory of international relations in the form of the democratic peace thesis. Since in such democracies, the civilian control over policy formulation is constantly contested by centralizing autocratic force inbuilt in the architecture of their armies and bureaucracies, democratically elected governments seldom have a say in the process of decision-making on sensitive issues such as war. In South Asia, Pakistan manifests as a classic case to represent this argument. The processes of democratic decision-making in Pakistan are largely stunted by the intrusive role of the army, especially in the sphere of defence and foreign policy (Fair, 2018, p. 25). Hence, by mapping the role of the army in the political processes of Pakistan, this book endeavours at understanding how a democracy in South Asia exhibits tendencies to make war, completely negating the postulates of the democratic peace thesis.

For this purpose, an attempt has been made here to demonstrate how Pakistan has made war while being ruled by a democratically elected government. The focus of this study is Pakistan's rivalry with India which has drawn the former into a belligerent military equation with the latter. However, while interrogating the working of the democratic peace thesis in South Asia, this book has considered the definition of conflict in terms of its conceptualizations as an 'asymmetric warfare or a sub-conventional conflict'. Pakistan was not under a democratic government during its first three wars with India; however, when the fourth war was fought at Kargil which treaded the midline between conventional and sub-conventional warfares, Pakistan had a democratically elected government. In any case, the emphasis of this study is Pakistan's asymmetric warfare which was initiated around 1989 when the insurgency in Kashmir intensified.

---

[5] For a theoretical treatment of the concept of 'democratic consolidation', see Huntington (1992, p. 263).

To do this, we seek to critique the democratic peace thesis for largely considering only the conventional definition of militarized conflict as part of its epistemology. It has been argued here that since the asymmetric conflict which is launched by Pakistan through its militant proxies is an institutionalized strategy directly involving the State machinery (Kapur, 2017, p. 2; Swami, 2007, pp. 3–4), any treatment of the democratic peace thesis must go beyond the mere conventional definition of warfare and consider the sub-conventional forms of conflict as empirical case scenarios. Further, the examination of the democratic peace thesis in South Asia cannot be done without considering the fact that the region is undergoing an unremitting spate of asymmetric conflicts because of the failure of nuclear deterrence. The overt acquisition of nuclear weapons by India and Pakistan has led to the intensification of the gravity of sub-conventional warfare. This has happened as Pakistan has gained the benefit of the stability/instability paradox.[6] Further, the acquisition of tactical nuclear weapons by the weaker power, that is, Pakistan, has magnified the complexities of dealing with the sub-conventional war for India, which is the stronger power. Considering this, it has been argued here that a study of India–Pakistan relations reveals that the notion of the interface between democracy and war tends to assume a positive relationship in the context of South Asia. The connection between democracy and war itself has been framed in an inverse negative relationship by the defenders of the democratic peace hypothesis. It is embedded in the neo-Kantian romance of liberal cosmopolitan idealism and has been enunciated in the epistemological context of the spatio-temporality of Cold War bipolarity. Michael Doyle, who is one of its proponents, invoked the Kantian philosophical abstraction of 'the perpetual peace', for providing an intellectual defence and moral high ground for the values of the liberal capitalist world (Doyle, 1986, pp. 1151–1161). In the post-Cold War setting, Francis Fukuyama recast the hypothesis and visualized the emerging international orders as the triumph of

---

[6] The phrase 'stability/instability paradox' was developed by Glenn Snyder. For Snyder, while the fear of nuclear conflict tends to bring in a kind of stability to the relations of adversaries that possess nuclear weapons, it also creates a kind of instability as nuclear weapons also create incentives for engaging in a low-intensity conflict (Snyder, 1965).

liberal international relations and designated the same as 'the end of history'. Through this, he attempted to reframe the democratic peace thesis not only to celebrate liberal values as the normative exemplar for ordering a post-Cold War international system but also to provide an intellectual defence for the newly emerging space for American leadership in a post-hegemonic international system (Fukuyama, 1992). Such an intellectual defence and hypostatizing of the ethical supremacy of liberal idealism in a world which was shaped by the leadership of the United States was also entrenched in the epistemological imperialism of the West and an exclusionary meta-history of the post-Westphalian international order (Kumar, 2020, pp. 344–345). However, the democratic peace thesis proposed by the liberal theory of international relations tends to imagine the functioning of international relations itself in terms of a hermetically sealed notion of spatial topography and temporal trajectory which is largely Euro-American in character. Such an ontic and epistemic vantage point of the West implies that South Asia does not emerge as an apt spatial-case scenario to prove the democratic peace thesis (Kumar, 2020, pp. 344–345). Locating ourselves on the foundations of this argument, an attempt has been made in this book to interrogate this phenomenon by examining the subcontinental security predicament involving the two nuclear-powered adversaries, India and Pakistan. This would be done through an idiographic deconstruction of the example of the crisis-prone equation that exists between India and Pakistan, by placing the same in the epistemological framework of the historical turn in international relations. The aim is to critique the epistemic foundations of the democratic peace hypothesis, by deconstructing its arguments in the geostrategic context of the South Asian regional security architecture. For achieving this task, we need to map the chequered history of relationship between India and Pakistan.

THE GENEALOGIES OF INDO-PAKISTAN ANTAGONISM

The choice of carrying out an interrogation into the dynamics of South Asian security in the context of India and Pakistan has been made after considering the fact that the relationship between the two countries has disconcertingly assumed a large space in the context of the study of the history and international relations of South Asia. If Pakistan's defence and foreign policies are largely shaped by perceptions regarding the security threats from India (Amin, 2010; Rizvi, 2004; Sattar, 2007), India accords primacy to Pakistan in moulding its security and foreign policy (Budania, 2001). Hence, as both India and Pakistan accord primacy to the equations between each other in their security and foreign policies and their relations form a key component of their respective domestic public opinion, India–Pakistan relations have drawn wider academic, strategic and policy interest both regionally and globally (Kumar, 2011, pp. 63–64). The onset of the nuclear dimension in the subcontinental strategic context has brought in an added urgency to the epistemic interest in the South Asian security architecture. The bilateral equations between the two countries have tended to magnify the security predicament to a considerable extent. Owing to this, the subregion of the Indian subcontinent becomes a significant spatial topos for understanding how the modes by which the trajectories of security, strategy and the contours of international relations in South Asia have tended to gain material embodiment (Kumar, 2010, pp. 35–36). In this sense, the Indian subcontinent becomes a kind of theatre, wherein the enactment of the everyday scenario of security predicament and the turbulent trajectory of international relations with regard to South Asia happen to be constantly rehearsed and staged (Kumar, 2014).

The troubled India–Pakistan relation has been considered here as a suitable template to determine the nature of conflict in South Asia because this intractable impasse does not merely represent a geopolitical dispute over cartographic claims. Rather, it exists as a manifestation of the multifaceted nature of conflict, representing a substratum of the ontology of divided geographies and the politics of imaging diachronic relationships of history in the synchronic connections of cultural assertions. Besides exhibiting an exegesis of the schizophrenic impact of the legacy of colonialism, India–Pakistan relations are deeply rooted in the psyche of fractured identities, perforated cultures, a strong sense of irredentism and a tinge of megalomaniacal sense of nationalism. Apart from this, the crises and dilemmas involved in the processes of State-making, nation formation and the deep-felt apprehensions regarding the construction of a regional identity have largely contributed in conditioning the ecology of their animosity. Viewed from this perspective, the ontic conditionalities that determine the nature of conflict between the two countries fall into the following broad rubrics. First is the geopolitical factor: primarily emanating out of the contest between the Westphalian and the primordialist conceptions of the State. This contest has locked the two neighbours in a state of unremitting hostilities regarding their claims over the territory of Jammu and Kashmir which has been one of the most protracted separatist movements of contemporary history (Osuri, 2017, pp. 2428–2429).

In this sense, the perceptions of both spill into divergent streams. For India, the idea of conceding any territory like that of Jammu and Kashmir to Pakistan amounted to the engendering of the fear of State disintegration. Pakistan, on its part, considered the accession of the disputed territory as an imperative to complete the process of the geopolitical construction of the nation state on the lines of the two-nation theory which clearly explains the reasons for its irredentist policy in this regard.[7]

In this context, status inconsistency in international relations also plays a vital role in inter-State conflicts (Midlarsky, 1975). This has factored deeply in determining the conflictual nature of India–Pakistan relations. Their perception and self-images of their power status vis-à-vis each other in regional as well as global context have been mutually so incompatible that their drive towards achieving these self-perceived status and positions brought them into armed conflict with each other (Muni, 1983, p. 49). To put this in terms of the argument of Buzan and Waever (2003, p. 71), it can be stated that the territorial conflicts between India and Pakistan cannot be visualized as a mere geographic dispute. Rather, it manifests as political tensions largely derived out of the complex history of colonialism in South Asia.

---

[7] According to Michael Hechter, 'irredentism involves the subtracting of a territory from one State and adding it into another. Irredentist movements are mostly initiated by States that are interested in annexing territories that they claim to be having large proportions of their co-nationals' (Hechter, 2000, p. 84).

Second, there existed ideological undertones to this political conflict. It manifested in the divergent affirmations of secularism and Islamic nationhood in the context of Jammu and Kashmir by India and Pakistan, respectively. For India, the existence of this Muslim-majority territory in the union was essential for providing credence to its nationalist ideology which contended that all minorities could live safely and progress under a secular pluralist State. The Pakistani ideology, on the other hand, which was largely predicated upon the conception of Islamic nationhood and the idea of Pakistan which was conceived as the homeland for the Muslims of South Asia, could not imagine the completeness of the process of State construction until the Muslim-majority Jammu and Kashmir formed part of its political territoriality. In this sense, both India and Pakistan pose systemic threats to each other. India's secular claim over Kashmir within the spirit of a secular federal multicultural polity challenges the two-nation theory, and due to this, Pakistan is threatened with dismemberment. On the other hand, Pakistan's subcontinental Muslim nationalism based upon the ideology of pan-Islamism and the two-nation theory is a peril for India's federal structure, geopolitical security of Jammu and Kashmir and its multicultural edifice. In this manner, the politico-strategic frictions between the two rivals over the status of Jammu and Kashmir which has been underpinned by a justification of their respective spheres of sovereign legitimacy facilitated the decision-makers on both sides of the subcontinental divide to manufacture fierce antithetical ideologies (McLeod, 2008, p. 65). Owing to this, the territory of Jammu and Kashmir has manifested as a semantic and semiotic materialization of the very essence of the conflict between India and Pakistan. Such an impasse between the two has largely been the product of intense jealousies and animosity which shaped the political processes in late colonial India (Gupta, 1967, p. 1).

The overt acquisition of nuclear weapons by both these subcontinental adversaries must also be visualized within the framework of such a contested terrain of power politics. On this count, it has been argued that the nuclear dimension in Indo-Pak bilateral dynamics tends to defy the conventional Cold War-centric explanation of the

State's desirability for weaponized nuclear power.[8] Rather, the entry of India and Pakistan into the group of countries possessing nuclear weapons capacity after the end of Cold War adverts our attention towards dealing with the issue from the perspective of a more non-traditionalist approach (Abraham, 2006, pp. 49–65). The necessity of such an epistemic departure becomes imperative as the conventional approaches seem to remain entrapped between constraints of structural realism and the advocacy of the non-proliferation policy (Walker, 1993).

Thus, to make sense of the semantic and semiotic significations of the quest for nuclear power by India and Pakistan, we need to transcend the conventional abstract models of non-proliferation, security studies and deterrence (Abraham, 2009, p. 3). Here, it has been stated that what actually binds both India and Pakistan together in their nuclear quest has been the linkage that exists between notions of nuclear power, national security and the legitimacy of the State. It is precisely this linkage that isolates the subcontinental experience with nuclear power, as compared to that of the other States.

THE NATURE OF CONFLICT IN SOUTH ASIA

The nature of conflict in South Asia has been examined from the perspective of its regional security substructure which is the Indian subcontinent. In this context, the colonially crafted redefinition of the cartographic idea of South Asia emerges as the epistemological starting point. This redefinition, we seek to argue here, has not only resulted in a horrendous cleft of organically integrated people but also led to an enduring conflict between two States, wherein the very idea of nation and nationalism became the source of conflict. The metastatic impact of this, as we maintain here, has been the nuclearization of conflicts in

---

[8] The institutionalized terror engendered by the great power rivalry between the United States and the Soviet Union has been considered by the traditional explanation as the immediate cause of States' urge to acquire nuclear weapons (Sagan, 1996, pp. 54–86).

South Asia. We attempt to dwell upon this phenomenon by situating India–Pakistan rivalry in this context.

As regards the nature of conflict in South Asia, it appears to be a psycho-pathological phenomenon because the image of the other is based on a distorted perception of reality, coupled with fear and suspicion. The unending conflict between the two subcontinental adversaries, India and Pakistan, which is located in deep-felt mutual threat perception, seems to be representing this aspect of conflict in the region. At the bottom of this lies the superimposed artificial character of the project of nation states, the imported values and institutional structures of governance and the divided geographies, all emanating out of the complex trajectory of South Asia's colonial past. In this sense, the pattern of conflict in South Asia thus has been shaped by the colonially crafted nation-building processes, the structures of governance built by the British empire and the trauma of partition. Although external forces have exercised considerable influence upon the regional affairs, however, the security dynamics of South Asia have been largely intra-regional in character (Hettne, 2007, pp. 47 & 53).

Such introverted regional security dynamics has been part of the imperial cartography and political history, a legacy carried forward by the succeeding native ruling classes (Hettne, 2007, pp. 47 & 53). Now, the trajectories adopted for achieving the goals of State formation, State construction and nation-building immediately after decolonization seem to have reached the point of exhaustion. If this situation is not addressed, the crisis may lead to perilous consequences (Neelsen & Malik, 2007, pp. 12–13). Situating ourselves in the context of such a predicament of the project of nation state formation, South Asia must be seen as a postcolonial territorial formation which has been plagued by internal conflicts which have got sustained due to the existence of inexorable socio-economic inequities. Due to its circuitous heterogeneity, the nature of conflict in the region has been marked by deeply embedded complexities.

Several cross-country connections and the trend towards regionalization of conflict advert a strong need for according a regional approach to understanding the patterns of conflicts in South Asia

(Hettne, 2007, p. 47). The lack of mutually acceptable frontiers among the States, the issue of river water sharing, the alarming growth of transborder migration and cross-border terrorism, and the unresolved status of diverse ethnic nationalities have cumulatively contributed to transform South Asia into a theatre of conflict.

Such a precarious situation marked by a turbulent chronology of violence has placed the processes of governance in the polities of South Asia at crossroads. This kind of governance dilemma tends to make the process of State formation, and State construction appears as though it is still in an embryonic stage (Jamil et al., 2013, p. 1). The exigency of the situation is so deep that countries like Pakistan have been often dismissed as a failed State (Islam, 2001, p. 1336). All this renders the notion of South Asian development and governance mechanism to appear as a puzzle, mainly because despite rampant corruption and extreme poverty, the region also tends to record high economic growth (Jamil et al., 2013, p. 2).

The nature of conflicts in the region may be categorized into two different variants. First, the intra-State conflicts stem from the lack of social cohesion among different groups of communities which inhabit a given territorial State. Second, there are the inter-State conflicts which have mainly been engendered by border disputes (Harshe, 2001, p. 19). Considering all this, it may be stated that the current politico-strategic pandemonium and the conflict-prone history of South Asia thus makes a strong case in favour of speedy exploration of amicable means to untangle the region's intricate problems. This is primarily because the two nuclear-powered adversaries, India and Pakistan, are still grappling to find amicable solutions to their long-standing disputes. With an ever-increasing intensity of cross-border terrorism and the continuing inability on the part of both sides to sustain the peace process, the South Asian security architecture appears very fragile. In a nutshell, South Asia has emerged as a tinder box, and the moderation of the highly charged-up atmosphere of the region has now become an exigency. Hence, adroit conflict management, speedy reduction of tension and rapid socio-economic progress, all acquire paramountcy when we visualize the current situation of the region.

The seriousness of the problem basically lies in the fact that not only authoritarian regimes but even those regimes which have been engaged in a constant but dilettantish experimenting in democratic governance have indulged in such activities which have had a blackball effect in accentuating the process of decadence which has pestered South Asia ever since the region got liberated from colonial fetters. In addition to this, the pressures of local geographical proximity adjacency are also potent for security (Buzan & Waever, 2003, p. 45). Besides, the international system for regions like South Asia situated in the Third World, unlike that of the West, is characterized by hierarchy rather than anarchy, and their domestic space is characterized by anarchy rather than well-defined hierarchy (Ayoob, 1995, pp. 1–20). On the other hand, States of South Asia are democratizing, with the process of State construction still in the nascence. This inevitably results in violence, as most of them recently emerged out of colonial fetters and are divided on the basis of diverse linguistic, cultural and tribal identities. It has also to be noted here that in the last part of the 20th century and at the dawn of the new millennium, there has been the globalization of South Asian security dynamics. This has been epitomized by the growing interference of outside powers in fashioning the geopolitical template of the region.

Signifying this, United States' security presence has been deep and pervasive in Pakistan, Afghanistan and some Central Asian countries, owing to the war on terrorism. Apart from this, the Anglo-American dyad also aided the Governments of Sri Lanka and Nepal in their endeavours at dealing with civil wars in their polities. Besides this, Norway was also actively involved in finding amicable ways to resolve the ethnic impasse in Sri Lanka, and Britain led the international initiatives to deal with the Nepalese quagmire. All this led to the erosion of the strategic autonomy of the countries of the region and made them prey to the global systemic pressures. Thus, South Asian security dynamics has been globalized under the aura of rampant spread of different forms of anti-regime activities which intensified the fear of widespread State failure and put the democratization process into shambles. Above all, the magnifying disquiet over the prospects of nuclear war between the two subcontinental rivals has brought in greater global activism in order to diffuse the tensions between them.

Owing to this, it can be argued here that at the epicentre of South Asia's conflict situation lie the two subcontinental adversaries. No other State of South Asia has been involved in any form of conflict with each other and, hence, we must locate the origin and development of the region's insecurity predicament in the vexed history of animosity between India and Pakistan. In the light of such a scenario, we must consider the chequered mosaic of conflict and the trajectory of disrupted peace which is embedded in South Asian geopolitics. While doing this, we are drawn towards ruminating over some of the dominant themes which tend to capture our attention. They include democratization and modernity, State construction and nation-building, independence and nationalism (a legacy of colonial past), the subtle but intricate linkages between religion and State (accentuated by the de-secularization of the political sphere), the complex linkages between globalization and nuclearization of regional security, and the overdeterminism of the subcontinental dynamics over the entire gamut of South Asian affairs. These themes are imbued deeply, and their pervasive influences considerably affect the politico-strategic dynamics of the region.

REFERENCES

Abraham, I. (2006). The ambivalence of nuclear histories. *Osiris, 21*(1), 49–65.

Abraham I. (Ed.). (2009). Introduction: Nuclear power and atomic publics. In *South Asian culture of the bomb: Atomic publics and the State in India and Pakistan* (pp. 1–19). Indiana University Press.

Amin, S. (2010). *Pakistan's foreign policy: A reappraisal*. Oxford University Press.

Ayoob, M. (1995). *The Third World security predicament*. Lynne Rienner.

Brecher, M. (1993). *Crises in world politics: Crises and reality*. Pergamon Press.

Breckenridge, C., & van der Veer, P. (1993). Orientalism and the postcolonial predicament. In *Orientalism and the postcolonial predicament: Perspectives on South Asia* (pp. 1–22). Pennsylvania University Press.

Budania, R. (2001). *India's national security dilemma: The Pakistan factor and India's policy response*. Indus Publishing Company.

Buzan, B., & Waever, O. (2003). *Regions and powers: The structure of international security*. Cambridge University Press.

Doyle, M. (1986). Liberalism and world politics. *American Political Science Review, 80*(4), 1151–1161.

Fair, C. (2018). *In their own words: Understanding the Lashkar-i-Tayyaba*. Oxford University Press.

Fukuyama, F. (1992). *The end of history and the last man*. Free Press.

Gupta, A. (1998). *Postcolonial developments: Agriculture in the making of modern India*. Duke University Press.

Gupta, S. (1967). *Kashmir: A study in Indo-Pakistan relations*. Asia Publishing House.

Harshe, R. (2001). Understanding conflicts in South Asia. In S. J. George (Ed.), *Inter and intra-state conflict in South Asia* (pp. 19–33). South Asia Publisher.

Hechter, M. (2000). *Containing nationalism*. Oxford University Press.

Hettne, B. (2007). Conflict dynamics and conflict management in South Asia. In J. P. Neelsen & D. Malik (Eds.), *Crisis of state and nation: south asian states between nation-building and fragmentation*. Manohar.

Huntington, S. P. (1992). *The third wave: Democratisation in late 20th century*. Oklahoma University Press.

Islam, N. (2001). Democracy and governance in Pakistan's fragmented society. *International Journal of Public Administration*, 24(12), 1335–1355.

Jamil, I., Askvik, S., & Dhakal T. N. (Eds.). (2013). Introduction. *In search of better governance in South Asia and beyond* (pp. 1–12). Springer.

Kapur, S. P. (2017). *Jihad as grand strategy: Islamist militancy, national security, and the Pakistani state*. Oxford University Press.

Krishna, S. (1994). Cartographic anxiety: Mapping the body politic in India. *Alternatives: Global, Local, Political*, 19(4), 507–521.

Kumar H. M., S. (2010). Internal dynamics of sub-continental security: Indo Pak tensions and the political response. *India Quarterly*, 66(1), 35–50.

Kumar H. M., S. (2011). The Pakistan factor in India's domestic politics. *South Asian Survey*, 18(1), 63–80.

Kumar H. M., S. (2014, 3 March). Reconceptualising deterrence: Nudging toward rationality in Middle Eastern rivalries (Review Article), *E-International Relations*. http://www.eir.info/2014/03/03/review-reconceptualising-deterrence/

Kumar H. M., S. (2020). Traversing the romance of a liberal international order: The democratic peace thesis and the regional security problematique in South Asia. *International Studies*, 57(4), 344–360.

McLeod, D. (2008). *India and Pakistan: Friends, rivals or enemies?* Ashgate Publishing Company.

Midlarsky, M. I. (1975). *On war: Political violence in the international system*. Free Press.

Muni, S. D. (1983). South Asia. In M. Ayoob (Ed.), *Conflict and intervention in the Third World* (pp. 38–72). Vikas Publishing House.

Neelsen, J. P., & Malik. D. (2007). South Asia–social fragmentation and political crisis in the periphery. In *Crisis of state and nation: South Asian states between nation-building and fragmentation*. Manohar.

Osuri, G. (2017). Imperialism, colonialism and sovereignty in the (Post)colony: India and Kashmir. *Third World Quarterly, 38*(8), 2428–2443.

Paul, T. V. (1994). *Asymmetric conflicts: War initiation by weaker powers.* Cambridge University Press.

Rizvi, H. A. (2004). *Pakistan's foreign policy: An overview, 1947–2004.* Pakistan Institute of Legislative Development and Transparency.

Sagan, S. (1996). Why do states build nuclear weapons? Three models in search of a bomb. *International Security, 21*(3), 54–86.

Sattar, A. (2010). *Pakistan's Foreign Policy 1947–2009: A concise history.* Oxford University Press.

Sethi, R. (2011). *The politics of postcolonialism: Empire, nation and resistance.* Pluto Press.

Snyder, G. (1965). The balance of power and the balance of terror. In P. Seabury (Ed.), *The balance of power.* Chandler.

Swami, P. (2007). *India, Pakistan and the secret jihad: The covert war in Kashmir, 1947–2004.* Routledge.

Van Schendel, W. (2007). The Wagah syndrome: Territorial roots of contemporary violence in South Asia. In A. Basu & S. Roy (Eds.), *Violence and democracy in India* (pp. 36–84). Seagull Books.

Walker, R. B. J. (1993). *Inside/outside: International relations as political theory.* Cambridge University Press.

Modernity and the Crisis of Democratization in South Asia

The idea of South Asia has undergone a drastic process of transfiguration as a product of the legacy of colonialism. Such a transfiguration lies at the bottom of what we designate here as the region's postcolonial predicament. It manifests in the dilettantish project of modernity and democratization, carried out by the polities of South Asia through flirtatious employment of received notions of metropolitan governance (Kumar, 2020, p. 276). Such a state of affairs, can be placed in the context of two epistemic trajectories. First is the situation of political development which can be designated in terms of what Samuel Huntington theorizes as political decay. The condition of political decay itself is marked by chaos and disorder engendered by the slower pace of the process of the modernization of political institutions as compared to that of the modernization of the processes of social structuration.[1] This implies that the rapidity of social development tends

---

[1] The term 'structuration' has been borrowed here from the social theory of the creation and reproduction of social systems, known as the theory of structuration. Its principal advocate is Anthony Giddens. For Giddens, structuration meant that social systems get constituted and tend to be constantly reproduced through a dialogue between both the agent and the structure. In this process, neither of the two are in any form of primordial position and, hence, mere application of either the micro or the macro analysis alone would be insufficient to understand the process by which social systems are constituted. Hence, the analysis of such interaction for Giddens must be situated in a post-empiricist framework of the analysis of the abstract forms of social relations. This would allow us to problematize ontology, viewed from the perspective of the human experience of space and time, in order to understand the nature of social relations. History in this sense becomes one of the primary ontological questions for decoding the complex patterns of social relations in distinct spatio-temporal circumstances (Giddens, 1984, pp. 3–11).

to transcend that of political development, consequently leading to a crisis in the functioning of political institutions (Huntington, 1968, pp. 386–430).

In postcolonial societies, this kind of crisis occurs, as the socio-economic forces tend to disrupt the equilibrium of the established political order (Fukuyama, 2011, p. 139). Social modernization, hence, engenders instability in the political order of postcolonial societies as political modernization does not mature in a temporary parallel with that of social modernization. As a consequence of this, the dominant indicators of social modernization such as increased urbanization, growing access to education, industrialization, rise in the per capita income and the gross national product, and the deepening role of the media do not get matched by the maturity and organizational efficiency of political institutions (Huntington, 1968, pp. 35–36).

Such a predicament deepens, as postcolonial States begin to inherit the imported narrative of neoliberal economic reforms. Such importations result in a kind of precariousness which can be designated in the words of Jurgen Habermas as the legitimation crisis. The legitimation crisis occurs, according to Habermas, when people begin to lose confidence in the functional capacity of the political leadership and mechanisms of policy formulation, execution and adjudication. In such a circumstance, the structures of governance are unable to demonstrate that their day-to-day practical functioning fulfils the roles for which they were instituted. This happens even as they continue to possess the legal authority to govern. Owing to all this, these institutions tend to confront a crisis of identity, as the people whom they govern do not seem to show adequate faith in them (Habermas, 1976, pp. 46–48).

At the root of the legitimation crisis for Habermas is the progressive displacement of the traditional moral and cultural values of a society which occurs with the growth of the structures of capitalist development. Such a displacement tends to engender structural problems for the State, insofar as its capacity to manage the social consequences of the rapidly expanding capitalist economy is concerned. It happens as there is a gradual erosion of the innate and established set of normative as well as cultural exemplars which not only can act as a restraint on unbridled consumer demand but also boost the society's work ethics (Plant, 1982, p. 341). Owing to this, the liberal capitalist States are confronted with a deep-seated internal conflict which manifests in the following form. On the one hand, as the priorities set under economic imperatives cannot be subjected to the discursive formation of the popular will, politics itself incarnates into the form of a vocation of the technocrats. On the other hand, it becomes increasingly difficult to exclude the more utilitarian questions by a depoliticized populous owing to the erosion of the traditional moral and cultural values (Habermas, 1974, p. 5). It is this very conflict within liberal capitalist societies for Habermas that leads to a chronic need for legitimation because the State apparatus is not merely concerned towards securing the general conditions of production, but it is also actively engaged in the same (Habermas, 1976, p. 36). Therefore, at the bottom of the legitimation deficit among liberal capitalist societies for Habermas not merely lie the concerns of the economy but they rather consist more of the problems relating to the political or cultural sphere (Plant, 1982, pp. 341–342).

Placing ourselves on the foundations of these two epistemic trajectories, we can attempt at examining the postcolonial project of democratization in South Asia. While doing this, the structuration process that emerges as a kind of triangulation must be decoded. Such a triangulation occurs between three factors. It involves the interactions between the two active agents; colonizing metropolitan elite and colonized native intelligentsia, the intersectionality of two historical epochs; the colonial and postcolonial, and the impact of the two epistemic trajectories; the received notions of metropolitan governance; and the morals of modernity in the form of neoliberal reforms upon the contours of postcolonial governmentality. Such a triangulation seems to have been explained in the theoretical treatment of spatial histories that is rendered by Huntington and Habermas in their concepts of political decay and the legitimation crisis. The process of structuration that is located in the triangulation between the three dialectically interacting phenomena renders the processes of social modernization and neoliberal economic transformation itself to become an exigency. Such an exigency is the product of a kind of structural fiasco, wherein the institutional mechanisms of governance reflect a deep sense of inability to negotiate the challenges imposed by the juggernaut of modernization. This kind of incapacity that manifests in the failure to device appropriate policy responses on the part of the governments becomes even more profound, as traditional moral and cultural values in their societies appear to be rapidly eroding.

DEMOCRATIZATION UNDER THE SHADOW OF POLITICAL DECAY AND LEGITIMATION CRISIS

The impact of the process of democratization on peace does not get limited to internal space of polities; rather, it permeates into the external space, destabilizing the regional security architecture. Thus, democratization involves the complex intercourse between internal peace and external peace in relation to the democratizing polities, with both feeding upon each other in a vicious cycle. In South Asia, the manifestation of this phenomenon is diverse and expressed in the ethno-political conflicts, communal tensions, terrorism, regional and linguistic chauvinism, which persist despite the polities of the region being engaged in processes of modernization and democratization. Situated conceptually, 'One of the main conditions for the emergence of a modern State is the rationalization of power and its accumulation and concentration in a rational fashion in proper institutions' (Hajjariyan, 2007, p. 14). The best way of accomplishing this task is rapid modernization of societies which will reciprocate by facilitating the democratization of political processes. That is, it will lead to a State's successful transition into a thriving liberal democratic polity.

It has been contended here that for the democratization process in South Asia to reach a fruition point, over all modernization of the societies of the region's polities is crucial. It means that the level of modernization will play a decisive role in determining the extent of success of democratic governance in the region. 'Modernisation brings democracy because once set in motion, it tends to penetrate into all aspects of life, bringing occupational specialization, urbanization, rising educational level, rising life expectancy and rapid economic growth' (Inglehart & Welzel, 2009, pp. 35–36). Apart from this, what actually matters is the socio-economic policies and governance strategy of a particular State (Grare, 2011, p. 164).

Compared to the West, South Asia is neonate in terms of its experience with democracy. Nevertheless, more than seven decades of experiment with democratic institutions seems to have not been enough for the polities of the region to transform into mature and stable democracies. The critical question that arises at this juncture is whether liberal democracy is only compatible to developed capitalist polities of the West and does not suit the developing societies? The capricious state of democracy in South Asia compels us to raise this question.

The establishment of a thoroughgoing democracy will in turn result in the rationalization of power and ensure proper accountability of the government towards the public. The developed capitalist societies of the West have been able to achieve the feat of maturing into full-fledged democratic States. However, the entire world has not been fortunate enough and still several countries in various parts of the globe are battling to transform into successful and stable democracies. South Asia stands out as one such region, where in the wheels of transition have yet to gain desired momentum.

This brings to the forefront the contention that despite the frenetic pace of modernization represented by corporate globalization, liberal democracy, considered to be an epitome of modernity, seems to have not yet succeeded in establishing itself as an unchallenged global phenomenon. Macro-regional forces antithetical to democratic values, such as ethno-cultural fanatics or linguistic chauvinists, have fiercely contested democratic processes and even the third wave of democratization merely has had a greater breadth than depth (Diamond, 1997, p. 15). Mainly because the euphoria of global democratization gave way to a number of sobering realities, it soon became apparent that democratic transitions were only half of the equation. Equally problematic were the dilemmas involved in democratic consolidation (Kamrava, 2000, p. 188).

Experience till recently demonstrates that in semi-modern societies, liberal democracy has manifested in heterodox forms. Outside the wealthy industrialized countries, liberal democracy tends to be shallow, illiberal and poorly institutionalized (Zakaria, 1997, p. 23). South Asia represents one such region, where in despite the advent of globalization, rampant destabilization of the democratic mechanism in its polities still persists. So, in spite of the widespread presumption that the positive relationship between democracy and globalization is becoming stronger, the antagonists of this notion are also increasing in number and they argue that globalization and democracy have not necessarily been complimentary and they have often produced ambiguous and conflicting implications (Moon, 1996, p. 10).

This phenomenon manifests in South Asia as the rapid spate of globalization tends to get impeded by the anti-modernist forces contesting for identity like the religious fanatics (Hindu, Islamic and the Sinhalese), linguistic chauvinists (Tamil or Marathi), or for that matter, the protagonists of caste-based politics, who have fractiously intervened in engendering a semi-modern society in the region. So, in the field of contemporary culture, we have become a witness to a contradictory but intertwined historical processes that are operating simultaneously. A globalizing tendency, where the economies and cultures around the world are getting embedded increasingly in a more and more pervasive global web; and a localizing tendency, expressed in its extreme form by a number of insurgencies on the basis of ethnic, religious and other local identities (Goonatilake, 1997, pp. 225–226).

Such a paradox encumbers the smooth democratization of the region and the resultant tumult has generated intense intra-regional tensions. Thus, it appears that democracy tends to be a compatible model only in limited parts of the world. All this, tends to convey here, what we wish to call the half-baked modernity syndrome that has marred democratic values and institutions in the region and has acted as a contravening force to globalization. This is mainly because for Anthony Giddens, 'modern processes entirely differ from previous sociocultural processes, due to its dynamism, the degree to which they under cut traditional habits and customs, and their global impact. However, these are not merely extensional transformations' (Giddens,

1991, pp. 1–3). Further for Giddens, modernity radically alters day-to-day social life and hence one of the distinctive features of modernity is in fact an increasing interconnection between extensionality and intentionality (Giddens, 1991, pp. 1–3). Besides this, 'modernity seeks to locate all creativity, including creative social action, in clear cut breaks with the past. Yet paradoxically, it strives hard to locate such breaks in history' (Nandy, 1983, p. 61). Clipped to this, the democratizing trends must not merely be seen as a predestined fate in politics, but its pervasive influence in cultural life as a whole is immense (Mannheim, 1992, p. 171)

A NEW FOUND HOPE IN SOUTH ASIA?

The climax of democratization process rests in the establishment of a consolidated and a matured democracy (Shin, 1994, p. 144).

> In a consolidated democracy, none of the political actors, parties, organised interest groups, forces or institutions consider that there is any alternative to the democratic process to gain power and no political institutions or groups have a claim to veto the actions of the democratically elected decision-makers. (Linz, 1990)

The existence of a totally opposite situation in some of the countries of South Asia has been a chronic phenomenon, which has proved to be highly destabilizing for the entire region. The problem for these South Asian countries has not been related to the establishment of democratic institutions, rather, the problem for them lies in the fact that they have not been able to consolidate the foundations of their democratic architectures and strengthen democratic values. It implies that South Asian countries with a probable exception of India and Sri Lanka have had fragile democratic systems and hence they have failed to sustain the same for a lengthy duration.

However, the year 2008 can be regarded as a watershed in the history of South Asia. Mainly because since this year, structural transformations towards the democratization of its countries were clearly visible. It was at this juncture that the region barged into a horizon of optimism, with a flurry of activities, symptomatic of move towards democratization in various parts of the region. The holding of general elections in Pakistan and Bangladesh, the move of Bhutan and the Maldives towards the establishment of electoral democracies, the dynamic process of democratization in Nepal, all reflected this phenomenon. However, this now seems to be an illusory situation that threatens to evaporate and is hidden with dangers of degeneration. The tumultuous process leading to the elections in Pakistan, the civic unrest in Bangladesh fountained by religious extremists in connivance with conservative political forces and the uncertainties that looms large over Afghanistan, all indicated the resurgence of instability in the region. At this juncture, it would be appropriate to take into cognizance the arguments made by Huntington (1992, p. 47) in his work on democratization. He argued thus,

> The third wave of democratisation reflected one glaring trend, that is democratisation proved to be advantageous for the powerful actors in the societies of those countries, where democracy was newly instituted. It meant that the transition from an authoritarian regime to a democracy, was beneficial for the already powerful groups in the society, as it facilitated them to consolidate and perpetuate their own dominance. (Huntington, 1992, p. 47)

This has exactly been the case in South Asia. The large measure of control that the military has exercised in Pakistan and Bangladesh over the democratic governments and also its repeated ascendance upon the citadel of political power mirrors this phenomenon. Hence, although the arduous restoration of democracy in Pakistan, the quivering process of democratization in Nepal and the Maldives and the bewildering transition of Bhutan into a democracy have generated an air of optimism, this new found hope appears menacingly ephemeral, considering the complexities and uncertainties that have marked South Asian dynamics. Hence, the intimidation of recrudesce of the sociopolitical tumult after a hiatus always looms large over the region. Above all, democracy's promise of a better world, based upon its emancipatory potential (Grugel, 2003, p. 236) has proved to be an empty signifier, especially if we consider the wide gulf separating the rulers and the ruled, the rich and the poor, in almost all of the South Asian countries.

Hence, the current sanguinity must not be considered to be interminable, as still, the situation appears to be very precarious. It is argued here that, South Asia is still passing through a scabrous phase and the positive developments that have transpired in Pakistan, Nepal, the Maldives and Bhutan, seem to be diaphanous. It has generated a sense of optimism among the people of the region, which appears not more than a hallucination. The unending trail of terrorist activities that has gradually encapsulated enormous spaces throughout the region, the unremitting ethno-political conflicts, the enduring left-wing insurgency and the stability/instability paradox in the subcontinent, caused due to the overt nuclearization of the two subcontinental adversaries; India and Pakistan all have driven the region into a horizon of perilous ambiguity.

HOW DEEP IS THE QUAGMIRE?

South Asian regional security architecture has constantly been fragile, as it tends to persistently be debilitated by strategic exigencies. Such exigencies seem to emanate out of politico-strategic instabilities and developmental bottlenecks that are both endogenous and exogenous in character. In this regard, the dominant factors that have eroded the politico-strategic stability of South Asia include the violence generated due to the emergence of armed non-State actors with independent objectives. To make matters worse, the growth of religious radicalism and the political and popular support that it tends to gain seem to have had a snowballing impact upon such a scenario. Besides, the proliferation and easy availability of narcotics and small arms and illegal movement of goods and people owing to porous borders in the region contribute to the intensification of cross-border terrorism that seem to be sustained by an element of support from rival countries. This kind of strategic environment not only pose sub-systemic threats to the security architecture of the region but has also brought in structuralist constraints that seem to raise existential questions pertaining to the legitimacy of States (Chandran & Rajamohan, 2007, p. 7). Owing to all this, there existed in the region a kind of a situation that could be dubbed as turbulent stalemate. It has been characterized by exasperated conflagration over issues such as Jammu and Kashmir, the stalemate over the ethnic unrest in Sri Lanka and the frenetic expansion of left-wing radicalism in various parts of the region, especially in Nepal and India. Now on account of the newly fountained democratization process in the region, a faint sense of optimism has dawned regarding the prospects of finding amicable solutions to the impasse over some of these contentious issues.

Contextualizing the Kashmir issue from this perspective, it may be envisioned that the democratization of Pakistan has brought a degree of optimism regarding the probability of a providential climax to what has been one of the most horrendous regional conflicts of contemporary history. It may be envisaged that two democratic States would strive to reduce tensions and the prospects of a permanent peace would become broader. However, the 1999 Kargil crisis has been a serious enough a predicament to create splinters in any fantasies of establishing a long peace in the region. In addition to this even after the reinstatement of the democratic political order in Pakistan in 2008, the intensity of militant activity has escalated dramatically in India in recent times. The terror strikes of 26 November 2008 on Mumbai and the attacks in Pathankot (2016), Uri (2016) and Pulwama (2019) have been some of the prominent instances. The result is the continuation of the deadlock on the issue of cross-border terrorism which has hampered the Indo-Pak dialogue process to a considerable extent. This has ultimately led to the torpedoing of all chances of an early and amicable solution to the Kashmir issue.

Above all, the turbulence that was generated due to the intensification of both Hindu and Islamic neo-fundamentalist movements on the issue of land transfer to the Amarnath Shrine Board also engendered a tempest in Jammu and Kashmir. Ever since the shrine board protests broke out, a cult of death flourished in Jammu and Kashmir, as both Hindutva groups and Islamists engaged in what they represented as a war for civilizational survival (Swami, 2008, p. 10). In addition to this, the abrogation of Article 370 has also led to a deep-seated political impasse. This has been a kind of macabre situation which threatened to sabotage the entire Indo-Pak peace process. This is because the domestic turmoil in Jammu and Kashmir tends to have a large impact upon Indo-Pak dynamics. Thus, as Kashmir remains to be an ignition point, tensions between the two subcontinental adversaries also do not seem to slacken.

THE NATURE OF DEMOCRACY IN SOUTH ASIA

To achieve a deeper cognition regarding the nature of democracy in South Asia, we have to go beyond the Western ideational transcripts that have merely eulogized democratic governance and democratic practices and explore the archaeology of socio-economic and political exploitation that democracies have unleashed. In this sense, democracy can be viewed as a dexterously crafted mechanism for engendering and sustaining a capitalist economic system and promoting the patently absurd individualistic connotation of a liberal society. Tinged with the sugar-coated self-extolling declamation of ethical supremacy, the democratic system of governance and its global manifestation; the liberal international order has acted as a concealing device for enshrouding capitalist exploitations, both within the domestic sphere in capitalist democracies and also in the realm of international politics.

Either in the form of State-engineered exploitation of the subaltern sections of the society or the acts merchandized by the Western capitalist powers in the name of saving democracy; be it the Cold War excesses in Korea and Vietnam or the post-Cold War overindulgence in Kosovo, Afghanistan, and Iraq, all exemplify the commonness of intention displayed by capitalism that is to hegemonize both domestic societies and global politics. The perpetual interweaving of these two strands of dominance meant that democracy merely emerged as a jack for hoisting the hegemonic designs of a long-established powerful class in the society.

However, while understanding the nature of democracy, there exists a need for analysing the situation of democratic governments from the perspective of the cultural differences of different regions. In this context, the pattern of the emergence of the democratic model of governance in Europe and then in South Asia demonstrates a clear asymmetry. While in the case of modern European societies, democracy emerged simultaneously and matured together in a temporary parallel development of other modern processes that include the rise of industrial capitalism, urbanization, rationalization and secularization. The concatenation of these forces configures together to form a modern society. Contrastingly, in South Asia, democracy has emerged as an anachrony. It was superimposed by the outgoing colonial administration in collusion with the dominant groups of the local societies. Colonialism thus brought in with it institutional forms of modern Europe and hence inflicted a capitalist model of State upon the postcolonial territories. The elite in South Asian polities emulated the historical and ideological trajectories of the former masters, hence, expediting the expansion of the industrial capitalist economic proto-types (Chatterjee, 1993, p. 31).

In this regard, Edward Said has argued that instead of liberation after decolonization, one simply gets the old colonial structures replicated in new national terms (Said, 1978, p. 107). 'As new nations emerged from the shadow of colonial rule, the older project of colonial modernity was renovated and then deployed as economic development' (Prakash, 1990, p. 393).

Through a subtle coalitional interdependence, the colonial powers and the dominant local groups crafted political formations in a manner that suitably guarded the interests of both: the continuation of the political influence of the colonizer and also the maintenance of domestic sociopolitical hegemony of the already powerful local elite. So a liaison that was peculiar and intricate but marked by shrewd reciprocity transpired between the erstwhile capitalist colonial masters and the nascent postcolonial political class. In this way, for the ruled, the colonial as well as the postcolonial structures of governance were imbricated in a complex double mimesis.

This has happened mainly because the political institutions which evolved as a result of the passive receptivity of the colonized periphery, emerging as elite constructions. These institutions were developed on the lines of the institutional approach, with the demotic conscious-ness remaining very much ignorant, and marginalized from this entire process. This ignorance ultimately led to an unequal socio-economic and political relationship between a tiny elite minority and the major-ity masses in the postcolonial State. This very inequality has been the subterranean molecular impulse that impeded the process of democratization and obviated the emergence of a strong State in the polities of the region. Such an organismic anarchy is underpinned by anti-modernist forces such as ethno-religious conflicts, caste-based social hierarchy, a predominant presence of feudal economic structures and language-based social tensions. These forces are used by the powerful groups in the society to assert their domination over those which are powerless, the source of their domination being derived out of their status as an ethnic or religious majority, a dominant linguistic group, the upper castes in the Hindu social order, or the owners of production in a predominantly agrarian economy. Even neo-institutionalist attempts at engaging the weaker groups in a participatory process of governance have merely been damage control mechanisms with the ontology of inequality still remaining divested of any therapeutic treatment.

Thus, the scenario for the powerless groups in postcolonial societies of South Asia remained static because decolonization ushered in the transfer of power in the newly created States only to the dominant native groups. The processes of decolonization thus made no meaning for the weak and marginalized sections. It happened because the process of colonial transition itself was a product of a mutually beneficial partnership between dominant native groups and the colonizing imperial power. In this condition, the people of the subverted groups merely existed as transhistorical mediated selves with an indeterminate sociocultural identity embedded in alienated structures of social relations. The established powerful groups, on their part, tended to invoke primordialist and perennialist claims over power to perpetuate their domination in the postcolonial State, issuing in with the marginalization of the powerless.

In this sense, South Asia's journey towards modernity, evident in its growth story, merely seems to reflect the material side of modernity and the entire process of democratization manifested in the existence of popular government appear only to have facilitated the perpetuation of dominant interests through a process of legitimization in the form of elections. In addition to this, it must be noted that modernity manifests in all aspects of social life as the basic characteristic and embodiment of the developmental process of modern society. It is a general concept concerning economy, politics, culture, society and many other factors. However, in South Asia, modernity seems to have assumed a dehumanizing materialistic character, owing to which subjectivity of one human individual to the other is still inbuilt in its system. Epitomizing this is the complex structure of domination and subjectivity characterized by the marginalization of minorities and other oppressed groups and the hegemony of the dominant groups in the sociocultural sphere. This pattern of subjectivity exists even as State possesses powers to guarantee sociocultural and politico-economic equality to the weaker sections through affirmative action.

All this ushered in a new form of internal colonization that was driven by the colonial ideologies of orientalism and liberalism. This implied that the traditional elite classes that acquired the reins of power in the newly decolonized societies began to internally colonize their own population. They did this by employing an oriental style argument, referring to their own domination as the legacy of traditional class superiority and by advancing a liberal judgement that called for the civilization of the inferior classes through the instruments of the State. In this regard, Gyan Prakash asks this pertinent question.

> If the Brown Sahibs imitation of the British was an Indian strategy of survival and even resistance; and if in spite of its clearheaded realpolitik, the modern Indian anti-colonial nationalism fell prey to a second colonization; then what is left of the neatly separated India and the West? (Prakash, 1990, p. 406).

Thus for Gyan Prakash, 'postcoloniality is not born and nurtured in a panoptic distance from history' (Prakash, 1992, p. 8). Rather for Gayatri Spivak, 'the postcolonial exists as an aftermath, as an after—after being worked over by colonialism' (Spivak, 1990, p. 228). This is what Homi Bhabha (1989, p. 112) calls an 'in-between, hybrid position of practice and negotiation' and Gayatri Chakravorty Spivak calls this as 'catachresis; reversing, displacing and seizing the apparatus of value-coding' (Spivak, 1990, p. 228).

Owing to this, democracy emerged as a tool of hegemony for the already dominant local groups in the societies of South Asia. The adventitious foisting of Western-style democratic governance also transpired as an ideological anachronism for the nascent States and hence domestic political incompetence in democracies has been a critical feature of South Asian polities. So, the autochthonous groups of these States that were already dominant such as the Punjabis, the most affluent community in Pakistan, the upper-class Hindu elite that enjoyed a hegemonic footing in the Indian or the Nepalese society for thousands of years, and the socially and economically stronger Sinhalese in Sri Lanka, became both benefactors and the beneficiaries of a democratic State. In this way, democratic elites in such nascent democracies do not always seem to actively try to or succeed in consolidating democracy culturally. The ensuing democratic system often ends up comprising largely isolated, elite groups whose main interests lie in securing their own positions within the new institutions of the democratic system (especially in the parliament or their own political party) rather than representing their constituents. So, democratic transition from above, in short, face the potential rather than inherent danger of resulting in elitist quasi-democratic polities that have all the institutional and structural trappings of democracy but lack a strong cultural component that would give them a strong resonance among the different strata of the society (Kamrava, 2000, p. 190).

Such a scenario demonstrates that paradoxical to the inception of democracy in the West, in South Asia, the polities seems to have anachronistically attempted to emulate the Western model of the democratic political process, by superficially imposing the Western style of democratic institutions without graduating through other modern processes. This seems to be one crucial factor that has rendered the democratization process into shambles. In a way, South Asia adopted the Western model of democratic governance, with their societies still possessing semi-feudal, semi-urban and semi-industrial characters. Putting things in this perspective, it may be argued that the democratization processes of the West and of South Asia exhibit asymmetric trends.

In the West, the democratic State was a product of multiple modern processes and got ensconced in a ripe modern society. In sharp contrast to this, in South Asia, democratic State has been the antecedent of modern society. So the democratic polities of the West flourished because of the existence of fully baked modern societies, whereas the State in South Asia emerged as the harbinger of modernity and was supposed to be the sole engine of social transformation and catalyst of various modern processes. In the context of India, Sunil Khilnani (1997, p. 41) has argued that

> after independence, the State was enlarged, its ambitions inflated, and it was transformed from a distant, alien object into one that infiltrated the everyday lives of Indians, proclaiming itself responsibility for everything that they could desire. Jobs, ration cards, educational places, security, cultural recognition. The State thus etched itself into the imagination of the Indians in a manner that no previous political agency had ever done before. (Khilnani, 1997, p. 41)

As pointed out by Deepak Malik,

> More than a mere economic actor and contrary to material theory, the State was not just a superstructure reflecting the underlying forces of material production and related social relations, but was itself supposed to become the principle actor in the transformation of the social and economic basis of the society. (Malik, 2007, p. 364)

An agent of modernization both in terms of industrial and social policy, it exercised a decisive influence on the evolution of the economy as well as the social configuration, including the balance of forces. It played this role independently of its political form through economic planning, resource allocation, educational and industrial policies which imply new economic opportunities impacting the labour market, social mobility and through it on class formation and value systems (Neelsen & Malik, 2007, pp. 22–23 & 26).

This pushed the region into the theatrics of a conflict between the modern liberal State with its reformative agenda and the deep-rooted and archaic sociocultural structures with their hegemonic tendencies. It generated immense social tensions and political friction, leading us to the notion that democracy must emanate inherently and cannot be simulated. Apart from this, the socio-economic underdevelopment of the region helped the dominant actors in the society to manoeuvre their way to the pinnacle of political power. Thus, a democratic State proved to be more advantageous for the powerful actors in the society, who nurtured motives for a quixotic perpetuation of their hegemony. This rendered the democratic State become an instrument for the maintenance of social hegemony by the powerful groups, resulting in subaltern discontent that fountained anti-regime sentiments, leading to frequent political destabilizations.

A modern representative State presupposes a modern class-based social order and not a social configuration based on collectively ascribed inequality and hierarchy such as caste. However, in South Asia, representative institutions were introduced not only without social struggles but also without the relevant social substratum of modern social class. In such conditions, the societal configuration does not correspond with the modern forms of the economy and the institutions of the State which provide the mould and the channels are provided through which power and privileges are accessed and distributed (Neelsen & Malik, 2007, p. 26). In the advanced capitalist countries, the State has developed in the wake of a single dominant class and the State institutions and powers have developed in keeping the needs and demands of that class, whereas the State in peripheral capitalist countries like those in South Asia tends to be subjected to neocolonial influences. Such influences deeply penetrate into the polity because of the persistence of the traditional coalitional interdependence between the metropolitan elite and the dominant groups of the periphery that tends to benefit both.

WHY MODERNIZATION PROCESS IN SOUTH ASIA IS DISSIMILAR TO THAT OF THE WEST

When we speak of modernity, it would be parochial to visualize the phenomenon purely from the Western perspective. To be precise, South Asia cannot modernize in the same fashion as that of the West. The simple reason is the sociocultural idiosyncrasy and different histories of the two regions. Thus, some lines of differentiation have to be delineated. This is because, as modernity permeates to wider spaces it assumes a more differentiated and plural character. Thus, there arises a necessity for a rethinking over the nature of modernity and simultaneously it should correspond with the reworking of the basic premises of sociocultural analysis (Giddens, 1991, p. 1).

A fitting illustration of the asymmetric nature of modernity in South Asia and the West must be traced in the foundations of social hierarchy in both societies. As regards the West, the social stratification is primarily based upon income, whereas in South Asian countries such as India and Nepal, the dogmatic orthodoxy of religion manifested in the caste system, determines the social hierarchy. Similarly, as far as the histories of the two regions are concerned, it may be noted that in the West, the notion of a modern nation state emerged in the era of renaissance and has been a product of religious reforms and secularization of politics. In the case of South Asia, the birth of the modern nation state was rather influenced by the anti-colonial movement. Hence, the process of modernization in South Asia must be disengaged from its encasement into the Western paradigm. Or to put it in the words of Chakrabarty (2000, p. 11), Europe can be provincialized provided if there is a recognition of the phenomenon that although THE origins OF modernity were European, its penetration into hitherto nonmodern non-European areas makes it get secluded from the roots of its origin.

So a search for alternative paradigms of modernity for different regions and the recognition of its multidimensional character becomes imperative. In this context, South Asia also exhibits uniqueness as a region and it demands recognition in accordance with its peculiar attributes. Its multi-ethnic character, long subjection to colonial rule, the religio-civilizational overlapping among the polities and the archaic nature of the cultures of different communities of the region, all beg a larger consideration and indicate the need for developing a South Asian conception of modernity. Hence, our alternative reading of the spatio-temporal dynamics of modern South Asia must be underpinned by the postcolonial criticism of the post-enlightenment assertion that it is the West which has been instrumental in the making of history (Prakash, 1994, p. 1475).

This, then, brings in the fundamental epistemic question regarding the significance of the concept of modernity, embedded in the epistemology of the post-enlightenment thought for the spatio-temporal archaeology of South Asia.

For Sudipta Kaviraj,

> The most influential Western theories on modernity have been developed by Marx and Weber. These theories contain two central arguments. First is that modernity is a single homogeneous process and is influenced by a single causal principle. In the case of Marx, it is the capitalist commodity production and for Weber, it is the abstract notion of rationalisation of the world. (Kaviraj, 2000, p. 137)

> Unlike some Western scholars who limit their interpretation of modernity and its source to conceptual cultural value and psychological dimensions, Marx pointed out that modernity came mainly through the modern production system. Starting from the historical context of his time, Marx explored various aspects of modernity and pointed out that modernity was inherent in the logic of capital, resided in the process of historical evolution, arose in social conflicts and segmentations and presented itself in a global horizon. The logic of capital, the historical viewpoint, the theory of contradictions and a global perspective are fundamental in the Marxist analysis of the problems of modernity. (Feng, 2006, p. 254)

Thus, Marxist interpretation of modernity is primarily materialist.

Contrary to this, Max Weber presents a non-materialist interpretation of modernity. He has presented a penetrating critique of modernity and has envisaged his own solutions to resolve the predicaments of what he calls institutional modernity. For Weber, 'the world was moving toward mechanised petrification' (Weber, 1958, p. 182) 'rule by administrators rather than by complete individuals' (Weber, 1946, p. 95), 'and control by the rational organic machine known as bureaucracy' (Weber, 1978, p. 1402). 'In this essentially modern condition, individual worth was lost. The individual was turned into a cog in the social machine' (Weber, 1946, p. 228). Weber's romantic solution to what he termed as this 'iron cage of modernity' is fundamentally combined with an epistemology that is essentially Kantian (Weber, 1949, p. 106).

Further for Weber, 'modernity has produced externalisation of reason', or what he called the 'mind objectified' (Koch, 1993, pp. 128–131). This for him,

> can bring in negative consequences for the social realm. The residue of rationalisation, industrialisation production, and bureaucratic organisation depletes the individual of spontaneous, creative character of human existence. Institutional life is rigid. Rigidity reproduces itself in the processes of social reproduction. Modernity comes to represent conformity and petrified existence. (Koch, 1993, pp. 128–131)

In Weberian terms,

> Answers to the pit falls of modernity lies in an interpretive understanding of social phenomenon by assigning importance to morality and values as the foundations of human relations and not instrumental rationality, as symbolised by a modern society governed by bureaucratic control and industrial production. (Koch, 1993, pp. 128–131)

In doing this, Weber resorts to the methodology of Kantian epistemology and the romantic tradition of 'Strum Und Drang' (Koch, 1993, pp. 128–131).

In this manner, both Marx and Weber tend to establish the homogeneous character of modernity and advocate a reductionist perspective to limit the interpretation of modernity in monocausal terms. It is acknowledged in this regard by Sudipta Kaviraj that

> Modernity has various distinct aspects. These include the rise of capitalist industrial economy, the growth of modern State institutions with the resultant transformation in the nature of social power, the emergence of democracy, the decline of the community and the rise of strong individualistic conduct, the decline of religion and the secularisation of ethics. These are all part of a historical structure animated by a single principle. (Kaviraj, 2000, p. 142)

A slightly different version of this approach acknowledges that these processes are distinct and can historically emerge quite independently. But it still claims that these processes are functionally connected to each other in such a way that the historical emergence of anyone tends to create conditions for others. Kaviraj states in this context that 'social individuation is a prior condition to the successful operation of the capitalist economy. All these processes of modernity either stand or fall together' (Kaviraj, 2000, p. 142).

Further for Kaviraj,

> The second idea usually accompanies the functionalist model of modernity. It is widely believed that as modernity spreads from the Western centers of economic and political power to other parts of the world, it tends to produce societies similar to those of the modern West. This belief further holds that modernity replicates Western social forms in other parts of the world. Where ever it goes, it produces uniform modernity. A corollary of this belief is that those societies, which are different from the Western models, are not sufficiently modernised and they remain traditional. (Kaviraj, 2000, p. 138)

However, it may be argued that the Western notion of modernity is ahistorical, in so far as South Asia is concerned. The track through which the West has moved towards modernity is very much specific to European history and geography, indicating that the understanding of modernity in the context of South Asia must be bereft of European ethno-centricism and should be guided by methodological agnosticism. However, modernity for the postcolonial South Asia is always interpreted in terms of the historical evolution that was marked by the advent of colonial modernity. This is because colonial intervention sought to rewrite the region's history on the foundations and premises of the Western experience with the era of modernity that began for them with the renaissance, emergence of the gun powder empires and industrial revolution. In this regard, the interpretation of South Asian history as backward in time and the forceful prescription of the Western values of modernity and metropolitan governance as a panacea have had long-lasting effects on the region.

Hence, Sudipta Kaviraj has argued that

> The conventional theoretical models regarding the structure of modernity and its historical extension across the world are faulty. To understand the historical unfolding of modernity, especially in the non-Western world, these theories need some revision. (Kaviraj, 2000, p. 137)

Modernity, therefore, is not a uniform process and do not determine a universal structure of the trajectory of history. The term modernity comes to us masking its origin in a distinct geographical space as well as an imagination almost entirely concerned with the change in Europe and America what we euphemistically refer to as the West. It is precisely because the term modernity is neither temporally nor geographically grounded, there is an increasing suspicion towards its relevance as a term to understand historical change (Menon, 2002, p. 1662).

In the geographic and historical sense, modernity, according to David Harvey, explicitly manifested in Europe and North America (see Harvey, 1989). Kaviraj further argues in this context that there are several reasons for modernity to be heterogeneous in character. Owing to such a character, the trajectory of modernity does not lead to the same kind of social process that would result in the reconstitution of institutions in all historical and cultural contexts in a similar fashion. This is because the advent of modernity is accompanied by a drastic transformation of sociocultural practices (Kaviraj, 2000, pp. 138–139). According to Kaviraj,

> Modern practices are not always historically unprecedented in the sense that the society was entirely unfamiliar with that kind of practice earlier. Most of the significant practices transformed by modernity seem to fall into the spheres of political power, State, economic production, education, science and even religion. It is true that modernity introduces a radical rupturing of the ways in which these social affairs are conducted. However, in all cases, the modern ways of doing things are not written on a clean slate. (Kaviraj, 2000, pp. 138–139)

Thus, it is incorrect according to Gusfield, 'to view traditional societies as static, normatively consistent or structurally homogeneous' (Gusfield, 1967, p. 351). Hence, any idea of modernity has to be understood in the historical and cultural contexts of its rendition (Menon, 2002, p. 1662).

In this context, it is significant to note that Anthony Giddens attempts to provide a revisory critique of modernity by arguing in favour of reflective modernity, based on the importance of intersubjectivity in human relations. For Anthony Giddens, modernity is mainly a Western project and has resulted in the erosion of traditional forms of life. The consequences of modernity have been accentuated, as it has become reflexive. Personal experiences of dislocation, uncertainty and choice, characteristic of modernity in general are yet more pervasive and constitutive of identity. Further for Giddens, 'modernity is a juggernaut, a runaway engine with enormous power which collectively as human beings we can drive to some extent but which also threatens to run out of our control and which could run itself us under' (Giddens, 1990, p. 139).

In this regard, it is pertinent to observe the notion of developing societies which is presented in studies relating to Third-World development by theorists of the modernization school, who adopted the structural–functional analysis and their neo-Marxist critiques belonging to the political economy school, represented by the dependency and the world economic system theorists. In the post-Cold War epoch, the modernization theorists reintroduced the studies relating to the institutions, values and class structures that make development possible. Their studies were predicated upon the reference to the dichotomy between two genres that described societies. The first was a traditional society which was underdeveloped and the second was the modern, developed, vastly industrialized and highly urbanized. According to this, the developing countries represent societies characterized by traditional cultures, indicating that cultural processes invariably intervene in the socio-economic process of development. For the dependency theorists, the phenomenon of this dichotomy was to be understood from the perspective of world capitalism which produced a relationship of dependency between the core capitalist countries, and the periphery which is the underdeveloped countries (see Frank, 1967). In the cycle of development, there emerges an intermediary stage that constitutes the conjuncture between tradition and modernity. For the world-system theorists, the structure of this conjuncture is called the 'semi periphery' (see Wallerstein, 1974).

However, one of the serious lacunas of the political economy school lies in their negligence displayed towards internal factors leading to development. A serious methodological error of this approach is to deprive local histories, their integrity and specificity (Smith, 1979, p. 257). It is only Cardoso and Faletto (1979, p. 145) who have taken serious reckoning of the internal dynamics through the class approach. Posing the question as to how do external factors of global capitalism affect internal structures of peripheral countries, they state that it is mainly through the interests and social practices of local groups and the dominating influence of a particular group. In such societies, the mode of production is indeterminate, with the simultaneous existence of the pre-capitalist, capitalist and transitional ones, with the State gaining a greater degree of autonomy because of the lack of balance of power among different groups (see Gold et al., 1975). In these societies, the overdeveloped State machinery had been created by the metropolitan power to control all the indigenous social groups (Alavi, 1972, p. 61). The postcolonial societies inherit this overdeveloped State apparatus and its institutional practices, through which indigenous groups are controlled (Ziemann & Lazendorfer, 1977, p. 147).

The roots of the limitations of the political economy school of development are embedded in their parochial interpretation of the Marxian notion of modernity. Although the concept of modernity did not appear evidently in his works, on the basis of his thorough exploration of the development of social history, Marx did expound ideas concerning modernity. His theory of modernity is a study of modern society, which in turn, is a capitalist society. Marx had stated that modernity came mainly from modern production and is inherent in the logic of capital, resided in the historical process of evolution. This should not be considered to imply that for Marx, the economy is the sole factor driving the process of modernity. Rather, he merely accentuated the effects of production on modernity and did not deem it as the only change agent. The political economy school of development only takes into account the Marxian conception of modernity as emanating from the forces of production and is inherent in the logic of capital. The dependency theorist's emphasis upon core/periphery relationship being shaped by core capital and the cycle of development laid down by the world economic system theorists based upon world capitalism provides credence to this phenomenon. Hence, this approach is inadequate to explain the essence of modernity and the problems of developing societies. Mainly because it does not take into consideration the internal sociocultural structures that factor in the process of development. As the basic characteristic and embodiment of the developmental process of modern society, modernity manifests in all aspects of social life. It is a general concept concerning economy, politics, culture, society and many other factors.

Thus, rather than visualizing Marx as the vindicator of modernity engendered by capitalist economic transformation, he should be viewed as the critique of the decadent effects of that modernity itself. To elaborate this, we should take note of various distortions according to Karl Marx which were produced by modernity. First is 'reification of social relations' which means that 'the exchange of commodities makes the relations among human beings appear as something alien to them, autonomous as a thing. In exchange value, the social connection between persons is transformed into social relations among things' (Marx, 1973, p. 157).

> The negative value and consequence of capitalist modernity ultimately concentrates in the full-scale reification of human beings. The capitalist mode of production not only produces poverty, exploitation and oppression, but also brings severe devastation and devaluation to the human world. Thus, it destroys both human life and cultural values. (Marx, 1973, p. 157)

It is thus clear by these statements that Marxian critique of modernity is fundamentally directed towards the negative impact produced in the form of the dehumanization of the society in the form of commodification and mechanization of human relations.

THE HISTORY OF DEMOCRATIZATION IN SOUTH ASIA: AN UNHEALTHY ACCOUNT

History is always in the making. It evolves through a complex and dialectical interplay between agency, structure, consciousness and action (Gill, 1993, p. 8). In an ontological sense, it represents a nexus between action and structure (Abrams, 1982, p. 14). History, in this sense, is a reflection of social change which can be explained through the interplay of social structure, social culture and social action. This kind of examination of the interplay between structure, culture and agency can provide a framework for the analysis of the factors influencing and the mechanisms through which history, as a marker of social change, unfolds (Uzelac, 2002, pp. 138–139).

Viewed in this sense, history involves a constant dialectical interaction between the objective material world and the subjective interpretation of the same, emanating out of human reason. This means that historical evolution symbolizes an interface between human consciousness and the material environment that operate around it. This interaction often produces a complex pattern of asymmetric interdependence which has manifested in various forms in diverse spatio-temporal topographies. One aspect relating to this is the coexistence of the upper and lower levels of civilizations which forces upon the historian, an illuminating dialectic. Implicit in this dialectic are the issues of epistemology and ontology (Gill, 1993, p. 8). One such representation of the modern epoch has been colonialism which signified an unequal relationship between the core industrial capitalist societies and the non-industrialized peripheral societies. This pattern of relationship created an imperial structure that was not merely politico-economic or military in character, rather it reflected a deep psycho-cultural influence upon the colonized societies.

Situating ourselves in the epistemological framework of such an idea of history, it has been argued here that due to the fractured trajectory of democratization, characterized by a crisis in the process of State construction, the countries of South Asia are still grappling to establish strong and stable States. This inadequacy has factored deeply in accentuating their external security dilemmas. To this effect, their bitter colonial past, coupled with the crisis of identity associated with their projects of nation-building, has contributed to exasperating this predicament. All this has come to a full circle with the absence of intra-regional cohesion, compounded by a mutual threat perception.

Here it needs to be understood that democracy has been recognized as a system constructed upon the notion that men have dignity enunciated in the forms of freedoms and rights. Construed in this sense, a democratic structure not only encompasses a liberal democratic system of governance but is also embedded in a just socio-economic order. Democracy in its entirety engrosses almost all the aspects of human life. Hence, it cannot be interpreted only from the sense of politics and governance, it has been emerging as a total philosophy of life. In the same way, democracy must not be understood within the preview of domestic politics, of late there has been a growing international realization that democracy is the essence of a just and fair international order. Equal dignity and status to all nations, just international economic order, absence of all kinds of domination that manifests in the form of imperialism or hegemony, and the existence of peace and security for all the members belonging to the family of nations are regarded as some of the primary conditions for making the world more democratic.

In this context, David Held states that democracy seems to have scored a historic victory over alternative forms of governance. Nearly everyone today professes to be a democrat. Political regimes of all kinds throughout the world claim to be democracies. Yet what these regimes say and do is often substantially different from one another (Held, 1993, p. 14). In this context, it can be asked here, in this contemporary world, how far democracy has been successful in establishing itself as a strong force both in its internal dimension as a system of political structure of a state and in its external dimension as a stable system of global governance? Have all the modern states managed to organize and sustain a vibrant and stable democratic structure of sociopolitical authority and a liberal and just domestic economic system? To what extent the countries of the modern world have been able to institute a just world order based on democratic values? All these appear to be mesmerizing questions and exploring answers to all of them may seem to be a pipe dream. Anyhow, for an examination of the status of democracy in the present context, it is pertinent to analyse the fundamental bottlenecks that have jeopardized the process of institutionalization of democratic principles in the socioeconomic and political spheres of nations both in their domestic and international dimensions.

In this regard, it has been argued that democracy has not functioned successfully in South Asia. Democracy is in a perilous condition in the region. Even though almost all the states of South Asia have tried to set up and run democratic political systems, their experience has shown that they are confronted by fractious sociopolitical authorities, which have always proved to be disruptive for the smooth functioning of democracy in the entire region. To comprehend the fundamental reasons for this, multicausal explanation having both internal and external dynamics can be broached. Since there is an integral relationship between domestic politics and foreign affairs of a country, it is crucial to understand the interlocking balances between the internal and external problems faced by democracies in South Asia.

Here, it is essential to highlight the fact that despite many policy and political changes which have taken place in South Asian countries, the degree and intensity of violence and unrest has dramatically escalated. Long-running conflicts in these countries became more deeply entrenched while new conflicts emerged, as a result, these societies faced an upsurge of ethnic violence, communal tensions, militant activities, misuse of political power, insecurity and criminality (Kumar & Khwar, 1996, p. 17). All these antecedents have directly or indirectly led to the wrecking of the democratic mechanism in the South Asian region. On the other hand, it may also be viewed here that failure of the democratic institution or democratic paralysis in the countries of the region seems to be one of the fundamental causes of their virulent socio-economic and political problems. Thus, it seems there exists a symbiotic and reciprocating relationship between the functioning of the democratic mechanism in South Asia and its exasperated and multidimensional problems. The problems rather than strengthening the democratic apparatus in these countries have proved to be counter-productive and has led to the weakening of the state's capacity to solve the problems effectively. Hence, due to such a syndrome that indicates domestic political incompetence in the democracies of the region, a cohesive regional order consisting of stable democratic polities has merely remained an imagination. The countries of South Asia seem to have established democratic regimes but they remain merely a parody. Even seven decades of arduous experiments in the democratic style of governance has been barely sufficient not only to bring socio-economic development but also to maintain a peaceful regional order.

An overview of the political history of South Asia across the last seven decades indicates a wavering trend for democracy in almost all the countries of the region. Although democratic structures were instituted, the turbulence in their external environment and internal turmoils rendered democracy in these South Asian countries either to collapse or to become handicapped. Hence, the stability of the democratic order in South Asia has been ephemeral. Right from the day in 1947 when India and Pakistan became independent states, the subcontinent has been battling to preserve a democratic system. Even though India and Sri Lanka have stayed well-nigh democratic during this period, but their democratic credentials cannot be seen as entirely unstained. Although the institutions of representative democracy have become deeply and socially embedded in India and Sri Lanka, none of the available evidence suggests that this has resulted in the magical transformation of the Indians and Sri Lankans from masses into liberal political subjects (Spencer, 2007, p. 72). Contrary to this, Pakistan, Bangladesh and Nepal have been struggling to remain democratic. This has happened as their domestic arena has been plagued by either of the problems such as ethnic tensions, left-wing insurgency and religious radicalism. Not only this, Pakistan and Bangladesh have had to counter civil and military conflicts, in which the military has not been hesitant to intimidate or veritably use force in order to clasp its hands upon the power structure of the state.

Most significantly, the region is nested in a web of internally governed and externally instigated fractious sociocultural and politico-strategic forces that have contemptuously intervened as instruments of abrasion, contributing towards the repeated decapitation of democracy. This process of disruption has been accentuated due to the fragility of South Asian Association for Regional Cooperation (SAARC), caused by internal dissonance. Hence, as democracy within a nation state or region requires democracy within a network of interwoven international forces and international relations (Held, 1993, p. 14), the SAARC debacle, seems to have had a corrosive impact upon South Asian dynamics.

A synoptic survey of the political history of South Asia depicts an ambiguous situation, as far as the state of democratic politics in various polities is concerned. Almost all the countries established the democratic style of governance, only to be hijacked by dominant groups in the society, either it may be the military-religious radicals in Pakistan and Bangladesh or the society infested by feudal structure and religious orthodoxy in Nepal. In Pakistan, the Mullah-military condominium has had a decisive role not only in the sociocultural dynamics and the economic affairs of the country but it also seriously affected the course of politics and governance (Markey, 2007, p. 87).

Similarly, democracy in the pre-popular movement phase of Nepal may also be seen as being merely an epitome of feudal-capitalist control over an impotent democracy, accentuated by the obtrusive role played by the palace. Thus, the palace-engineered deportation of politics in February 2005 and the subsequent political instability was an apparent manifestation of the vulnerability of Nepal's democracy to an obstinate complex of self-seeking royalists and their aids in the democratic government. Anyhow, contemporary Nepal is passing through a more optimistic phase, but perspicuously, it is merely a dubious optimism. Pakistan on its part has moved towards a horizon of hope, with the installation of a democratically elected government and the end of military rule. But could this transition be construed as irreversible? This question remains significant due to the tainted history of Pakistani polity. Similarly, in Bangladesh, the political parties, such as the Bangladesh National Party (BNP), have struck an unholy alliance with the Islamic radicals using the rhetoric of the phrase of 'home-grown democracy' in order to masquerade their nefarious intentions (Hossain, 2006, p. 791).

In this line, Sri Lanka has figured somewhat better than its other South Asian neighbours, with India being an exception, in terms of the performance of the democratic political order. However, like all other South Asian countries, Sri Lankan democracy, has also not remained popular in the true spirit. The democratic processes tend to be hijacked by the Sinhalese nationalists, the socially and economically powerful ethnic group in Sri Lanka. The two major national political parties in Sri Lanka, the United National Party (UNP) and the Sri Lanka Freedom Party (SLFP), have built their political image as the political guardians of the Sinhalese interests. Both have attempted during elections to dexterously play the ethnic card and project themselves as the best choice for the Sinhalese, for being ensured of the safety of their interests. This has been the worst kind of political misdemeanours associated with competitive politics. Neil DeVotta has called the broad framework of this process 'ethnic outbidding' (Uyangoda, 2007, p. 41). These messianic endeavours of the two political parties have had a catalytic impact in widening the schisms in Sri Lanka's multifarious society, pulverizing the ethnic foundations of the country's politics. It is this politics of ethnic outbidding, electoral competition between UNP and SLFP to persuade Sinhalese voters that they are the best equipped to ensure Sinhalese dominance that marginalized the Tamilians from the State, reinforced the ideology of Sinhalese ethnic and political supremacy and eventually created conditions for Tamil separatist insurgency. The politics of ethnic outbidding thus generated a pan-Sinhalese consensus, for Sinhalese hegemony in the polity. Thus, Sri Lanka may be called a democracy that has facilitated the hegemony of the fringe (Uyangoda, 2007, p. 41).

Finally, as regards India, it is not only the largest, the most developed country having a better military capability compared to its South Asian counterparts, but it is also a multicultural, multi-ethnic and multireligious society accommodating the population of all the religions to which South Asia is home to. Apart from this, it is the most successful democracy in the region. However, Indian democracy has not remained fully untainted. It has been successful in so far as the sustenance of the democratic architecture is concerned, through regular, free and fair elections. However, the polity has exhibited a gradual decline, in so far as the capacity to deal with pressing problems is concerned. Such a predicament that is encountered by the postcolonial polity in India has been the product of the perpetuation of the domination of the feudal-capitalist structures over the contours of the political economy. The nature of such a structure of the political economy is bolstered by an intrusive role of the bureaucracy which is still rooted in the mental fetters of its colonial roots.

A LAYERED PROCESS OF DEMOCRATIZATION?

Normally, the democratization process goes through four stages: decay of authoritarian regime, transition to democracy, consolidation of democracy and maturity of democracy (Shin, 1994, pp. 143–144). The polities of South Asia are undergoing different stages of democratization and the entire region is not passing through the same stage. Hence, the pace of democratization of the region is rather sluggish. A glimpse at the current political dynamics in different polities of the region will indicate this phenomenon.

To begin with, the Maldives, Bhutan and Afghanistan have just crossed the first stage, that is, the decay of authoritarian regime. Since independence, the Maldives has been governed by two successive authoritarian regimes, the first one led by Ibrahim Nasir who ruled from 1968 to 1978 and Maumoon Abdul Gayoom who ruled since 1978. Recently, the democratic process was initiated and the country moved closer to liberal governance by adopting its constitution in 2008. But the legal system in the Maldives is still Islamic in character. Afghanistan has been the most unfortunate country in the region, as political stability has always been an illusion. Either it has been a battleground for big powers, or it several times got enmeshed in the cross-fire of conflict between indigenous groups contesting for greater sociopolitical space. The most horrendous aspect of this quagmire was the Talibanization of the country.

Although Taliban was dislodged by US intervention in 2001, Afghanistan failed to achieve democratic stability. This has been the case, mainly due to the resurgence of the neo-Taliban movement in the country. Such resurgence seems to have reached a fruition point with the capturing of power by the Taliban forces in August 2021. As the last US soldier left the Afghan soil, the Taliban began to infiltrate into all the registers of the country's sociocultural and politico-economic life by a coercive imposition of religious fundamentalism upon the people. Thus considering this, it may be stated here that the most significant obstacle to the process of democratization in Afghanistan and the Maldives has been the inertia towards modernization exhibited by the conservative Islamic forces. This stems from their aversion to the Western model of development and the belief that Islam and democracy cannot be reconciled (Bashiriyeh, 1993, p. 143). Hence, for the democratization of Afghanistan and the Maldives, secularization of politics is crucial. The imperative is to bring reforms in Islam to make it more progressive and compatible with modern liberal society. However, there have been positive signs, as progressive Islamists around the world are struggling to find viable answers to the question of compatibility between democracy, modernity and Islamic beliefs (Wright, 1996, p. 77).

Further, Pakistan, Bangladesh and Nepal are at crossroads, having to pass through dual stages of democratization, that is, the transition to democracy and consolidation of democracy. All these countries have been frequently oscillating between democratic and authoritarian regimes. Hence, the consolidation of democracy is the major problem that these countries are grappling with. It is obvious that the democratization of a political system depends upon the presence and absence of many social and political variables in a country. It needs political leaders who are committed to democratic principles and practices of government (Parry & Moran, 1994, p. 5). A democratic political system requires an electoral process to transfer power from one party to another without violence and intimidation. The transition to a democratic political system and consolidation requires a consensus among its dominant elites on the basic tenets of the democratic system. As democratic consolidation is defined in terms of broad consensus or at least elite consensus, on a certain set of norms as to how politics should be conducted (Chowdhury, 2003, p. 3).

Democracy is consolidated according to Peceny, 'when it is perceived by actors as one legitimate, just or at least the normal way to do politics and when the daily practice of democratic rules reinforces their normative legitimacy' (Peceny, 1999, p. 98). Considering this, it may be stated that it is difficult to conceive of a democratic political system without having a consensus on the fundamental components of the same (Chowdhury, 2003, p. 3). In this regard, the question that Apter has posed is that

> can democracy be made functional if democratic values are not domesticated and internalized, their meaning constituting some kind of consensus prior to the practice of democracy itself and especially among those responsible for administering if not those on whose behalf it is administered? (Apter, 1991, p. 476)

Hence, the adoption of democratic values by the leaders and people is very important to build up democratic institutions in a political system (Chowdhury, 2003, p. 4).

For Linz and Stepan,

> behaviorally, a democratic regime in a territory is consolidated when no significant social, national, economic, political or institutional actors spend significant resources to achieve their objectives by creating a nondemocratic regime or seceding from the State. (Linz & Stepan, 1996a, p. 29)

Further for them,

> Attitudinally, a democratic regime is consolidated when a strong majority of public opinion, even in the midst of major economic problems deep dissatisfaction with incumbents, holds that democratic procedures and institutions are the most appropriate ways to govern collective life and support for anti-system alternatives is quite small and is more or less isolated from the prodemocratic forces. (Linz & Stepan, 1996a, p. 29)

Finally for Linz and Stepan,

> Constitutionally, a democratic regime is consolidated when Governmental and non-Governmental forces alike become subject to and as well as habituated to the resolution of conflicts within the bounds of the specific laws, procedures and institutions that are sanctioned by the new democratic process. (Linz & Stepan, 1996a, p. 29)

Linz and Stepan (1996b, p. 29) specify five basic requirements for the consolidation of democracy. 'A vibrant civil society, autonomous political society, neutral bureaucracy, rule of law and institutionalized economic society'. The broad inadequacies engendered by the lack or disruption of these attributes have stifled the consolidation of democracy in Bangladesh and Pakistan. The military takeover of Bangladesh in 1975 meant that liberal democracy got doomed in its embryonic stage. The return to democracy after 1991 has been a traumatic political journey wherein the concept of home-grown democracy has become a tool of rhetoric to veil the authoritarian and whimsical character of the popular political class. In a sense, the term democracy had lost almost all of its liberal characteristics in the country (Hossain, 2006, p. 791). Despite satisfying the elementary conditions of a minimalist democracy, it had not made significant progress towards the consolidation of the democratic institutions. Mainly, because the democratically elected leaders behaved in an autocratic manner and used State power to patronize their supporters and subvert their opponents.

The leaders of the two main political parties, Begum Khaleda Zia of the BNP and Sheikh Hasina of the Awami League, had turned the country into scaffolding to decapitate the democratic architecture by their involvement in fierce political confrontation. During the second stint of democratic governance, the country witnessed an opera of dynastic feuds between the Awami League and the BNP. More perilous has been Begum Khalida Zia-led BNP's attempts at bracing its position through a massive Islamization drive that tore apart the secular fabric of Bangladesh's society since 2001. This not only impaired the modernization process but it has also considerably enfeebled the democratic institutions of the country.

Hence, all these developments spawned a tumultuous situation in Bangladesh, which saturated into a political impasse of the highest order in 2006 and drove the country nearly into a massive civil war. In this predicament, the military was compelled to take the centre stage, again demonstrating the political bankruptcy of the country's democratically elected leaders. This fittingly illustrates the reasons for the failure of democracy in Bangladesh. The values that impelled the national movement in 1971 and the people's movement against the military regime in 1991 were thrown into thin air by a fractious political class and its unholy alliance with the conservative religious extremists, leaving adequate space for the military to meddle in civic affairs. Huntington's statement that he made for third wave democracies aptly fits to describe the lamentable state of democracy in Bangladesh. He viewed that

> Threats to third wave democracies are likely to come not from generals and revolutionaries who have nothing but contempt for democracy, but from the participants in the democratic processes itself. These are political leaders and groups who win elections, take power and then manipulate the

mechanisms of democracy to curtail or destroy democracy. (Huntington, 1992, p. 8)

In any case, democracy has been reinstated in Bangladesh and its future and stability is yet to be predicted. This is mainly because the radical religious forces have managed to gain a wider canvas to exercise their influence over civil society. Such leverage has been granted to them by vested political interests in the polity, who have sought to consolidate their position by radicalizing the religious sensibilities of the populous. The results of such endeavours have been apparent. They were demonstrated during the civil unrest, caused due to the activities of the Jamaat-e-Islami in the wake of the protests over the issue of punishing war criminals of the 1971 war under the guidelines of the International Crimes Tribunal. In any case, the significant cause for the state of Bangladesh's politics seems to be the severe economic inequalities that have bedevilled the country ever since its independence. Poverty has been a bane on its society that has bridled modernization process. More than four decades of bad governance did not help the cause of liquidating poverty, in turn it has had a metastatic influence upon the entire polity. Even transition to democracy proved worthless because the success of a democracy lies in the reduction of income inequalities.

In addition to this, the whimsical character of its democratic governments has ridiculed the popular movement that affected the transition to democracy. This has further baffled the public and they are now confronting a civic dilemma whether to oppose the military intervention in favour of a moral claim for democracy or support the military-backed establishment in its cathartic reform agenda, in order to deal with the putrid state of the country's democracy. The military's reform agenda also appears to be dubious, because the army also contemplated the notion of building Bangladesh's own brand of democracy. All this does not augur well for the prospects of constructing a liberal democracy in Bangladesh. As Linz (1990, p. 157) argues, 'the lack of a constitutional spirit and of an understanding of the centrality of the constitutional stability, has been one of the weaknesses of many illiberal third world democracies'. This statement aptly sums up the condition of democracy in contemporary Bangladesh.

A review of the state of democracy in the Maldives, Bangladesh, Afghanistan and Pakistan reflects upon the fact that Islamic extremism has been a common denominator in all the countries when we attempt to identify the key factor that has retarded the process of democratization. Islamic extremism has acted as a countervailing force to modernization and it has contributed significantly to the half-baked modernity syndrome existing in these countries. Modernity in its cultural, political and economic dimension is assumed by the contemporary Islamic fundamentalists to have caused the gradual decline of Islam, or its virtual disappearance as an active force in international and State affairs. The institutions and concepts of secularism and liberalism, nationalism, Marxism and democracy, are blamed for eroding the religion of Islam, leading them to forsake its way of life to other ideologies and other Western models (see Choueri, 2003). Thus, Islamic fundamentalism advocates antithetical versions of the contemporary paradigm of modernity and this tendency has jeopardized the democratization process in the Maldives, Bangladesh, Afghanistan and Pakistan to a considerable extent. This is primarily due to the omnibus influence that Islamic extremism exercises in the socio-economic and political spheres of these countries.

Now, let us consider yet another country that has struggled to consolidate democracy. Nepal, the tiny Himalayan country, has been witnessing political instability for decades which has smothered the process of democratization. The most crucial hurdle in this regard has been the ideological friction between the liberalism of the democrats and the authoritarianism of monarchy and other conservative forces. This strife usually ended in the regime being transformed into a royal autocracy, by the declaration of emergency and royal takeover of all executive powers. At the time of emergency, the royal Nepalese army was endowed with enormous powers, resulting in all the dissenting voices being pummelled severely. The most nefarious thing here has been the contradiction of perceptions that existed among the three claimants of power, the monarchy, the Maoists and the democrats, regarding the character of a democratic State. Hence, the existence of competing and radically incommensurable ideals of democracy, that is, the clash of visions contributed significantly to the civil war (Gellner,

2007, p. 50). However, the morass has been ended by the people's movement of 2006 and now the country is passing through a phase of tectonic transformation.

Further, if we look at Sri Lanka, it may be stated that the most crucial impediment that has been in the way of democratization is the ethno-cultural dichotomy and the resultant conflict. For Daniel, 'the cultural construction of Sri Lankan ethnic identities can be located within two dispositions towards the past, history and heritage. The former associated with Sinhala identity is sharply defined and clearly instantiated, the other is vague, though rich potentially' (Daniel, 1996, p. 27). So, ethno-nationalistic strife's has been one predominant force that shaped the contemporary domestic and foreign affairs of the country. In this regard, Daniel has stated that 'the excess of violence endured by Sri Lankans in the late Twentieth century, takes us to the very limits of culture and its significations' (Daniel, 1998, p. 68).

The key cause for the ethno-cultural divide has been the hegemonic designs of a fringe of Sinhalese, whose overall economic status has been markedly better than others which majorly include the Tamils or the Muslims. The control over material resources facilitated the Sinhalese to get a stronghold upon the political sphere and also translate it into a position of hegemony. As Marx and Engels have stated:

> The ideas of the ruling class are in every epoch the ruling ideas, i.e. the class which is the material force in the society, is at the same time its ruling intellectual force. The class which has the means of material production at its disposal has control at the same time over the means of mental production, so that thereby generally speaking, the ideas of those who lack the means of mental production are subject to it. (Marx & Engels, 1974, p. 64)

It is this kind of dominant position that has enabled the Sinhalese to act as a major pressure group in Sri Lanka and worked towards determining the contours of national politics for their own advantage, that is, to perpetuate the hegemony of the Sinhalese in the socio-economic and political spheres of the country. The political use of Buddhist ideology by the Sinhalese nationalists to foist the hegemony of a fringe has polarized Sri Lankan society (see Tambiah, 1986 & 1992). All this significantly contributed to the radicalization of Tamil political aspirations and also eroded the foundations of the liberal polity in the country.

The futility of the endeavours to explore a political solution to the ethno-political impasse and the abrupt military intervention to untangle the morass reflects upon the fragility of the democratic institutions in Sri Lanka. Ethnicity and religion have played a critical role in engendering internal cleavages in the polities of South Asia, and also have steered-up fierce international tensions at the regional level. The repercussions of the ethno-religious conflicts have been catastrophic; be it the violence unleashed at the time of India's partition, or the India–Pakistan conflict over Jammu and Kashmir; all indicate the hideous impact that religio-civilizational divergences have produced.

Pakistan on its part emerged as a Zionist political idea wherein, new land was promised in the name of nationalism for the subcontinental Muslims. It came with an assurance of allaying the fears of majoritarian persecution that was rightly or wrongly perceived by the Muslim minority of the Indian subcontinent (Devji, 2013, p. 3). However, as a complete departure from its foundational goals, the idea of Pakistan seems to have unfolded as an elite construction, proving to be beneficial only to the condominium of a landed aristocracy, the bureaucracy and the army. With the domination of this oligarchy, the common masses appear to be getting waned away from the very ontic and epistemic idea of Pakistan itself (Alavi, 2002, p. 5123). Pakistan in this sense, seem to be confronting a kind of nationalist impasse, as the contemplated notion of Muslim nationalism appears to be collapsing under the weight of ethno-cultural cleavages. It is manifest in the disenchantment with the very idea of Pakistan, expressed first by the Bengalis and now it is the other non-Punjabi population such as the Baloch, Sindhi and Mohajir (Siddiqi, 2012, p. 1). On this count, the foundations of nationality upon which the idea of Pakistan was sought to be constructed, appear to emerge as merely a kind of exclusionary notion of nationalism that is devoid of inclusiveness even for the Muslims (Devji, 2013, p. 8).

Such a problem of exclusion got compounded as the country has experienced a tumultuous history of imbalance in civil–military relations. The incapability of the State to deal with the strains of modernization has led to the destabilization of the process consolidating the authority in the structure of a strong State. This kind of crisis of authority and structural incapacity led to the intermittent takeover of the institutions of governance by the military (Geller, 1982, p. 45). To make things more complex, the political decay in Pakistan is being exasperated by the menace of radical Islamic extremism. A political flashpoint that tended to deepen as Pakistan ambitiously attempted to tread the path of neoliberal economic reforms since the 1980s.

This precariousness has intensified the legitimation crisis in Pakistan. It has been evident in the dogmatic influence of radical Islamic ideology over the functioning of sociopolitical institutions. It has not only been a major hindrance to both the processes of political modernization and economic development but its omnibus presence has resulted in the unfolding of a persistent threat of a Taliban-like Islamic takeover of Pakistan. This situation has resulted in a political and cultural crisis that has led the Pakistani citizenry into a conundrum, where they may have to make a choice between a weak democratic government, always vulnerable to the extremist pressures, or support a military regime, which may be authoritarian but considered to be a potential hedge against the extremists.

Hence in such a predicament, the civil society comes to an ineluctable conclusion that it would be better to support a military rule which would at least prevent the worst-case proposition of State collapse and an Islamic takeover, rather than commiserate a fragile democratic establishment under which their existence itself may be in jeopardy (Zaidi, 2007, p. 26). On this count, in the domain of the political sphere of Pakistan, the civic obligation tends to be channelled more towards an extra-constitutional authority like the army, rather than getting directed towards a legitimately elected government. Such a political and cultural crisis can be assigned to a kind of negative dialectical interplay of neoliberal economics and radical Islamic ideology that symbolizes the state of political decay and legitimation crisis in Pakistan.

In India, the endeavour of the nascent postcolonial State to bureaucratize the narrative of development and social transformation allowed the bureaucracy to retain its ontic behaviour that was rooted in colonial psychology. Owing to the bureaucratic over determinism of the governmental function that was meant for social change, the bureaucracy managed to exercise an enormous influence upon the everyday socio-economic and political processes in the country (Kaviraj, 2010, p. 154). Such an ontology of the bureaucracy continued, despite many policy reforms. Even after the introduction of the policies of market liberalization leading to the shrinking of the public sector due to the withdrawal of the State, it appeared that there was a scant reduction in the colonial behaviour of the bureaucracy. It still did not seem to have been liberated from the colonial psyche (Kaviraj, 2010, p. 147). Hence, anthropologists researching on the Indian State have noted that the State behaviour in India does not correspond with that of the State behaviour in the developed West (see Gupta 1998, 2012; White, 2004).

In addition to this, decades of experiments with planned economy and State regulation, rather than obliterating the castist conundrum that haunts India's political economy and society seems to have exasperated the same (White, 2004, p. 179). The castist predicament still tends to bedevil India's post-reform political economy that had come with an immense promise of rational organization of economy and society (White, 2004, p. 177). The continuing caste-based violence, humiliation and marginalization, hence, renders the neoliberal reforms in India's political economy to appear merely as a representation of transformation in the lives of the middle class and the capitalists, with the underprivileged still remaining untouched by its benefits (Corbridge, 2010). Such a scenario is inbuilt with the portents of an imminent legitimation crisis in India.

This implies that India is still in the process of a search for the maturity in its democracy. It has not yet succeeded in reaching a stage, wherein it may be perspicuously termed as a flawless and full-fledged democracy. Such a situation signifies the condition of political decay in India. However, in the ultimate analysis, the report card of Indian democracy is relatively better than its South Asian neighbours. It has been successful in holding on to its democratic institutions and has checked any chance of degeneration to any kind of civilian or military autocracy. There are several other anti-modernist forces such as religious fundamentalism and linguistic Chauvinism which have not been mentioned above. Their influence upon the process of democratization also has been one of regression, but the detrimental impact of the factors discussed above seems to be irretrievable. They appear to have suffocated Indian democracy, right at the stage when it was about to attain complete maturity and development.

CONCLUSION

Inability to achieve a fully baked modern society has been an instrumental force in retarding the process of democratization in South Asia. It has made the process more excruciating and also prolonged the solution of numerous other problems of the region. The crises of democratization in South Asia manifests in the weakness of the democratic system of governance in Pakistan, Bangladesh, Afghanistan and Nepal, the centralized character of the polity in the Maldives, the unresolved ethno-cultural divide in Sri Lanka that may exhume at any time, the immature democratic institutions in Bhutan and the existence of a crisis of governability in India manifest in the internal security conundrums and the predicaments of socio-economic inequalities. Thus, the problems of democratization in South Asia manifests at three main levels, structural, institutional and cultural, but their intensity varies from country to country (Chowdhury, 2003, p. 6).

Hence, modernization by ending traditional structures of social hegemony is the pressing requirement for peace, security and stability of South Asia. Until this happens, prospects for the democratization of the region appear nebulous. Significantly because the traditional forces of dominance have fiercely contested the doctrines of modernity with adherence to archaic sociocultural framework and politico-economic principles. This has rendered the polities of South Asia to be mired in history and squinted their national visions. Prioritization of parochial loyalties such as caste, religion or language over that of the nation state, has produced catastrophic consequences. This tendency ultimately has strongly deterred the process of democratization by affecting sociocultural transformation which is an urgent imperative for modernization. Above all, the existence of asymmetry in the levels of techno-economic development and diverse kinds of sociocultural dichotomies among the polities of South Asia has rendered the overall democratization of the entire region into a sought of cognitive complexity.

REFERENCES

Abrams, P. (1982). *Historical sociology*. Open Books.

Alavi, H. (1972). The state in postcolonial societies: Pakistan and Bangladesh. *New Left Review*, 1(74), 59–81.

Alavi, H. (2002). Social forces and ideology in the making of Pakistan. *Economic & Political Weekly*, 37(51), 5119–5124.

Apter, D. (1991). Institutionalism reconsidered. *International Social Science Journal*, 129 (August), 463–482.

Bashiriyeh, H. (1993). *Aqldar Siyasat (reason in politics)*. Negah-e Moaser Publication.

Bhabha, H. (1989). The commitment to theory. In J. Pines & P. Willemen (Eds.), *Questions of the third cinema* (pp. 112–131). BFI Publishing.

Cardoso, F. H., & Faletto, E. (1979). *Dependency and development in Latin America*. California University Press.

Chakrabarty, D. (2000). *Provincialising Europe: Postcolonial thought and historical difference*. Princeton University Press.

Chandran, S. D., & Rajamohan P. G. (2007). Soft, porous or rigid? Towards stable borders in South Asia. *South Asian Survey*, 14(1), 6–21.

Chatterjee, P. (1993). *The nation and its fragments: Colonial and post-colonial histories*. Princeton University Press.

Chowdhury, M. H. (2003). *Democratisation of South Asia: Lessons from American institutions*. Ashgate Publishing Company.

Corbridge, S. (2010). The political economy of development in India since independence. In P. R. Brass (Ed.), *Routledge handbook of South Asian politics* (pp. 305–320). Routledge.

Daniel, V. E. (1996). *Charred lullabies: Chapters in an anthropography of violence*. Princeton University Press.

Daniel, V. E. (1998). The limits of culture. In N. Dirks (Ed.), *Near ruins: Cultural theory at the end of the century* (pp. 67–91). Minnesota University Press.

Devji, F. (2013). *Muslim zion: Pakistan as a political idea*. Harvard University Press.

Diamond, L. (1997). Introduction: A search for consolidation. In L. Diamond, M. E. Plattner, Y. H. Chu, & H. M. Tien (Eds.), *Consolidating the third wave democracies: Regional challenges* (pp. 13–47). Johns Hopkins University Press.

Feng, Z. (2006). A contemporary interpretation of Marx's thoughts on modernity. *Frontiers of Philosophy in China, 1*(2), 254–268.

Frank, A. G. (1967). *Capitalism and under development in Latin America.* Monthly Review Press.

Geller, D. (1982). Economic modernisation and political instability: A casual analysis of bureaucratic-authoritarianism. *Western Political Quarterly, 35*(1), 33–49.

Gellner, N. N. (2007). Democracy in Nepal: Four models. *Seminar, 576,* 50–56.

Giddens, A. (1984). *The constitution of society: Outline of the theory of structuration.* Polity Press.

Giddens, A. (1990). *The consequences of modernity.* Polity Press.

Giddens, A. (1991). *Modernity and self identity: Self and society in the late Modern Age.* Polity Press.

Gill, S. (1993). Gramsci and global politics: Research agenda. In *Gramsci: Historical materialism and international relations* (pp. 1–18). Cambridge University Press.

Gold, D., Lo, Y. H., & Wright, E. O. (1975). Recent development in Marxist theories of capitalist state. *Monthly Review, 27*(5), 29–43.

Goonatilake, S. (1997). The self wandering between cultural localisation and globalisation. In J. N. Peiterse & B. Parekh (Eds.), *The decolonisation of imagination: Culture, knowledge and power* (pp. 225–239). Oxford University Press.

Grare, F. (2011). Pakistani pursuit of democracy. In R. Kalia (Ed.), *Pakistan: From the rhetoric of democracy to the rise of militancy* (pp. 160–176). Routledge.

Grugel, G. (2003). Democratisation studies: Citizenship, globalisation and governance: Government and opposition. *International Journal of Comparative Politics, 38*(2), 235–251.

Gupta, A. (1998). *Postcolonial developments: Agriculture in the making of Modern India.* Duke University Press.

Gupta, A. (2012). *The Red Tape: Bureaucracy, structural violence and poverty in India.* Duke University Press.

Gusfield, J. R. (1967). Tradition and modernity: Misplaced polarities in the study of social change. *The American Journal of Sociology, 72*(4), 351–362.

Habermas, J. (1974). *Theory and practice.* Heinemann.

Habermas, J. (1976). *Legitimation crisis.* Heinemann.

Hajjariyan, S. (2007, 15 May). The nature of a modern state. *harkdaily.*

Harvey, D. (1989). *The condition of postmodernity: An enquiry into the origins of cultural change.* Basil Blackwell.

Held, D. (1993). Democracy from city states to cosmopolitan democracy. In *Prospects for democracy* (pp. 13–50). Stanford University press.

Hossain, M. (2006). Home-grown democracy. *Economic & Political Weekly, 41*(9), 791–782.

Huntington, S. P. (1968). *Political order in changing societies.* Yale University Press.

Huntington, S. P. (1992). *The third wave: Democratisation in the late 20th century.* Oklahoma University Press.

Inglehart, R., & Welzel, C. (2009). How development leads to democracy. *Foreign Affairs, 88*(2), 33–48.

Kamrava, M. (2000). *Politics and society in the developing world* (pp. 4–48). Routledge.

Kaviraj, S. (2000). Modernity and politics in India. *Daedalus, 129*(1), 137–162.

Kaviraj, S. (2010). *The imaginary institution of India.* Permanent Black.

Koch, A. M. (1993). Rationality, romanticism and the individual: Max Weber's modernism and the confrontation with modernity. *Canadian Journal of Political Science, 26*(1), 123–144.

Khilnani, S. (1997). *The idea of India.* Hamish Hamilton.

Kumar, R., & Khwar, M. (Eds.). (1996). *Internal conflicts in South Asia.* SAGE Publications.

Kumar, Sanjeev H. M. (2020). The colonial genealogies of political decay and legitimation crisis: An enquiry into the predicament of state-construction in post-colonial South Asia. *India Quarterly, 76*(2), 276–293.

Linz, J. J. (1990). Transitions to democracy. *The Washington Quarterly, 13*(3), 145–158.

Linz, J. J., & Alfred, S. (1996a). *Problems of democratic transition and consolidation: Southern Europe, South America and the post-communist Europe.* Johns Hopkins University Press.

Linz, J. J., & Alfred, S. (1996b). Towards consolidated democracies. *Journal of Democracy, 7*(2), 14–33.

Malik, D. (2007). The political economy of communalism: A response from the left. In J. P. Neelsen & D. Malik (Eds.), *Crisis of state and nation: South Asian states between nation-building and fragmentation* (pp. 363–398). Manohar.

Markey, D. (2007). A false choice in Pakistan. *Foreign Affairs, 86*(4), 85–102.

Marx, K. (1973). *Grundrisse.* Penguin Books.

Marx, K., & Engels, F. (1974). German ideology. In *Selected works* (Vol. 1). Lawrence and Wishart.

Menon, D. M. (2002). Religion and colonial modernity: Rethinking belief and identity. *Economic & Political Weekly, 37*(17), 1662–1667.

Nandy, A. (1983). *The intimate enemy: Loss and recovery of self under colonialism.* Oxford University Press.

Neelsen, J. P., & Malik., D. (2007). South Asia-social fragmentation and political crisis in the periphery. In J. P. Neelsen & D. Malik (Eds.), *Crisis of state and nation: South Asian states between nation-building and fragmentation* (pp. 10–36). Manohar.

Parry, G., & Moran, M. (1994). Introduction: Problems and democratisation. In *Democracy and democratisation*. Routledge.

Peceny, M. (1999). The social construction of democracy. *International Studies Review*, 1(1), 95–102

Prakash, G. (1990). Writing post-oriental histories of the Third World: Perspectives from Indian historiography. *Comparative Studies in Society and History*, 32(2), 383–408.

Prakash, G. (1992). Postcolonial criticism and Indian historiography. *Social Text*, 31/32, 8–19.

Prakash, G. (1994). Subaltern studies as postcolonial criticism. *American Historical Review*. 99(5), 1475–1490.

Said, E. W. (1978). *Orientalism*. Wintage Books.

Shin, D. (1994). On the third wave of democratisation: A synthesis and evaluation of recent theory and research. *World Politics*, 47(1), 143–150.

Siddiqi, F. H. (2012). *The politics of ethnicity in Pakistan: The Baloch, Sindhi and Mohajir ethnic movements*. Routledge.

Smith, T. (1979). The underdevelopment of development literature: The case of dependency theory. *World Politics*, 31(2), 247–288.

Spencer, J. (2007). *Anthropology, politics and state: Democracy and violence in South Asia*. Cambridge University Press.

Spivak, G. C. (1990). Poststructuralism, marginality, postcoloniality and value. In P. Collier & H. Geyer-Ryan (Eds.), *Literary Theory Today*. Polity Press.

Tambiah, S. J. (1986). *Sri Lanka: Ethnic fratricide and the dismantling of democracy*. Chicago University Press.

Tambiah, S. J. (1992). *Buddhism betrayed: Religion, politics and violence in Sri Lanka*. Chicago University Press.

Uyangoda, J. (2007). Sri Lanka: Democracy and the hegemony of the fringe. *Seminar*, 576, 39–49.

Uzelac, G. (2002). The morphogenesis of nation. In S. Malesevic & M. Haugaard (Eds.), *Making sense of collectivity: Ethnicity, nationalism and globalisation* (pp. 138–166). Pluto Press.

Wallerstein, I. (1974). *The modern world system: Capitalist agriculture and the origins of the European world economy*. Academic Publishers.

Weber, M. (1946). *From Max Weber: Essays in sociology*. (E. Shils & H. Finch, Trans. and Ed.). Free Press.

Weber, M. (1949). *The methodology of the social sciences*. (E. Shils & J. Finch, Trans. and Ed.). Free Press.

Weber, M. (1958). *The protestant ethic and the spirit of capitalism*. Scribner.

Weber, M. (1978). *Economy and society*. University of California Press.

White, B. H. (2004). *India working*. Cambridge University Press.

Wright, R. (1996). Islam and democracy: Two visions of reformations. *Journal of Democracy*, 7(2), 71–97.

Zaidi, A. S. (2007). Pakistan a democracy? *Seminar, 576,* 13–27.

Zakaria, F. (1997). The rise of illiberal democracy. *Foreign Affairs, 76*(6), 22–43.

Zakaria, F. (2003). *The future of freedom: Illiberal democracy at home and abroad.* W. W. Norton.

Ziemann, W., & Lazendorfer, M. (1977). State in peripheral societies. In R. Miliband & J. Saville (Eds.), *The socialist register 1977* (pp. 143–177). Merlin Press.

Political Decay and the Legitimation Crisis in South Asia

Underlying the different case scenarios of South Asia has been the inability of the decolonized periphery to successfully adopt the institutional values imported by the imperial metropolis during the age of colonial transition (Halvorson, 2013, p. 19). This ultimately resulted in the syndrome of what has been termed as the postcolonial predicament in South Asia. It is in the context of this very postcolonial genealogy that we must map the interactions between the precolonial native traditions, colonially imposed morals of modernity and the processes of State-making, State-construction and economic development in the polities of South Asia. The deconstruction of such a linkage holds the key for understanding why colonial psychology[1] has penetrated deeply in the political imagery of South Asia, paving way for the engendering of a complex trajectory of the scenario of political decay and legitimation crisis among the States of the region.

---

[1] The term 'colonial psychology' has been borrowed here from Ashis Nandy who employs psychoanalysis in postcolonial theory (Young, 2016, p. 341). For Nandy, colonialism is a shared culture which emerges as a product of the interaction between the colonizer and the colonized. It manifested as the psychological dominance of the European middle class in the colony (Nandy, 1983, p. 44). As an ideology, the influence of colonialism does not end with the formal departure of the colonizers from the erstwhile colony. Rather, its impact lives beyond the epoch of colonial rule and is visible in many sectors of the life of postcolonial societies. In this way, colonialism manifests as an enduring psychological state (Nandy, 1983, p. 2). Hence, for Nandy, 'colonialism is a matter of consciousness and needs to be defined in the minds of men' (Nandy, 1983, p. 63).

The entropy that the political system of Pakistan has undergone due to the crises of State-making can be considered a crucial example to substantiate this phenomenon. Such entropy of the postcolonial society has been exasperated by the omnibus influence of the military–bureaucratic oligarchy upon political processes. This has happened because of an alignment struck by the military–bureaucratic oligarchy with the indigenous bourgeoisie, the metropolitan neocolonialist bourgeoisie and the landed aristocracy. Such an alignment ushered in with the creation of what Hamza Alavi describes as the 'over-developed State' (Alavi, 1972). Such an influence of the overdeveloped State persists even as the per capita number of civil servants in both these subcontinental States is very limited. As compared to the North American or European democracies where the number of civil servants per capita is much larger, South Asian bureaucracies do not possess such numbers. Besides, unlike the Euro-American democracies, bureaucracies in South Asia have less information about the citizenry and are also not connected deeply to the general public.

However, on this count, the fundamental epistemic question that arises is as to how an overdeveloped or a controlling State has tended to sustain its functional value in postcolonial South Asia, despite such an anomaly. Such an overbearing presence of the controlling State in postcolonial South Asia can be accredited to the region's colonial genealogy. In South Asia, it has now been established that the bureaucracy which is a key instrument of the controlling State still functions according to the whims of colonial psychology. During the British Empire, the colonial State had expected to make the bureaucracy as an instrument of governance that would act as an intermediary between the minority elite governors of the metropolis and a largely uninformed and unconcerned majority population of the governed periphery. This colonial intention was made very clear in Lord Thomas Macaulay's agenda of the oriental plan of education that was laid out in his minute on India's education, presented to the Governor-General-in-Council or the Indian Council at Calcutta on 2 February 1835. Lord Macaulay stated thus:

> We must at present do our best to form a class who may be interpreters between us and the millions whom we govern, a class of persons, Indian in blood and colour, but English in tastes, in opinions, in morals and in intellect. The fulfillment of the British connection with India then involved nothing less than the complete transformation of India's culture and society. Its' outcome would be the creation of an India politically independent, but one that embodied an imperishable empire of our arts and of our morals, our literature and of our laws. (Macaulay, 1835, p. 240)

Such a plan of education, hence, aimed at creating a class of rulers from within the native populous who would act as mediators between the colonial authority and the native populous. The main objective was to divide the polity itself into a class of loyalists who would control their population under the directions of a foreign government. The repercussions of the colonial creation of such a class in South Asia are apparently being felt in the experiences of State construction in postcolonial polities of the region. It is on the foundations of this assessment of the emergence of an overdeveloped or a controlling State as a product of the colonial legacy; we must understand the multilayered and multifaceted contours of political decay and the legitimation crisis in the Indian subcontinent. By drawing instances from Pakistan and India, we intend to show here how colonial ontology of spatial history and temporal geography tend to knit together the sociocultural and political genealogy of the countries of the Indian subcontinent. It is this very genealogical connection that lies at the bottom of the making and sustenance of the overdeveloped or a controlling State in the countries of this subregional formation. Pakistan and India in this regard must be seen as two countries whose sociopolitical genealogies can be traced to the ontic and epistemic structures that are embedded in the ontology of India's colonial history.

However, while doing this, the question arises here as to why unlike in India wherein, the bureaucracy and the armed forces have been kept under stringent machinery of checks and balances, Pakistan has not only failed to manage the contours of civil–military relations, but also been unsuccessful to regulate the extra-judicial sway of these institutions in a similar manner. In India, the broadening of the State-building processes through the creation of statutory bodies such as the Lokpal, Lokayukta and the central vigilance commission and stringent democratic control over the armed forces resulted in the regulation of any form of overdeterministic role of these institutions that is beyond the normative exemplars laid down by the constitution. This has not been the case with Pakistan which has demonstrated a deep-seated incapacity to achieve such forms of checks and balances. It has been argued in this regard that the multiple claims of power and a lack of consensus over the nature of political institutions to be evolved in Pakistan resulted in the emergence of a weak and unstable State. This is exactly the reason for the insinuating influence of these institutions and the erosion of the contours of democratic governance in Pakistan. It is this very condition that we seek to designate as political decay and legitimation crisis.

Besides, unlike India that has emerged to be a status quo developmental State,[2] Pakistan has evolved into a revisionist security State.[3] Such a divergence in the trajectory of State construction has happened, despite both emanating out of the common historical genealogies that were characterized by the shared legacy of the complex processes of colonial transition, decolonization and the pressures of postcolonial State-making. However, the responses of India and Pakistan to the contemporary implications of the structures and processes of such shared historical experiences were antithetical to each other. On the one hand, India endeavoured to strengthen the liberal norms of democratic decentralization, civilian control over the defence forces and

[2] For Leftwich,

> The developmental state or interchangeably state development capitalism refers to a model of capitalism in which state acquires more independence, autonomy and political power in order to drive and control the economic growth. This kind of state is characterized by having strong state intervention as well as extensive regulation and planning. (Leftwich, 1995, pp. 400–427)

[3] According to Dandeker,

> Security state constantly enlarges its military and policing capabilities and uses intelligence, secrecy, and surveillance, both overtly and covertly, to control, administer and safeguard sovereign power and lives of its citizens. This kind of a state usurps unbridled and extraordinary power, legitimized by the external or internal threat perception, through which the paradigm of security is made as a primary and normalized condition. (Dandeker, 1990, pp. 45–47)

adequate checks and balances between the three principal agencies of the government; the legislature, executive and the judiciary. India also not only rigorously maintained the functioning of procedural democracy via regular free and fair elections[4] but also attempted to reach the goal of transforming the country into a substantive democracy[5] by constantly advancing policies to boost the welfare, social security and human rights of its citizens. Thus, the track record of India in its efforts to deepen democracy has been quite satisfactory. However, India still grapples with the challenges of bureaucratic intrusion and caste hierarchies that have hampered its evolution into a mature democracy. In this sense, India confronts its own challenges in terms of what has been designated as the political decay and the legitimation crisis.

On the other hand, the bitter memories associated with the inaugural moment of Pakistan that was engendered by the mass communal pogrom and the militarization of the Kashmir imbroglio penetrated deeply into the political consciousness of the Pakistani elite. It convinced the leaders like General Mohammad Ayub Khan to assume that Pakistan's survival largely depended upon the possession of a well-trained, well-equipped and well-led army (Khan, 1967, p. 2).

[4] Procedural democracy is a form of democracy which is about particular kinds of rules and procedures such as free, fair and regular elections, fair competition among political parties, political equality, universal adult suffrage, etc., which produce electorally legitimate government. Robert A. Dahl, in his 1989 book *Democracy and Its Critique,* characterizes a 'perfect procedural democracy' having five key elements: 'political equality, effective participation, enlightened understanding, agenda control, and power to demos' (Dahl, 1989, p. 20).

[5] Substantive democracy is not just about democratic elections; it requires a whole range of institutions that provide meaningful checks and balances on power, and all the authorities of state must be subjected to legislative and judicial scrutiny. In general, electoral outcomes are representative of the people, and democratic governments must function in the interest of the people. In other words, the will of the people is significant for any government in their political affairs. As David Held notes in *Models of Democracy* (2006),

> Substantive democracy implies denial of any form of totalitarianism or absolutism and the supremacy of fundamental rights, dignity and autonomy of people above any kind of political, social, cultural, and economic power. Thus, substantive democracy brings people at the centre of the governmental agendas and democratic governance. (Held, 2006, p. 14)

One leader in the early 1950s also went to the extent of making a melo-dramatic assertion that he would starve before allowing the defences of Pakistan to be weakened (McGarr, 2013, p. 21). All this led towards the evolution of Pakistan as more of a security State (Rais, 2017, p. 4) rather than a developmental State (Ayoob, 1991, p. 281). It meant that the primacy of the security problematique of the State was put above all considerations of political development and human emancipation (Samad, 1995, p. 128).

In addition to this, Pakistan's entanglement with India in a militarized conflict on the issue of Jammu and Kashmir right at the beginning of assuming formal Statehood, allowed the army to penetrate deep into the corridors of political power in the country (Rizvi, 1974, pp. 161–165). The contested territoriality of Jammu and Kashmir has factored deeply in determining the contours of the irredentist security and foreign policy of Pakistan. It happened as Kashmir became the symbolic representation of the idea of Pakistan (Cohen, 2004, p. 52). The issue of Jammu and Kashmir has largely been responsible for the making of Pakistan into a revisionist State that is guided by the principle of cartographic fundamentalism. Subsequently, the first Kashmir war became the defining moment in the history of the evolution of the identity of Pakistan, as it enforced upon it, the compulsions of revisionism and cartographic fundamen-talism to protect that very identity (Zaheer, 1998, p. 63). Owing to this, Pakistan focused on increased defence spending by sidelining the pressing developmental imperatives (Jalal, 1995, p. 74).

This laid the foundation for the building of a military-dominated State in Pakistan that has been variously designated as the praetorian State (Talbot, 1998, p. 3), an overdeveloped State (Alavi, 1972, pp. 59–81), a garrison State (Ahmed, 2013), a parallel State (Aziz, 2008), and a State pivoted upon a political economy of defence (see Jalal, 1990 & 1995). In this entire process, the civilian bureaucracy acted as a junior partner to the army (Jalal, 1995, p. 65). Pakistan in this manner excessively militarized the motto of its postcolonial political development and transformed itself into what T. V. Paul described as the warrior State (Paul, 2014, p. 2).

The first Kashmir war of 1947–1948 that happened at the very inaugural moment of the State formation in Pakistan, thus fomented the process of the transformation of the polity into a war-making State (Swami, 2007, p. 26; Ziring, 2003, pp. 40–41). To put it in the perspective of Charles Tilly, war made a war-making State (Shah, 2014, p. 13). Since then, the army has constantly justified its civilian presence in the name of national security and defended its extra-constitutional role by emphasizing on the incompetence of the country's political class (Wilcox, 1958, p. 142).

THE POLITICAL DECAY AND LEGITIMATION CRISIS IN PAKISTAN

In the making of Pakistan, religion has been the determinant of nationality (Jalal, 1994, p. 1). Till today, this factor has deeply underpinned the trajectory of the structuring of the nation-building process in Pakistan. To complicate the situation, Pakistan is not only armed with nuclear weapons, but it is also heavily infested with a growing mass of domestic radical Islamists. Owing to all this, Pakistan has been famously designated as one of the most dangerous places on earth. At the bottom of such a quagmire, lies a feudal political establishment that is largely interested in promoting and preserving its own narrow class interests. This class has displayed a gross sense of inability and unwillingness to seriously address the emergent threats the country faces (Schmidt, 2009, p. 26). Until these dynamic changes, Pakistan would be unable to stop the spread of radical Islam within its own borders.

Unfortunately, the country has nothing in the nature of Pakistani political culture nor in the performance of its political class since the founding of the State that provides any grounds for optimism (Schmidt, 2009, p. 26). This clearly explains as to why Hamza Alavi, way back in the 1970s, dubbed Pakistan as an overdeveloped State. Week political institutions operated by self-seeking feudal class facilitated the military–bureaucratic complex to gain enormous influence over the civic affairs of the country. Lack of visionary leaders and a constant struggle for power among various sections of the political class resulted in the army emerging as the most organized and influential component of the Pakistani polity.

Due to this, Pakistan manifests as a praetorian quasi-democratic State (Hagerty, 2020, p. 5). Presently, the civilian government led by Imran Khan appears to be a hybrid regime,[6] with the military strongly dominating vital sectors of society and politics (Shafqat, 2021, p. 183). Pakistan has been designated as a hybrid regime because it has emerged to be neither autocratic nor democratic, but manifests as a combination of both, with the military having a definite edge over any other State institutions (Oldenburg, 2017, pp. 6–7). This demonstrates that even as the civilian governments are in office, there tends to be an indirect rule of the military and its associated organizations such as the Inter-Services Intelligence (ISI; Mukherjee, 2017, p. 178).

This has been the trajectory of political processes in Pakistan, even as the country has witnessed an unprecedented course of democratic transition. For the first time in the history of Pakistan, it has witnessed three successive democratic regimes assuming office, with two consecutive peaceful transitions, a kind of change that has been unprecedented in the political history of Pakistan. By virtue of this, presently Imran Khan's right-wing Pakistan Tehreek-e-Insaf (PTI) is heading the civilian government. However, the questions still remain as to whether Pakistan is moving towards democratic consolidation and has it gained the capacity to mature into a substantive democracy? Or will the fulfilment of the lowest minimum bar of a procedural democracy which is the holding of elections, lead towards the inception of an autonomous civilian government (Sehmitter & Karl, 1991, p. 78).

Indicative of this, the army still enjoys the same clout which it has successfully sustained right from the formation of the State of Pakistan, despite the processes of democratic transition that occurred due to the holding of elections. Even the Imran Khan-led PTI won the elections only because the military/judiciary alliance backed up the party (Congressional Research Service, 2020). Such a hegemonic position of the army endures as it remains the strategic alternative intermediary

[6] For a theoretical treatment of the concept of 'hybrid regimes', see Diamond (2002, pp. 21–35).

for maintaining proper channels of communication with the foreign countries, non-State actors and political leaders belonging to different ideological and organizational dispensations. All this allows the army to execute a politburo style of political functioning (Shafqat, 2019, p. 50). This kind of position of the army which has been designated as the military hegemony facilitates it to not only control domestic politics but also regulate crucial spheres of the country's international affairs like defence and foreign policy (Shafqat, 1997, p. 7). Owing to this, the army has been designated as the parallel State in Pakistan wherein, the military identifies itself with the State, rather than acting as a subset of the broader governance structure (Aziz, 2008, pp. 1–3).

A critical cause that has factored deeply in the degeneration of the structure of the Pakistani polity has been patronage politics perpetuated by its self-seeking politicians. The fundamental problem of Pakistan's political parties is that they have failed to aggregate national interest and deeply pursue personal rather than collective agendas. They do not tend to develop robust party platforms; indeed, they are more interested in servicing patronage networks than promulgating and shepherding effective policies (Fair, 2011a, p. 95). Owing to this, democracy has been battling to survive in Pakistan. It was one of the two States that emerged out of the breakup of the British colonial empire in the Indian subcontinent. It was created as an imagined homeland for South Asian Muslims (Dhulipala, 2015, pp. 1–3).

However, ever since the day of its genesis, Pakistan's social and political dynamics have been in deep turmoil, mainly because of the chronic institutional crisis that has debilitated the processes of nation-formation, State-making, State-construction and democratization (Ganguly, 2010, pp. 81 & 83). The major signifiers of such a scenario manifest in a complex concoction of State failure, fears of the implosion of its territorial integrity, military domination, Islamic fundamentalism and a fragile liberal democratic architecture (Jalal, 2014, p. 3). Hence, even almost after more than seven decades of existence, Pakistan still remains an enigma. It was born as a homeland for the Muslims of the Indian subcontinent, with a staunch rejection of theocracy. However, since its early days, the country has been caught up in between the pulls of political Islam vs Western constitutionalism and democracy vs military authoritarianism. As a result of this, the country has been constantly bedevilled by the uncertainty of defining itself as a nation, with the very idea of Pakistan itself getting subjected to plural interpretations. The ultimate challenge for Pakistan hence has been the conundrum of forging a coherent national identity (Shaikh, 2009, p. 1).

Owing to such a conundrum, Pakistan gradually began to develop a kind of an ambiguous relationship with Islam that led to the emergence of a kind of complex concoction between Islam, nationalism and the ideas of territorial sovereignty and the politics of democratic governance. Such a concoction has been deeply problematic and it undergirds the ideological uncertainty that is tormenting the polity in contemporary Pakistan (Shaikh, 2009, p. 2). As a product of this ideological uncertainty, a deep-seated political vacuum seems to have been created in Pakistan. A void that has allowed the extremist Islamic forces to expand their sway and as a consequence of this, everywhere in Pakistan, the Islamic forces have grown in strength. Presently, they are operating with impunity and considerably control the cultural life, social psyche and political processes in the country (Bajpai, 2011, pp. 77–78). On this count, Pakistan is now in a state of cognitive dissonance and the difficulties of transformation from this state emanate out of the paucity of political vision and cohesive social action. It is precisely because of this, the question of political stability has been particularly a critical one for Pakistan and the army has exploited this unsettled situation and wielded considerable influence over the country's domestic politics and foreign affairs (Jalal, 2014, p. 4).

A MILITARIZED DEMOCRACY?

The army has been at the epicentre of the postcolonial crisis of the nation state in Pakistan. It assumed such a role when the country was still in the embryonic stage of the formation of the contours of its State and the nationalist imagery (Newman, 1959, pp. 18–33). The failure of the civilian political elite to control the competing visions pertaining to the modes of nation state formation, allowed the army to intrude into the civilian affairs and engage itself in the interpretation of the idea of Pakistan and its nationalist imagery (Wilcox, 1965, pp. 142–163). Owing to this, it appears that the issue of democracy as against authoritarianism in Pakistan still remains unresolved.

In just over seven decades of its history, Pakistan has witnessed the demolition of democratic architecture on four occasions, each time to be substituted by an autocratic military regime. In between eras of military dictatorship, the rare periods of civilian governments that Pakistan has experienced since 1958 have been pseudo-democratic intervals during which the military kept pulling the strings allowing the civilians only a narrow political space to manage current affairs and making sure that nothing considered essential for the military remained outside its control. The civilian elites on their part neither endeavoured at consolidating democracy nor did they attempt at providing good governance. They also lacked respect for the basic values of a democracy (Grare, 2011, p. 161).

However, it must be noted that it is not just the unpopularity of the political class that intermittently brings the army to the political scene, but its long-established image in Pakistan and its importance as an employer, educator and development agency that makes the army a potent force to be reckoned with (Talbot, 2000, p. 6). The army has incarnated into such a multifaceted role and has deeply penetrated the multilayered strands of the Pakistani polity because it has not merely remained confined to the contours of defence policy. Rather, it has expanded its business activities into the spheres of banking, business firms, real estate, insurance, transport and entertainment (Siddiqa, 2007, pp. 145–150). It has also spread its sway in the field of education by establishing schools and universities (Rahman, 2004, pp. 53–56). Such an enormous sociocultural and economic penetration of the army that has been acquired by decades of control over the structures of the State is an incentive for its persistence at the helm of political affairs (Zaidi, 2005, p. 5177).

Besides, the Pakistan army like any other established organization has also acquired a deep-seated sense of class consciousness which it has sought to protect by investing heavily in all the sectors of the Pakistani polity. Driven by its class consciousness, the army has gained a heightened sense of self-recognition and feeling of difference, by developing a corporate identity of its own (Nasr, 2005, p. 186). It is the very class consciousness emanating out of the discipline, regimentation and professionalism inbuilt in the army that also tends to guide its political behaviour (Janowitz, 1977, p. 146). Hence, the interests engendered by the Pakistani army's corporate identity have played a significant role in shaping its inclinations towards interventions in civic affairs (Aziz, 2008, pp. 66, 83–88 & 93–96).

By virtue of this, the military has never faced resistance while assuming power. Rather, political parties and the public at large have invited the military. In fact, for all practical purposes in Pakistan, no political institution has the steam to circumvent any decision of the army (Zaidi, 2007, p. 27). The popular support that General Musharraf was able to commend, especially from the urban elite, in October 1999 after he dislodged the incompetent democratic establishment of Nawaz Sharif and assumed to himself all executive powers, provides credence to the above argument. It can also be noted here that history is witness to the fact that military regimes in Pakistan have not been thrown out of power by a mass movement, but they tend to retire from politics when they run out of steam (Zaidi, 2007, p. 31). Above all, the public and the intelligentsia have often approached the army to bail out the country from the quagmire created by the incompetence of the civilian leadership. The Army Chief has been expected to put pressure on the prime minister to avoid engaging in corruption, nepotism and even criminality (Musharraf, 2006, p. 137).

This totally ridicules what Linz has argued regarding a consolidated democracy, where none can veto the decisions of the democratically elected decision-makers. In Pakistan, it is the other way around; nobody seems to be in a position to challenge the decisions of the army. The futile endeavour of the democratic government to bring the ISI under the purview of the interior ministry perspicuously establishes this phenomenon. Hence, it is quite clear that the civilian rulers of Pakistan do not have the ability to exert real control over the ISI or the army (Guruswamy, 2008).

To place it in the prism of Foucault's erudite proclamation which stated that 'power is exercised and not possessed', it may be argued that although the democratic establishment possesses power it does not exercise it. Rather, it is the military establishment that actually exercises power in Pakistan. Hence, in admiration of Foucault's words, it may be stated that in Pakistan, the possessor of power may not hold a pivotal position as compared with those who actually exercise it.

Pakistan army also harbours the belief that it is the only institution capable of not only protecting the State but also managing its political and administrative affairs (Fair, 2014a, p. 21). A large swath of popular opinion has also given into this belief (Siddiqa, 2014). This is because of the enduring weakness of the civilian political class and the sustained confidence of the army to consider itself as the centre of gravity, in so far as the survival and stability of Pakistan is concerned (Shah, 2014, p. 23). Hence, the army is the most visible organization, when it comes to the issue of the setting not only the agenda of Pakistan's defence and foreign policy but also, in shaping the organizational contours of domestic politics. The rise and sustenance of Islamism as a foundational driving force in the politics of Pakistan has also been an integral component of such a process of agenda setting. In pursuit of this, the military has often shown a willingness to partner with the Islamists in order to dominate domestic politics (Markey, 2007, p. 85).

This is the greatest threat that contemporary Pakistan is facing, mainly because of the fact that the basis of nationhood in Pakistan is Islam and when the State proclaims a religious identity (a cultural construct) in addition to assuming a religious vocation (a political factor), it is bound to clash with those who traditionally organize religious life (Boquerat & Hussain, 2011, pp. 177 & 190). Such a syndrome has not only retarded the modernization process, much due to the wrecking tactics of the Islamists, but it has also enhanced the public dilemma in an exponential manner. It was largely due to their unflinching faith over the army as a saviour against the tempest of Islamic extremism and their growing disenchantment towards the democratic institutions. This is exactly the situation of legitimation crisis for Pakistan wherein; people have tended to show more faith in the army as compared to that of the elected government.

The army on its part has dexterously camouflaged the existence of the army/Islamists condominium by projecting itself as the sole protector of the State from an imminent Taliban like Islamic takeover

(Waseem, 2007, pp. 191–192). Besides, it has also successfully engendered the threat of existential crisis in the context of India and Afghanistan (Shah, 2014, p. X). To deal with this, the army argues that Pakistan lacks adequate strategic-depth. Hence, in such a scenario, it is the army that emerges as the ultimate guardian of Pakistan (Fair, 2011a, p. 97). Such a concocted mix of issues in the sphere of both domestic and international politics for the army makes up a formidable justification for its extra-constitutional involvement in the institutions managing the country's domestic and international politics, and the mechanisms that motor the organizational actions of social structuration (Fair, 2011a, p. 97). Owing to this, the military in Pakistan operates as what has been called the deep State (Kalia, 2011, p. 39).

On the basis of this, it may be observed that the enduring crisis situation of Pakistan has been characterized by three stages of evolution: regime crisis, crisis of the State and crisis of society. Since the regime of General Muhammad Zia-ul-Haq, these have evolved simultaneously. Thus, the Pakistani crisis is complex and cannot merely be reduced to the crisis of the State and democratic order (Weidemann, 2007 p. 97). Owing to such a complex trajectory of State-construction and sociocultural transition, Anatol Lieven (2011) has designated Pakistan as a 'Hard Country'. The key problem for Pakistan however has not been establishing democracy, but it has been the problem of its consolidation. In Pakistan, the military has always fancied its chance of acquiring control over civilian institutions, whenever the democratic institutions have become flimsy due to the incompetence of the political class. However, recent experience indicates towards a horizon of hope, with the installation of a democratically elected government and the end of military rule in Pakistan. But the caveat here is that whether this transition is irreversible? Significantly due to the bespattered history of Pakistan, where ulterior control over the government by the military has been an apparent phenomenon.

THE ISLAMIZATION OF THE PAKISTANI PUBLIC CULTURE

The political scenario of Pakistan tends to have got compounded with the fractious engagement of right-wing politicians in Islamizing the public culture by employing religion as an instrument of political populism. This was done by endeavours of rulers like Zia-ul-Haq who transformed Pakistan's traditional society into a bastion of religious fundamentalism and terrorism (Neelsen & Malik, 2007, p. 13). The process of decadence began with the assassination of the first prime minister Liaquat Ali Khan in 1951, after which Pakistan has been confronted with a continuing and open regime crisis. This was a point of departure from the liberal and democratic foundations of the State and a transformation towards an Islamic State.

The objectives resolution of 12 March 1949 formulated by the constituent assembly, left the debate on whether Pakistan should be a constitutional democracy or an Islamic State, wide open for multiple and devious interpretations (Rais, 2017, p. 14). Acting as the constitutional grundnorm or a kind of preamble to the future constitutions, the Objectives Resolution laid down the idea of Pakistan as a State and the role of Islam in the sociopolitical affairs of the country. It was a monumental influence upon the constitution-making processes in Pakistan before it finally became the operative part of the constitution in 1985 (Binder, 1961, pp. 116–153; Zafar, 2001, pp. 31–32). For the Islamists, the inclusion of this resolution as the preamble of the constitution, justified the definition of Pakistan as an Islamic State because the inaugural formula states the absolute sovereignty of Allah and the limited authority of the State. In 1985, Zia made it a constitutional requirement for all laws and legal acts to be in concurrence with the Quran and the Sunnah (Weidemann, 2007, p. 94).

Further under Zia, rigorous steps such as the creation of sharia courts, the levying of the Islamic charity taxes, the introduction of the punishments that were based on the Quran and the authentic sunnah and the expansion of the madrassa system of Islamic education were introduced (Haqqani, 2005, pp. 131–157; Talbot, 1998, pp. 270–283; Ziring, 2003, pp. 164–165, 171, 183, 184–185). In any case, during the regime of Zia ul-Haq, it was the army that was at the centre of the Islamization drive in Pakistan (Khan, 1999, p. 167). When General Zia took over as Chief of Army Staff, he introduced purely an Islamic vocabulary to define the motto of the army (Jalal, 2008, pp. 274–275). It consisted of *iman* (faith), *taqqwa* (piety) and *jihad-fi-sibilillah* (holy war in the name of god; Nawaz, 2008, p. 384). Zia justified such a State-sponsored Islamization drive in the belief that Islam was the raison d'être of Pakistan. It has been argued in this regard by Khan that

> For the first time, a Maulvi, a deeply religious person, was the head of the State, head of the Government and the army chief—a frightening combination and he seemed determined to recreate the Islamic legal and social order that originated centuries ago in tribal Arabia. (Khan, 2000, p. 94)

After this, the officer core tended to be considerably Islamized (Rizvi, 2000, pp. 208–210).

This resulted in the creation of a powerful group of Mullahs, who began to exert considerable influence over the politics and society of Pakistan. Owing to this, the Muslim State that the founding father Quaid-e-Azam Mohammed Ali Jinnah envisioned before the partition in 1947 is very much different from the Pakistan we see today. During its short history, the country has grappled with a continuous process of defining and redefining the idea of Pakistan in which the place of Islam has acquired a pivotal position. Such a process of interpretation and the reinterpretation of the idea of Pakistan seemed to be most explicit during the rule of General Zia-ul-Haq (Bokhari, 2011, p. 85). Presently, Pakistan faces a major threat to its very existence from radical Islamists which its self-absorbed political culture is ill-equipped to resist. Over the last two decades, the forces of radical Islam have constituted a rising tide that now threatens even to wash over the Pakistani ruling establishment (Fair, 2011a, p. 97). This fact gains credence with the rapid expansion of the Pakistani Taliban and the way in which the group besieged the country during electoral processes. The Taliban in Pakistan intends to perpetuate the state of instability in the country through their subversive activities.

In addition to this off-late, the country has also confronted insurgency fomented by the Tehrik-i-Taliban Pakistan (TTP) which mainly operates in the Pashtun dominated areas of the Federally Administered Tribal Areas (FATA) and parts of the Khyber Pakhtunkhwa. The organization comprises several Deobandi-affiliated organizations that draw their members from a raft of Deobandi militant groups such as the Sipah-e-Sahaba (SSP), Lashkar-e-Jhangvi (LeJ),

Jaish-e-Muhammad (JeM) and the Harkat-ul-Jihad al-Islami (HUM). These Deobandi militant groups are also tied up to the Deobandi Islamist political parties such as the factions of the Jamiat Ulema-e-Islam. Pakistan's ability to decisively eliminate these groups is limited by the fact that Pakistan still seeks to protect groups like JeM (Fair, 2011b, p. 110).

Besides, the support that the Pakistani State has rendered to Lashkar-e-Tayyiba (LeT) which is now operating in the name of Jama'at-ud-Dawa (JuD), after its attack on Mumbai on 26 November 2008 has increased rather than getting diminished. Pakistani security managers also believe that the JeM would reorient against India and become an ally one day, rather than remaining a potential foe of the State (Fair, 2011a, p. 100). Owing to all this, although Pakistan is characterized as a failing State the reality is much more complex (Schmidt, 2009, p. 26).

The sweep and influence of the radical Islamic ideology over Pakistan's polity can be gauged by the results of the following survey data. It was conducted in 2009 with 6000 respondents belonging to all the four provinces of the country (Fair, 2010). Nearly one-third of the respondents felt that Pakistan was governed on the basis of Islamic principles. Nearly 70 per cent of respondents believed that Sharia should play a larger role in Pakistan's legal/juridical process, whereas only 1 in 10 wanted it to play a smaller role. Sharia meant good governance which would translate into greater access to justice and reduction of corruption. Pakistanis remain divided on the best ways to deal with the Pakistani Taliban. Large swaths of Pakistanis support peace deals with them and they have also deeply torn apart regarding the idea of the use of military force to defeat them (Fair, 2011a, p. 93). The ramifications of this are very much apparent and get reflected in the systemic crisis that Pakistan is going through. If Pakistan cannot abandon Islamic militancy as an external power projection, its ability to eliminate its internal threat will be very limited (Fair, 2011a, p. 101). Here, we can take into cognizance the cogent argument of David Gilmartin. He has argued thus:

> The reconciliation of a mediatory democracy with the public assertions of the Islamic community continues to preoccupy many Pakistanis. This is

because the legacy of both empire and Islam have shaped the history of Pakistani State and society. (Gilmartin, 1988, p. 232)

A PUNJABI PAKISTAN?

Another significant hurdle in the nation-building process of Pakistan has been the domination of the Punjabis over all registers of the country's affairs. The entrenched institutional dominance by a mainly Punjabi army and federal bureaucracy has on repeated occasions frustrated democratic processes in Pakistan (Bose & Jalal, 2004, p. 180). The hold and power of the Punjabis are expressed through their omnibus demographic presence and strong and deep-rooted ethnic geography which socio-historically and psycho-culturally, makes them the most powerful component of the Pakistani society, both in terms of social capital and ideological influence. It manifests in their unchallenged control over the economy, the political structure, the armed forces and services, the higher education and to a considerable extent, the media (Weidemann, 2007, p. 91).

Owing to this, the country is wrestling with foundational issues such as the role of Islam in the State, who is a Pakistani and who is not and what kind of Islam should Pakistan follow as a State (Weidemann, 2007, p. 92). Pakistan has a troubled history of ethnic feudes, sectarian bloodshed and linguistic politics that has stemmed the process of national cohesion. The country's rule by the dominant Punjabi elite has alienated other provinces and ethnicities. In this regard, the Bangladesh fiasco signified the culmination of the political rather than the military failures of the defence establishment of Pakistan (Jalal, 1995, p. 63). A failure that was largely impelled by the Punjabi ethnicization of the project of the military/bureaucratic/Islamist hegemonic control over the domestic politics, defence strategy and foreign policy of Pakistan (Malik 2001, p. 208). All this lie at the bottom of the political alienation of East Pakistan and its eventual disintegration from West Pakistan (Jahan, 1972, p. 166).

In any case, the lesson of Bangladesh had a completely reverse effect. Instead of drawing the people of Pakistan into a tighter, more coherent entity, fissiparous tendencies intensified. The separatist

Sindhi, Baloch and Pashtun movements, feeding upon the feeling of economic exploitation and political discrimination, have questioned the viability of Pakistan's federal framework (Weinbaum, 2011, p. 226). The lingering Pakhtunistan dispute had been given a new vitality with the 1973 seizure of power in Afghanistan by Sardar Daud. A Baluchi liberation organization was active in Baluchistan. If these frontier troubles were not enough, the country was also faced with a Sindhu Desh movement which was directed against both the Muhajirs and the Punjabis, who since independence had acquired large land-holdings in the irrigated sectors of the province (Ziring, 1982, p. 6). So even after the defection of its Eastern wing, Pakistan has failed to design a political system in which the minority ethno-political groups would not suffer a deep sense of deprivation (Gupta, 1988, p. 22). The simple logical explanation for this may be found in the hegemonic tendency of the ethnically powerful community in Pakistan that is the Punjabis. As the largest demographic component and traditionally the more influential ethnic group in Pakistan, the Punjabis have been perceived by the minorities as monopolizing the power and wealth of the country (Callard, 1975, p. 184).

All this symbolizes a deep-rooted identity crisis in Pakistan. The struggle between civil society and military rule, the enlightened liberal sections and the radical Islamic forces is an unavoidable result of the failure of the national State in Pakistan (Weidemann, 2007, pp. 87–88). Thus, the question of the Pakistani self-perception is an enquiry into the Pakistani identity which till today is shaped by the historical heritage (Jalal, 2000, p. 10). There are many reasons for this situation. Beyond the historical deficits in its self-perception, the major causes responsible for the difficulties of national identity rests with the social and political structures of the new State, in its political system and not least in the politics and power struggle of the ruling groupings. The concentration of power in the hands of a small oligarchy is also considerably responsible (Weidemann, 2007, p. 89).

Hence, addressing the fundamental challenges mentioned above which are being confronted by Pakistan appears to be an uphill task. This is because the political parties lack the capacity to do so. Mainly because they not only face structural problems and lack intra-party democracy, but also the civil society in the country is unable to pressure them to act in a positive direction (Fair, 2011a, p. 96). On account of this, the future of Pakistan cannot be gauged by the current dynamics in its political affairs. Rather, history should be a telescope to understand the micropolitics of democratic governance in that country. Pakistan is still encapsulated in the firm grip of its army and as long as the US interests in the Middle-East and Central Asia remain, there exists a wider scope for the Pakistan army to be mollycoddled by Washington. Until the US strategists and policymakers are obsessed with the notion that a benign military ruler is the only obvious bulwark against a broader State failure in Pakistan, keeping the candle of hegemony kindled would be an easy task for the armed forces.

This has led the people of Pakistan into a quagmire wherein they have been left with few choices. General Pervez Musharraf's drive of enlightened moderation also has been an empty signifier, considering the magnifying influence of the Islamists on society and politics (Boquerat & Hussain, 2011, pp. 177 & 190). The assassination of Benazir Bhutto and the failed assassination bid on Musharraf himself two times by the extremists exemplify the gravity of the situation. After examining the state of democracy in Pakistan, it may be argued that the country is now experiencing a crisis of nationhood. Indicative of this, Musharraf had made a shocking admission in his book *In the Line of Fire* that the degree of disintegration of Pakistan is reaching such a severe level that uniting the entire country even in the time of a threat to national security seems to be difficult (Musharraf, 2006, p. 19). Hence, purgation of the scourge of Islamic extremism is an exigency for strengthening the process of democratization in Pakistan.

Akmal Hossain has outlined four major characters of the crisis of the State and democratic order in Pakistan which still appears relevant. (a) The distinction between the political and the repressive apparatus of the State tend to be deeply eroded. Political and social mediation is not performed by the organizations representing the interests of the people but it is done by organizations that commend a narrow social basis and are driven by their own specific interests. All this leads to growing tension between different social groups. (b) The State which is dominated by its repressive apparatus is highly centralized wherein the weaker ethno-nationalist groups who are at the margins do not gain recognition. (c) The official interpretation of the religion by the ruling establishment is a mere camouflage to pursue their specific class interests and also to justify the repression of anybody questioning their legitimacy. Owing to such a crisis of the State, the political class has lost the capacity to stay in power without the use of force. This has paved the way for the army to interfere in the civic life of Pakistan. (d) A lengthy military rule has sabotaged the balance between institutions of the State such as the army, bureaucracy and the judiciary. It has resulted in an institutional crisis in particular and a crisis of the State in general. By virtue of all this, the problems of Pakistan emerge to be systemic in character (Hossain, 1985, p. 225). Hence, as Stephen Cohen has stated, when the internal stability of the State is lost, neither the instruments of the State nor the rule of the military is in a position to reclaim it. A long period of military rule, the usurpation of the functions of the State by the men in uniform and the self-proclamation of the military to be the State has not only discredited the army, but it has also brought much disrepute to the State as an institution (Cohen, 1985, p. 299).

Such a scenario of postcolonial State building in Pakistan has been characterized by Veena Kukreja as a trajectory of the decay of the process of political institutionalization, owing to which there was a kind of legitimation crisis. She further states that the course of post-colonial political development in Pakistan resembles Huntington's model of praetorian society,[7] wherein conditions of underdevelopment and the politicization of the processes and structures of the society created a conducive environment for intermittent military interventions (Kukreja, 1991, p. 45). This becomes evident when we analyse Pakistan's political history wherein, three most prominent rulers of the country who definitively shaped the State construction process in the formative decades of the postcolonial polity, constantly endeavoured

---

[7] For Huntington, in a praetorian society, the polity does not accept the political institutions and leaders as legitimate. The political intervention of the army in such a situation is predicated upon its perception that it is the only legitimate arbitrator among the political actors and even a substitute to the non-existent social forces (Huntington, 1968, p. 196).

towards establishing a personalized control over the State. A political manoeuvre that has been designated by Khalid bin Sayeed as 'Bonapartism'. The two military rulers, Field Martial Ayub Khan and General Zia and the civilian leader Zulfikar Ali Bhutto for Sayeed, attempted at transforming Pakistan into a 'Bonapartist State' in which emphasis was laid upon creating a centralized state under a strong single leader.[8] In this way, both the military and the civilian leaders of Pakistan represented an aberration to the Weberian conception of 'politics as vocation'.[9] Thus, the Pakistani politician failed to strike a balance between what Weber calls 'the ethic of moral conviction and the ethic of responsibility'.[10]

Putting this in terms of the theoretical perspective of Gunnar Myrdal, Pakistan can be designated as the 'soft State'. For Myrdal, a soft State represents the kind of politics that is characterized by a deep sense of social indiscipline. Such a condition of social indiscipline manifested for Myrdal in the form of the deficiencies in the political processes of law-making, enforcement and adjudication. It also expresses itself in the functional inadequacies of the bureaucracy and the propensity of the public officials to collude with the powerful

[8] The 'Bonapartist State' was characterized by the exercise of complete domination over all the sociopolitical structures and processes by a leader that was done with an intense urge for the aggrandizement of one's own personal power (Bin Sayeed, 1980, p. 91).

[9] 'Politics as Vocation' is a classic essay written by the German economist and sociologist Max Weber. One of the striking features of this essay is the argument Weber advocated in favour of the States' legitimate right to use violence. In this sense, for Weber, 'Politics as a vocation is nothing but the pursuit of power over the State' (Weber, 2015, p. 136). Apart from this, it also categorized authority into three pure types. These are described by Weber as 'traditional, charismatic and rational legal' (Weber, 2015, pp. 137–138).

[10] The most significant aspect of Weber's essay is his description of the nature of a politician (Weber, 2015, pp. 178–179). For him, a politician should always be in a position to maintain a balance between an ethic of moral conviction and an ethic of responsibility. The ethic of moral conviction, on the one hand, implies towards a politician's deeply held ethical beliefs that are unshakable. On the other hand, the ethic of responsibility refers to the routine imperatives coming in the way of politicians that necessitate them to use violence in the interest of society at large. Every politician, according to Weber, confronts profound challenges that impel them towards making constant compromises between these two types of ethics (Weber, 2015, pp. 181–182).

sociopolitical groups (Myrdal, 1970, p. 268). At the bottom of such a social indiscipline for Myrdal has been the colonial destruction of the traditional models of power and influence which are hitherto operational in the colonial periphery and the failure of the metropolis to construct viable alternatives to these processes of sociopolitical structuration. Conjoined to this was the development of an attitude of disobedience by the native population to any authority that was pivotal to the nationalist politics of resistance. An attitude, according to Myrdal, persisted even after the postcolonial transition and the institution of native governments in these polities. It is this kind of soft State in South Asia that has been incapable to impose the right kind of developmental policies, ensuring transparency in governance and being strict on corruption at all levels (Myrdal, 1968, 1970).

Due to such a political ecology of its domestic space, Pakistan has shown that there is a deep-seated legitimation crisis in the country. This is evident in the fact that the confidence of the people seems to be with the army as compared to that of the legitimately elected government. The intrusion of the army in the civic space hence symbolizes the legitimation crisis wherein the popular consciousness supports the non-civic institutions to protect them from the fear of social fragmentation. Such a lack of confidence in civic institutions completely belies the foundations of civil science and indicates that people's preferences in terms of security can ultimately lead to an erosion of confidence in the legitimate political institutions itself. Such an irony that indicates towards a paradox wherein people do not wish to bestow faith in those institutions that are meant for their security can be regarded as the actual legitimation crisis in Pakistan.

Hence, the question of whether democracy can ever be consolidated in Pakistan is still an open-ended one, reflecting a kind of collective myopia (Grare, 2011, p. 174). As Huntington notes, the problems of communal conflicts and foreign war and social decay that were produced in some measure by the process of democratization, join the many other problems that new democracies inherit from the previous authoritarian regimes (Huntington, 1992, p. 7). The crisis of democratization that Pakistan has undergone is associated with similar problems that Huntington has elaborated.

THE CASE OF INDIA

Similarly, if we consider the example of India and compare it in the context of the contours of the regional dynamics of political development in South Asia, it may be stated that the country emerges to be the largest and the most developed, having a better military capability compared to its South Asian counterparts. It is also a multicultural society accommodating the population of several indigenous and immigrant religious communities. In addition to this, diverse linguistic cartography and ethnic geography lie at the foundation of the constitution of its society.

In any case, with all such affirmed attributes and assertions of possessing a stable democracy that is underpinned by a strong and stable State, the normative and structural aspects of India's democratic and developmental processes have not remained fully untainted. India has been successful in so far as the sustenance of the democratic architecture is concerned, through regular, free and fair elections. However, the polity has exhibited a gradual decline, in so far as the ability of the State to deal with multiple voices of dissent in the process of constructing and executing the narrative of development is concerned. This has happened as the developmental policies appear to have failed to disseminate to the least advantaged sections of society. Rather the benefits of the instrumental value of the State's legitimate intervention seem to be trickling down only to an elite minority (Chandhoke, 2008, p. 254).

Hence, it has been argued that the functioning of the democratic State in India is replete with conundrums. The structural/functional intricacies of the architecture of its administrative mechanism and political processes do not unveil themselves for an easy judgement. On the one hand, the notion of political equality has been strongly enshrined into the polity through the mechanism of social contract which is manifest in the country's constitution. However, on the other hand, the country appears to be a dismal failure when we look at how the idea of political accountability has become fragile due to the weakness of the institutions of policy formulation, execution and adjudication. Such a scenario makes us think that the processes of

State formation, consolidation and the project of nation state building in India still appear to be in process (Desouza, 2007, p. 33).

Such an enigmatic connotation of Indian democracy has largely been the product of what Frantz Fanon designates as 'false decolonization'.[11] For the ideology of colonial nationalism, the colonizer was to be treated as an 'intimate enemy' (Nandy, 1983). On this count, the struggle between the colonizer and the colonized was an ethical one wherein, colonial authority and the resultant form of politics was to be questioned purely for the reasons of morality and not be contested on politico-military grounds. Such questioning embodied the nonviolent modes by which freedom was achieved, hence represented more of a moral victory rather than that of a political gain. This kind of victory that was crafted through an interface between politics, power and ethics, largely contributed towards the making of the public culture in independent India. At the heart of this newly crafted public culture, rested the ancient concept of 'dharma' (duty) which emerged to be the connecting string between politics, power and ethics (Kanes, 1946, pp. 241 & 825–829; Nandy, 1970, p. 67).

However, the postcolonial predicament (Breckenridge & van der Veer, 1993) that had thrown up the challenges of making a new polity that ought to be dictated by the notion of Statist fundamentalism, emerged to be a kind of the predicament of culture (Clyfford, 1979; Nandy, 1973, p. 130), a crisis of tradition (MacIntyre, 1988) and an epistemological crisis (Vajpeyi, 2012). Such a predicament

---

[11] Frantz Fanon talks about the 'false decolonization and the pitfalls of national consciousness and the weakness of spontaneity in order to draw our attention to the historically and politically specific nature of nationalist movements'. With this he attempted to alert us to nationalism's class-specific and liberating potentials (Bannerji, 2000, p. 902). For Fanon, the falsity of decolonization is directly connected to the ideological control exerted by the national bourgeoisie, or more accurately, the petty bourgeoisie, on the ideological and organizational processes of the nationalist movement. To the extent that these ruling classes were able to deflect the movement outside of the left popular directive, the project of decolonization became false (Bannerji, 2000). Hence, decolonization demands a sustained, quotidian commitment to the struggle for national liberation, for when the high heady win of revolution loses its velocity, there is no question of bridging the gap in one giant stride. The epic is played out on a difficult day-to-day basis and the sufferings endured far exceed that of the colonial period (Fanon, 2004, p. 90).

was manifest in what Rajni Kothari designates as a structural crisis of postcolonial polity. Independent India encountered this because of the resurgence of the messy diversity and the contingent factionalism that was integral to the country's archaic social order. The nationalist romanticism of the colonial era had subsumed all such factions that were potent to throw up dissenting voices of resistance. However, the new structural formations of democracy and development created adequate spaces for the return of these forces with an added political vigour (Kothari, 1967, p. 165). All this had brought to the fore the classic Weberian contention regarding the need for a politician to balance the ethics of moral convictions and the ethics of responsibility in the context of the postcolonial political development in India.

The ethical dilemmas encountered by the postcolonial political leaders in India can be visualized from the perspective of the classic question raised by Jean Hampton that 'can political philosophy be done without metaphysics'? (Hampton, 1989, p. 791). Such a question takes us to the notion of the post-Gandhian emphasis on the conception of politics in India as an amoral vocation (Erikson, 1969). The post-Gandhian conception of politics was premised on the imagery of India as a nation and politics as a vocation that should be underpinned by a sense of deontological virtue. Such a conception began to be shaped by the philosophy of the constitution and the prevalent left-of-centre ideological consensus of the Nehruvian era (Kothari, 1976, p. 52). This kind of conception of politics was completely different from the idealistic vision of Gandhian politics that manifested as a Jamesonion utopia which could be resorted to as an escape from the hard world of the politics of material power (Jameson, 2004). The contest between the idealist and realist vision of politics in India was largely engendered by the decline of Nehruvian romanticism which paved the way for the emergence of the era of realpolitik. This was epitomized in Indira Gandhi's style of functioning. The division of the Indian National Congress, the imposition of national emergency and the subsequent relegation of tall leaders like Nijalingappa or Kamraj Nadar to the back seat, signified the erosion of the Gandhian idealist vision of politics (Brass, 1984, pp. 89–90). In a way, this was a serious setback to early postcolonial India's most celebrated axiological

framework of the Gandhian-style-politics which Morris-Jones designated as saintly tradition. He considered it as one of the unique idioms
of politics in India, in addition to two others that are tradition and
modernity (Morris-Jones, 1964).

This happened as the imagery of the Indian republic dreamt by
a small metropolitan elite in the colonially tableted spatiality was
exposed to an imperially mediated imperfect modernity. The attitude
of the elite towards the dream of the Indian republic during the freedom struggle was riddled with confusion and contradictions. On this
count then, the postcolonial Indian republic is not only at crossroads.
Rather, it is in fact at a historical impasse, still in search of a road. One
factor that contributed towards the engendering of such a stalemate
has been the erosion of the Gandhian style of politics. It happened as
postcolonial India had witnessed the politicization of a fragmented
social structure that was being engendered by the penetration of
immigrant political formations, values and ideologies.

This was also a time when the immutability of social institutions
was considered to be an ontological condition to the systemic structure
in India (Weber, 1958). The psycho-cultural foundations of such a
genealogy and archaeology considerably tended to mediate an interaction between the immigrant political formations and the intransigent
traditional forces (Nandy, 1970, p. 57). Owing to such an interface, it
was expected that the newly emergent political formations would not
only derive formative power of structuration but were also expected
to considerably alter those very traditional archaeology and put the
polity in the path of modernization (Desai, 1959). In a way, it was
expected that modernity and tradition would be involved in a complex
process of symbiotic interaction that could be deterministic to the
modes by which the systemic contours of the postcolonial polity in
India was to be shaped.[12] In a nutshell, the idea was to Indianize the

---

[12] In their work *The Modernity of Tradition: Political Development in India*, Lloyd
Rudolph and Susanne Hoeber Rudolph attempt to demonstrate as to how modernity
and tradition infiltrate and transform each other. The authors here do not conceive
modernity and tradition as radically contradictory as conceptual categories. Rather,
they argue that modernity and tradition are involved in a dialectical interaction with
each other. Through such an interaction, the authors hold that both modernity and

very discourse on politics and to explore as to how Indians were looking at the modern animal called 'the political' (Kothari, 1970, p. 89).

Such an idea was evolving in an ontic spatiality and temporality wherein, Indian politics itself was witnessing drastic structural transformations with the coming of the new phenomenon and actors. The end of the one-party dominant system or what has been called the Congress system, coming of the green revolution and the emergence of a new agrarian middle class which Rudolph and Rudolph have designated as the bullock capitalists (1987) and the student unrest that was engendered by the JP movement, all formed part of this transforming political terrain (Brass, 1984, p. 92). Here, the interpenetration of caste and class acted as the critical intermediary in engendering the politics of social transition and structuration (Brass, 1985, p. 3).

The operationalization of the interpenetration of class and caste was happening in a milieu wherein political institutions of the postcolonial State were evolving as a product of two elite agents. First was the colonially trained bureaucracy and the second was the Indian National Congress with its bourgeois character, which now commanded the engine of political authority. The combination of these two agents as the primary vehicle of governance in the early postcolonial era dominated the large public space of India that was characterized by a vacuum in terms of the absence of a popular imagery of the phenomenon of political itself, a vacuum that can be traced back to colonial genealogies which also transgressed India's postcolonial political spatialities. By virtue of this, the contours of modern sociopolitical institutions rather than being created with the help of mass participation that was motored by a social revolution got formulated as structures of colonial superimposition (Kaviraj, 2010, p. 154).

This postcolonial political vacuum has been the product of two major factors. First, the postcolonial leadership of the Indian National Congress that comprised of both the English educated elite and the traditional elite of the patrimonial order were quick to transform the organization in order to demobilize it from a militant political form

tradition jointly contribute towards the significant process of political modernization (Rudolph & Rudolph, 1968, pp. 3 & 5).

to an ordinary instrument of ministerialism. It means that the ontic structural/functional constitution of the Congress drastically metamorphosized from being an agent of revolution to an electoral machine. Second, the colonially cultured English educated bureaucracy that became large in size and gained enormity of function owing to the postcolonial programme of welfare and accounting gradually began to be bedevilled by the shadows of class and culture. This manifested on the one hand in the large gulf that separated the upper-level bureaucrat who was running the policymaking institutions and the local village-level clerk, in charge of routine implementation, both of whom utterly failed to comprehend the semantics and semiotics of each other's administrative vocabulary. Both also lacked unanimity in so far as their ontic and epistemic cultural topographies, leading to divergent perceptions of the social world. Such a dichotomy of interpretations questioned the very logic of rationalization and democratization. Besides, the narrative of development advocated by the metropolitan centre confronted stiff resistance from a coalition of provincial Congress elite and local bureaucracy (Kaviraj, 2010, pp. 155–156).

Besides, there was the simultaneous existence in postcolonial India of an elite political culture of the metropolis operating from Delhi and the mass political culture which characterized the structuration of the strands of peripheral politics at the district level (Weiner, 1963, pp. 114, 138 & 149–151). This kind of duality is interpreted by Edward Shils as the simultaneous presence of the national and parochial cultures (Shils, 1965). It is integral to the systemic ontology of the postcolonial political economy in India which has been described by Rudolph and Rudolph, in terms of an interaction between two contrasting models designated as the 'command politics and the demand politics'.[13] Above all, the traditional Indian culture that was deeply

[13] According to Rudolph and Rudolph (1987), the spatial topography of the postcolonial political economy in India can be explained in terms of an interaction between the increased activities in the sphere of political mobilization and the changing capabilities of the Indian State. This has been framed by Rudolphs in the theoretical framework of the interaction between the model of demand politics which treats citizens as sovereign consumers in a competitive market economy and the model of command politics wherein the State emerges as the undisputed sovereign which is differentiated, autonomous and authoritative. According to them, both models tended to

aristocratic and repressive, engaged in structured violence against the oppressed (Kaviraj, 1981, p. 5).

All this can be regarded as a fundamental reason for the marginalization of the masses from the everyday evolution of the imagery of the notion of politics. Such a precariousness resulted in the engendering of several dilemmas of the modern State. They included first the modern legislations emerged as elite constructions, with the demotic consciousness remaining very much ignorant and marginalized from this entire process. Such an ignorance that was the product of the passive receptivity of the demotic consciousness ultimately led to an unequal socio-economic and political relationship between a tiny elite minority and the majority masses. This very inequality has been the subterranean molecular impulse that impeded the process of democratization and obviated the emergence of a liberal social order.

In this regard, Sunil Khilnani (1997, pp. 16–17) argues,

> democracy is a type of Government, a political regime of laws and institutions. But its imaginative potency rests in its promise to bring alien powerful machines like the State under the control of human will, to enable a community of political equals before the constitutional law to make their own history. Like those great democratic experiments inaugurated in eighteenth century America and France, India became a democracy without knowing really how, why or what it meant to be one. Yet the democratic idea has penetrated the Indian political imagination and has begun to corrode the authority of the social order and of the paternalist State. Democracy as a manner of seeing and acting upon the world is changing the relations of the Indians to themselves. (Khilnani, 1997, pp. 16–17)

Similarly, Hansen (1999, p. 57) has stated, 'The trajectory of modernity and democracy in India so clearly demonstrates how democracy makes the political dimensions of the society crucial, productive and deeply problematic.' The ontologies of such a predicament of postcolonial political development in India can be traced to the focal point of difference between the developed democracies of the West and the

dominate the landscape of India's political economy at different epochal phases of the country's postcolonial history (Rudolph & Rudolph, 1987, pp. 14, 227–228, 240, 395, 399–400).

developing democracy of India which is rooted in the country's history. To understand this, some aspects of colonial transition in India must be considered here.

THE ONTOLOGIES OF
A FEUDAL POLITICAL ECONOMY

The administrative success of the colonial metropolis in the Indian subcontinent represented the skilful manipulation of the twin dialectics that marked the subcontinental history of internal struggles to integrate its geographical and political frontiers. These twin dialectics was constituted on the one hand by the antithetical formulations of the authoritarianism of centralism and the secessionist inclinations of regionalism. On the other hand, it manifested in the contested expressions of the notion of an all-inclusive nationalism and an exclusionary conception of communalism (Jalal, 1995, pp. 12–16). One of the most crucial factors that facilitated the British to colonize India with the help of the manipulation of these twin dialectics was the existence of a structure of social property relations that was based on land ownership. However, the question of whether to designate such a structure as feudalism has been a severely contested one.

In this context, we can take into cognizance the problems of interpreting Indian history from the perspective of borrowed European theories and the kind of controversy that it has generated among Indian historians. Here, we can bring in the cogent argument of Burton Stein who states,

> Although the notion of intermediate historical period has proven as legitimate and useful in India as it is in Europe, there are reasons still to question the identification of shared detailed characteristics or common origin. The attempt to transfer feudalism from Europe to India has been principally problematic because in Europe or at least in some parts of Europe and at some times, it is a totalizing system of political, social and economic institutions and ideas. However, whether there was a coherent system of feudalism in India, continues to be contested among historians. (Stein, 1998, p. 106)

For instance, S. A. Dange in his book *India: From Primitive Communism to Slavery* attempted to show that the ancient Indian society moved in a single file from primitive communism to slavery (Dange, 1949). In a similar tone, Ranajit Guha, the founder of subaltern studies, unequivocally declared that India had a feudal society before the establishment of British colonialism (Guha, 1998, p. 12). These generalizations were however criticized and reformulated by other Marxist Historians, who demonstrated the irrationality of generalizing Indian history by conceptualizing it in the framework of slavery or feudalism.

In this regard, R. S. Sharma sought to demonstrate the invalidity of understanding the precolonial socio-economic system in India from the perspective of mere Western conceptualization of feudalism and tried to even use African patterns of socio-economic transitions to understand the same. He did not have problems in the use of the word feudalism, but his contention was to indicate the distinctness of origin and nature of Indian feudalism, as compared to that of the European case. His focus is to explain this from 700 to 1200 AD and seeks to call it the Early Medieval Indian history. Sharma argued that 'unlike in Europe, feudalism in India began with the land grants "Bhumidana", made first to the priestly class and then later on to the warrior class' (2005, p. 4), whereas Irfan Habib totally rejected the very use of the word feudalism and instead preferred to call the pre-colonial socio-economic system as 'the Medieval System' (Habib, 1963, p. 43). Harbans Mukhia has attempted to demonstrate the structural differentiations between the Indian feudalism and the European type. According to him, 'European feudalism emerged from the changes at the base of the society, whereas in India the establishment of feudalism is attributed by its protagonists to State actions in land grants' (Mukhia, 1981). However, Mukhia questions the possibility of establishing a complex social system like feudalism by administrative and legal procedures. He thus made an outright rejection of the existence of Indian feudalism (Mukhia, 1981).

D. D. Kosambi, however, sought to differ from these scholars and supports the existence of feudalism in early Medieval India. According to him, 'the transfer of fiscal and Administrative rights over the land by the Kings to their subordinate chiefs changed the social and economic relations among the people' (Kosambi, 1956, p. 296). With this, he put forth a two-stage theory of feudalism in

India (Kosambi, 1956, p. 296). According to Kosambi, in India, feudalism existed at two levels.

> Firstly, feudalism from above meant that a State wherein an emperor or a powerful king levied tribute from subordinates who still ruled in their own right and did what they liked within their own territory. As long as they paid the paramount ruler. On the other hand, the second stage of feudalism meant that a class of landowners developed within the village, between the State and the peasantry, gradually to wield armed power over the local population. This class was subject to military service, hence claimed a direct relationship with the State power, without the intervention of any other stratum. (Kosambi, 1956, pp. 295–296)

In this regard, R. S. Sharma has argued that

> The political essence of feudalism in India rested in the organization of whole administrative structure on the basis of land' its economic essence was predicated in the institution of serfdom in which the peasants were attached to the soil held by the landed intermediaries placed between the king and the actual tillers who had to pay in kind and labour to them. (Sharma, 2005, p. 1)

During the epoch of colonial transition, such a situation suited both Britishers and local feudal lords in conserving their respective interests. For the Britishers, the continuation of an agrarian society with a feudal order was advantageous for them because capitalist economic transformation meant that the entire substructure of their colonial policy was froth with perils. The feudal class on the other hand were interested in preserving the status quo which was derived out of a nexus with the colonial administration and this proved to be highly beneficial in their endeavours to perpetuate the traditional structures of feudal authority. Their collaborative endeavours thus helped the persistence of feudalism in the country. Due to this feudal/colonial condominium, the modernization process was drastically affected as the Indian psyche was severely influenced by this cultural legacy even after the postcolonial transition. Thus, it must be noted here that the birth of a modern democratic State in India was not coincided with the ending of feudalism, implying that the archaic hegemonic sociocultural structures crafted for the perpetuation of the dominant groups in the society and a feudal structure of political-economy also continued to exist.

All this meant that the onus of bringing capitalist economic transformation was left to the nascent democratic State. So different to that of the West, the democratic State in India became the primary source of modernity. This is contrary to what has happened in the West. The democratic State in the West has been the product of modernity, dissimilar to the Indian case, where the democratic State was expected to invigorate the process of modernization. In the West, democracy entered after capitalist economic transformation reached a fruition point and the society became fairly wealthy. The industrial working force was much larger than that of the agricultural sector. Comparatively, Indian democracy at the outset encountered an agrarian society with a much smaller industrial sector and a high degree of poverty. So, democratic politics primarily became a tool for advancing the cause of promoting the grant of subsidies for agriculture, rather than contemplating upon building a thriving industrial-capitalist economy (Varshney, 1999, p. 19). This also facilitated the newly crafted politico-bureaucratic architecture to gain excessive control over the realm of public affairs. Situating ourselves on this, we can attempt at mapping the scenario of political decay and the legitimation crisis that the postcolonial state in India has tended to experience.

THE FAILURE OF THE PROJECT OF NEOLIBERAL REFORMS?

The symptomatic reflections of political decay and the legitimation crisis began to be evident during the 1970s–1980s. First, in the 1970s, it manifested in the form of a conflict between the industrial and agricultural interests that was centred around the models of development to be followed by the government, the modes of implementing the same and as to who should benefit out of such programmes of development. Such a conflict resulted in intra-party tensions, leading Indira Gandhi to embark upon a path of populism. This kind of trajectory of political populism was adeptly exploited by the well-to-do peasant cultivators (Gupta, 1998, pp. 15–16). This period witnessed deepening socio-economic distress that was engendered by the agrarian revolution, the J. P. movement and the subsequent student unrest, and the predicament of political authority and civic obligation induced by the declaration of national emergency.

Similarly, during the 1980s, the situation expressed itself in the impending crisis of State security, owing to the Khalistan movement and the Kashmir uprising. All this led to what Atul Kohli designated as the crisis of governability. By examining the notions of political order and change in India during the period between the 1960s and the 1980s, Kohli argues that despite being one of the more successful countries in the cartography of the developing world, the nation during this period experienced a deep-seated crisis of order and stability. During this period, he contends that the institutional mechanisms designed for the resolution of conflicts got considerably debilitated owing to the greater politicization of the civil and police services. Also as part of this crisis, the policy-executing agencies began to lose innovative imagination to implement effective plans for economic development. Kohli hence described such a crisis of governability as the growing incapacity of the Indian State to govern which he framed in the Huntingtonian metaphor of 'political decay' (Kohli, 1990, pp. 16 & 30).

In view of this, it has been argued by Sudipta Kaviraj that

Tangible institutions of the State may be helpless against the intangible force of historically sedimented cultural understandings of ordinary people. Long-term memories and time-tested ways of dealing with power of the political authority took its revenge on the modern State, bending the straight lines of rationalist liberal politics through a cultural refraction of administrative meaning. The logic of new legislations was twisted to produce strange travesties. (Kaviraj, 2000, p. 41)

At the root of such a scenario, lie several factors that constitute what can be designated as India's postcolonial predicament. One reason that has been widely discussed in this regard has been the introduction of a planned economy that was shielded by various protective laws. In accordance with such economic policies, the government sanctioned the creation of a large public sector of core industries that led to the enormous expansion of bureaucratic influence over the developmental affairs of the country (Potter, 1986, p. 61). Planning itself became a kind of an embodiment of divinity that was supposed to drive the universe of the postcolonial developmental state in India (Inden, 1995, p. 247). This kind of an over-emphasis on planning and economic policies of protection facilitated the newly crafted bureaucratic architecture in the postcolonial State, to gain excessive control over the realm of India's political economy (see Chibber, 2003; Frankel, 1978; Rudolph & Rudolph, 1987).

This is because the bureaucracy, which is one of the principal instruments of the modern State, behaved in ways very different from its European counterpart. The nature of bureaucracy in India presents itself as altogether different from the theoretical picture of behaviour constructed so powerfully by the Weberian model of rational-legal authority. Under the pressures of modernity, the Indian State however has gone through serious stages of successive elaboration, but it is hard to be confident that it is coming to resemble the model of Weberian bureaucratic State (Kaviraj, 2000). The result of this is what Foucault called the governmentalization of the State which has emerged as the major characteristic of the contemporary regime of power (Foucault, 1991, p. 87).

Here, it can further be noted that the recent policies of market liberalization and neoliberal reforms have merely been a sought of damage control exercise. This is because for Neelsen and Malik,

> Structural reasons are responsible for the importance attached to the State even under conditions of neoliberal globalization with its primary emphasis on the market. There is first of all the under development and fragmentation of the economy in general, of the private sector, not least the private capital, in particular. The concentration of material resources in the hands of the Government, made it the primary agency of development in the early years of independence, even independently of the ideological foundations of the Statist development strategy. (Neelsen & Malik, 2007, p. 22)

Such a phenomenon has emerged because the caste system has demonstrated an immaculate potency for adaptability to the changing contours of the nature and structure of India's political economy. This is because the antiquarian, undemocratic nature of the social structure manifest in the *Varna* (Hindu) order may be declining but it still has a strong latent presence in the subterranean domain of society and culture. Owing to this, the benefits disseminating out of the reforms in the nature and structure of political economy gets locked up to the upper castes or a tiny elite minority among the lower castes (Brass, 2010, p. 18). Further in this regard, it has been argued here that caste as a religiously sanctioned system of resource transfer may be declining in importance. However, it remains a potent marker of political identity and signification of symbolic and social capital (Jeffrey, 2001, p. 218). Although in a limited urbanized spatiality, caste does not tend to exist as an agent of cultural mobility or social control (Beteille, 1997, p. 450). In any case, if we look at the scenario of the majority of India's cultural cartography, caste as a sociocultural category has been able to sustain itself, despite the metamorphosis that has occurred due to its de-ritualization and the subsequent de-institutionalization as a religiously mandated social sanction.

On this count, with the erosion of rituality and religiosity, the support system that caste as a social category enjoyed, got debilitated considerably in a modernizing and liberalizing India. This has rendered caste to now survive as merely a kinship-based cultural community. In any case, it operates in a newly emergent system of social stratification which is entirely different to its genealogies (Sheth, 1999, p. 2502). Due to such continuity in the history of the sociocultural structure of stratification, the caste system in India has its own impact on modern politics or vice versa, modern politics in India has tended to condition itself in accordance with a caste-oriented society. Henceforth, caste and politics seem to be inextricably linked up with each other.

Casteism in politics and politicization of caste are dialectically intertwined with each other in a vicious cycle. Its impact has been mordacious, resulting in the polarization of Indian society. This trend is still a part of modern India, despite neoliberal reforms, directed towards achieving the prodigious goal of becoming a mega industrial-capitalist economy. The ending of caste-based social inequalities was one of the foremost challenges for post-Independence India and the constitution attempted at constructing an egalitarian society through affirmative action by making provisions for positive discrimination in favour of the lower castes (see Galanter, 1984). However lamentably, the existence of caste-based social disparities is still a hard reality and subaltern emancipation has remained as a fictitious dream. This is because the policies of the developmental State tend to lose their innate character, as they actually reach the stage of implementation (Kaviraj, 1988, p. 2440). On this count, it has been stated that there exists a significant gap between the legal rhetoric and actual conduct that eventually tends to slow down the ameliorative project of the policy of reservation, rendering it to be an empty signifier.

In this sense, the affirmative action seems merely to have granted a kind of formal ritualistic citizenship to the lower sections of the Indian society and the State appears to have failed in its task of imparting an effective redistribution of dignity and incomes (Kaviraj, 2005, p. 288). As a marked contrast to this, caste has become a crucial political weapon, in post-Independence Indian politics and has been instrumental in determining political equations in the process of shaping and sharing power. Rather than getting eroded due to the juggernaut of modernization and neoliberal reforms, caste as a social category has emerged to be the primary marker of individual identity, community recognition, group difference and a major theatre upon which popular resistance gets staged and enacted. Owing to this, caste has become a potent electoral instrument through the process of caste succession (see Brass, 1985). It now manifests as a new idiom of clientelism and a means to politicize the masses, a scenario that has tended to transform India into a patronage democracy (see Chandra, 2004).

In this context, Barbara Harris White has argued that although it is contended that economic liberalization means that the economy is freed from political control. But India offers itself as an entirely contrary example. In terms of the trajectory of its political economy, it has been noted here that owing to the historical continuities in the social structures of accumulation, there has merely been a change in the nature of political control over the economy rather than its withdrawal in India (White, 2004, p. 16). In this sense, the economy does not tend to get released from the hold of politics (White, 2004, pp. 65–66). The traditional social category of caste becomes a significant intermediary instrument that tends to foment the sustenance of such a control. This kind of complex trajectory of political economy wherein sociocultural and political formations get intertwined with each other to determine the nature of power-sharing among the communities has been described by Mushtaq Khan as a clientelist State (Khan, 2000, pp. 91–95). Such a trajectory of political economy has been engendered in India because caste renders a gargantuan influence upon the chemistry of sociocultural relations among the communities.

This happened as the caste hierarchy is antiquity; hence, it preceded the birth of a modern State in India. It is now established that traditionally, social stratification in India was based upon caste hierarchies and an individual's identity has been inextricably linked up with his caste affiliation. The modern State with its social emancipatory potential was expected to act as a modernizing force and an agent of social change. Establishing an egalitarian society free of the scourge of the caste system was one of the foremost challenges of postcolonial State in India. However, the caste system still exists as a dominant discourse and a source of hegemony and any expression against this dominant discourse is largely considered as an anathema.

Considering this, it may be argued here that the caste system exists as an anti-modernist force, retrograding the process of building a modern liberal society. It is so deeply entrenched in Indian culture that despite State-initiated processes of modernization, leading to conspicuous transitions in the modes of production, the caste system did not undergo drastic changes in its form, content and meaning (Bahl, 1997, p. 1336). So, such a circumstance makes way for occidental criticisms that oriental civilizations including India have not seen any basic change in their social structure, despite the advent of European political, economic and industrial revolution (Wittfogel, 1957, p. 80). One significant representation of such a phenomenon has been the castist trajectory of electoral politics in India. It has been a fact that in successive elections both at the level of the assemblies and that of the Parliament, Dalit candidates rarely succeeded in getting elected on unreserved seats. Hence, when we consider the relationship between caste and politics, the vicious equation between the two tends to suspend history and a modernizing society neither becomes fully modern nor remains utterly traditional. It merely is able to shunt from the thresholds of tradition and modernity. In the course of which, there occurs a metamorphosis in both the traditional social structures, belief systems and also the modern institutions of governance and social control.

On this count, it can be noted that the emergence of the modern State in India did not mean that the traditional social structures entirely disappeared. In turn, archaic social structure, determined by the caste system began to impose itself upon politics and social dynamics. In this context, Rajni Kothari has argued that institutions of governance do not tend to be situated in vacuity. Rather, they get deeply entrenched and subsequently, get profoundly influenced by the long-established societal structures and elements of culture. Such a sociopolitical arrangement may give rise to new cultural forms and patterns of social relations that possess the capacity to transform the ontology of legal and political institutions themselves. This has been exactly the case with the hegemonic structure of the caste system. It has tended to assume new forms of cultural assertion and social polarization, even as the modernizing influence of the structures of politics are becoming deep and pervasive (Kothari, 2001, p. 21).

Rather, such politico-administrative structures of modernization seem to have tended to get enmeshed in the quagmire of these new forms of caste-based cultural assertions and social polarization. The legitimate authority, such as the bureaucracy, seems to be mired in the quagmire of such forms of cultural assertions. The bureaucratic determinism that was inbuilt in the functional attribute of the State hence exists as a farcical reflection upon the failure of constitutionalism in post-Independence India. Hence, the neoliberal reforms in

India merely manifest as an elitist transformation, with the masses still confronting a structured trajectory of inequality (Corbridge & Harriss, 2000, p. 43). The major irony that is evident is that a large size of the masses is also ignorant about the structural transformations that are being engendered by the reforms in India's political economy (Varshney, 2000). As regards the negative effects of reforms, Stuart Corbridge argues that since the economic reforms, social and spatial inequalities have deepened in India. There has been an increase in bad inequalities wherein, certain groups of people tend to be kept away from various paths of gaining human capital and other transferable skills. This may happen due to social cleavages such as the caste-based social order that persists as an endemic source of marginalization in India. The caste system has been one of the most dominant strands of bad inequalities in India (Corbridge, 2010).

CONCLUSION

South Asia's tryst with democratization has been an unhappy political experience because the processes of nation-formation, State-making and democratization in the region have been based on received colonial wisdom and imported institutions of metropolitan governance. Due to this, the structural formations and the institutional character of the State and its agencies of the polities in the region appear to be a mere farcical simulation of the values of the colonial metropolis and the postcolonial models of economic development that are being transmitted from that very metropolis. Such a process of top-down transmission tended to transform the native political consciousness of the periphery into a mere mimetic expression of received notions of politics and government. The absence of the native agency to affect a bottom-up institutional process of value formation and the authoritative dissemination of the same to the wider population resulted in the fractured structural/functional models of governance that the postcolonial states of South Asia have inherited.

Owing to this, the functional capacity of the State itself seems to be in jeopardy, despite the semblance of sovereignty and legitimate authority that these States tend to display. Implying that although States in South Asia tend to possess the legitimate authority to govern their population and advert sovereign allegiance from their population, the examination of their everyday functioning exhibits that the institutions of the State merely appear as burlesque imitations of borrowed metropolitan formations that are rooted in colonial genealogy. The political decay and the legitimation crisis that Pakistan and India have experienced tend to substantiate this phenomenon. By virtue of its inability to deal with the crises of sovereignty, legitimacy, authority and political obligation owing to the twin phenomenon of military-autocracy and Islamic extremism, the State in Pakistan has experienced a complex trajectory of political decay and legitimation crisis. Similarly, owing to the perpetuation of the colonial ontology of the bureaucracy and the enduring structured domination of the caste system over sociocultural life, India tends to have suffered a crisis of governability. In this very process of degeneration, the neoliberal reforms in both countries seem to have deepened the primordialist forms of inequalities, thereby, widening the traditional sociocultural cleavages.

REFERENCES

Ahmed, I. (2013). *Pakistan: The garrison state: Origins, evolution and consequences.* Oxford University Press.

Ayoob, M. (1991). The security problematique of the Third World. *World Politics,* 43(2), 257–283.

Aziz, M. (2008). *Military control in Pakistan: The parallel state.* Routledge.

Bahl, V. (1997). Relevance or irrelevance of subaltern studies. *Economic & Political Weekly,* 32(23), 1333–1344.

Bajpai, K. (2011). Pakistan's future: Muddle along. In S. P. Cohen (Ed.), *The future of Pakistan* (pp. 71–82). Oxford University Press.

Bannerji, H. (2000). Projects of hegemony: Towards a critique of subaltern studies resolution of the women's question. *Economic & Political Weekly,* 35(11), 902–920.

Beteille, A. (1997). The family and the reproduction of inequality. In P. Uberoi (Ed.), *Family, kinship and marriage in India* (2nd ed., pp. 435–451). Oxford University Press.

Binder, L. (1961). *Religion and politics in Pakistan*. California University Press.

Bin Sayeed, K. (1980). *Politics in Pakistan: The nature and direction of change*. Praeger.

Bokhari, L. (2011). Radicalisation, political violence and militancy. In S. P. Cohen (Ed.), *The future of Pakistan*. Oxford University Press.

Boquerat, G., & Hussain, N. (2011). Enlightened moderation: Anatomy of a failed strategy. In R. Kalia (Ed.), *Pakistan: From the rhetoric of democracy to the rise of militancy* (pp. 177–193). Routledge.

Bose, S., & Jalal, A. (2004). *Modern South Asia: History, culture, political economy*. Routledge.

Brass, P. R. (1984). National power and local politics in India: A twenty-year perspective. *Modern Asian Studies, 18*(1), 89–118.

Brass, P. R. (1985). *Caste, faction and party in Indian politics: Vol 2. Election Studies*. Chanakya Publications.

Brass, P. R. (2010). Introduction. In *Routledge handbook of South Asian politics* (pp. 1–24). Routledge.

Callard, K. (1975). *Pakistan: A political study*. George Allen and Unwin.

Chandhoke, N. (2008). Exploring the linkages between rights and security in South Asia. In N. C. Behera (Ed.), *International relations in South Asia: Search for an alternative paradigm* (pp. 253–270). SAGE Publications.

Chandra, K. (2004). *Why ethnic parties succeed: Patronage and ethnic head counts in India*. Cambridge University Press.

Chibber, V. (2003). *Locked in place: State-building and late industrialization in India*. Princeton University Press.

Clyfford, J. (1979). *The predicament of culture: Twentieth century ethnography, literature and art*. Harvard University Press.

Cohen, S. P. (1985). *The Pakistan army*. University of California Press.

Cohen, S. P. (2004). *The idea of Pakistan*. Oxford University Press.

Congressional Research Service (2020, 5 March). *Pakistan's domestic political setting* [Report No. IFI0359]. https://fas.org›sgp›crs›row

Corbridge, S., & Harriss, J. (2000). *Reinventing India: Liberalism, Hindu nationalism and popular democracy*. Polity Press.

Corbridge, S. (2010). The political economy of development in India since independence. In P. R. Brass (Ed.), *Routledge handbook of south asian politics* (pp. 305–320). Routledge.

Dahl, R. A. (1989). *Democracy and its critics*. Yale University Press.

Dandeker, C. (1990). *Surveillance, power, and modernity*. St Martin's Press.

Dange, S. A. (1949). *India- From primitive communism to slavery: A Marxist study of ancient history in outline*. People's Publishing House.

Desai, A. R. (1959). *Social background of Indian nationalism*. Popular Publications.

DeSouza, P. R. (2007). The Indian common sense of democracy. *Seminar*, 576(August), 33–39.

Dhulipala, V. (2015). *Creating a new Medina: State power, Islam and the quest for Pakistan in late colonial North India*. Cambridge University Press.

Diamond, L. (2002). Elections without democracy: Thinking about hybrid regimes. *Journal of Democracy*, *13*(2), 21–35.

Erikson, E. H. (1969). *Gandhi's truth*. W. W. Norton.

Fair, C. C. (2010, March). *Roots of militancy: Explaining support for political violence in Pakistan* [Working Paper]. www.princeton.eduHns/papers/FMS_2009_The_Roots_Of_Mtancy.pdf

Fair, C. C. (2011a). Addressing fundamental challenges. In S. P. Cohen (Ed.), *The future of Pakistan* (pp. 91–107). Oxford University Press.

Fair, C. C. (2011b). The militant challenge in Pakistan. *Asia Policy*, *11*(1), 105–137.

Fair, C. C. (2014a). *Fighting to the end: The Pakistan army's way of war*. Oxford University Press.

Fanon, F. (2004). *The wretched of the Earth*. (R. Phicox, Trans.). Grove Press.

Foucault, M. (1991). Governmentality. In G. Burchell, C. Gordon, & P. Miller (Eds.), *The Foucault effect: Studies in governmentality*. Chicago University Press.

Frankel, F. R. (1978). *India's political economy, 1947–1977: A gradual revolution*. Princeton University Press.

Galanter, M. (1984). *Competing equalities: Law and backward classes in India*. Oxford University Press.

Ganguly, S. (2010). Pakistan: Neither state nor nation. In J. Bertrand & A. Laliberte (Eds.), *Multination states in Asia: Accommodation or resistance* (pp. 81–102). Cambridge University Press.

Ghoshal, B. (2008). Ask no question. *Times of India*, 18 November.

Gilmartin, D. (1988). *Empire and Islam: Punjab and the making of Pakistan*. University of California Press.

Grare, F. (2011). Pakistani pursuit of democracy. In R. Kalia (Ed.), *Pakistan: From the rhetoric of democracy to the rise of militancy* (pp. 160–176). Routledge.

Guha, R. (1998). *Elementary aspects of peasant insurgency in Colonial India*. Oxford University Press.

Gupta, B. S. (1988). *South Asian perspectives: Seven nations in conflict and cooperation*. B. R. Publishing Corporation.

Guruswamy, M. (2008). Financing terror: The Lashkar and beyond. *The Hindu*, 5 December.

Habib, I. (1963). *The agrarian system of Mughal India*. Asia Publishing House.

Halvorson, D. (2013). *States of disorder: Understanding state failure and disorder in the periphery*. Ashgate Publishing Company.

Hampton, J. (1989). Should political philosophy be done without metaphysics. *Ethics, 99*(4), 791–814.

Hansen, T. B. (1999). *The saffron wave: Democracy and Hindu nationalism in modern India.* Princeton University Press.

Haqqani, H. (2005). *Pakistan: Between mosque and military.* Carnegie Endowment.

Held, D. (2006). *Models of democracy.* Stanford University Press.

Hossain, A. (1985). Crisis of the state in the Pakistan experience. In M. A. Khan (Ed.), *State of Religion* (pp. 221–242). Zed Books.

Huntington, S. P. (1968). *Political order in changing societies.* Yale University Press.

Huntington, S. P. (1992). *The third wave: Democratisation in the late 20th century.* Oklahoma University Press.

Inden, R. (1995). Embodying god: From imperial progresses to national progress in India. *Economy and Society, 24*(2), 245–278.

Jahan, R. (1972). *Pakistan: Failure of national integration.* Columbia University Press.

Jalal, A. (1990). *The state of martial rule: The origins of Pakistan's political economy of defence.* Cambridge University Press.

Jalal, A. (1994). The sole spokesman: Jinnah, the Muslim League and the demand for Pakistan. Cambridge University Press.

Jalal, A. (1995). *Democracy and authoritarianism in South Asia: A comparative and historical perspective.* Cambridge University Press.

Jalal, A. (2000). *Self and sovereignty: Individual and community in South Asian Islam since 1850.* Routledge.

Jalal, A. (2008). *Partisans of Allah: Jihad in South Asia.* Harvard University Press.

Jalal, A. (2014). *The struggle for Pakistan: A Muslim homeland and global politics.* The Belknap Press of Harvard University Press.

Jameson, F. (2004). The politics of utopia. *New Left Review, 25*(1), 35–54.

Janowitz, M. (1977). *Military institutions and coercion in the developing nations.* Chicago University Press.

Jeffrey, C. (2001). A fist is stronger than five fingers: Caste and dominance in rural North India. *Transactions of the Institute of British Geographers, 26*(2), 217–236.

Kalia, R. (2011). Jinnah's Pakistan. In *Pakistan: From the Rhetoric of democracy to the rise of militancy.* Routledge.

Kanes, P. V. (1946). *History of dharmashastra* (vol. 3). Bhandarkar Oriental Research Institute.

Kaviraj, S. (1981). Political culture in independent India: An antiromantic view. *Teaching Politics, 7*(3/4), 1–22.

Kaviraj, S. (1988). A critique of the passive revolution. *Economic & Political Weekly, 23*(45/47), 2429–2444.

Kaviraj, S. (2000). Modernity and politics in India. *Daedalus, 129*(1), 137–162.

Kaviraj, S. (2005). On the enchantment of the state: Indian thought on the role of the state in the narrative of modernity. *European Journal of Sociology, 46*(2), 263–296.

Kaviraj, S. (2010). *The imaginary institution of India*. Permanent Black.

Khan, J. D. (1999). *Pakistan leadership challenges*. Oxford University Press.

Khan, M. A. (1967). *Friends not masters: A political autobiography*. Oxford University Press.

Khan, M. H. (2000). Rent-seeking as a process. In M. H. Khan & K. S. Jomo (Eds.), *Rents, rent-seeking and economic development: Theory and evidence from Asia* (pp. 70–144). Cambridge University Press.

Khan, R. (2000). *Pakistan: A dream gone sour*. Oxford University Press.

Khilnani, S. (1997). *The idea of India*. Hamish Hamilton.

Kohli, A. (1990). *Democracy and discontent: India's growing crisis of governability*. Cambridge University Press.

Kothari, R. (1967). Party politics and political development. *Economic & Political Weekly*, 2(3/5), 163, 165, 167–169, 171–173, 175, 177–178.

Kothari, R. (1970). *Politics in India*. Little, Brown & Co.

Kothari, R. (1976). *Democratic Polity and Social Change*. Allied.

Kothari, R. (2001). *Caste in Indian politics*. Orient Longman.

Kosambi, D. D. (1956). *An introduction to the study of Indian history*. Popular Book Depot.

Kukreja, V. (1991). *Civil–military relations in South Asia: Pakistan, Bangladesh and India*. New SAGE Publications.

Leftwich, A. (1995). Bringing politics back in: Towards a model of the developmental state. *Journal of Development Studies*, 31(3), 400–427.

Lieven, A. (2011). *Pakistan: A hard country*. Penguin.

Macaulay, T. B. (1835; 1972). Minute on Indian education. In J. Clive & T. Pinney (Eds.), *Thomas Babington Macaulay: Selected writings*. Chicago University Press.

MacIntyre, A. (1988). *Whose justice? Which rationality?* University of Notre Dame Press.

Malik, D. (2007). The political economy of communalism: A response from the left. In J. P. Neelsen & D. Malik (Eds.), *Crisis of state and nation: South Asian states between nation-building and fragmentation* (pp. 363–398). Manohar.

Malik, I. (2001). *Ethnic conflict, international dispute*. Oxford University Press.

Markey, D. (2007). A false choice in Pakistan. *Foreign Affairs*, 86(4), 85–102.

McGarr, P. M. (2013). *The cold war in South Asia: Britain, The United States and the Indian subcontinent 1945–1965*. Cambridge University Press.

Morris-Jones, W. H. (1964). *The government and politics of India*. Hutchinson University Library.

Mukherjee, K. (2017). Military governments, the ISI and political hybridity in contemporary Pakistan: From independence to Musharraf. *Journal of Intelligence History*, 16(2), 172–193.

Mukhia, H. (1981). Was their feudalism in Indian History? *Journal of Peasant Studies*, 8(3), 273–310.

Musharraf, P. (2006). *In the line of fire*. Simon and Schuster.

Myrdal, G. (1968). *Asian drama: An enquiry into the poverty of nations* (3 Vols.). Pantheon.

Myrdal, G. (1970). *The challenge of world poverty*. Vintage Books.

Nandy, A. (1970). The culture of Indian politics: A stock taking. *The Journal of Asian Studies, 30*(1), 57–79.

Nandy, A. (1973). The making and unmaking of political cultures in India. *Daedalus, 102*(1), 115–137.

Nandy, A. (1983). *The intimate enemy: Loss and recovery of self under colonialism*. Oxford University Press.

Nasr, V. R. (2005). National identities and the India–Pakistan conflict. In T. V. Paul (Ed.), *The India–Pakistan conflict: An enduring rivalry* (pp. 178–201). Cambridge University Press.

Nawaz, S. (2008). *Crossed swords: Pakistan, its army, and the wars within*. Oxford University Press.

Neelsen, J. P, & Malik, D. (2007). South Asia: Social fragmentation and political crisis in the periphery. In J. P. Neelsen & D. Malik (Eds.), *Crisis of state and nation: South Asian states between nation-building and fragmentation* (pp. 10–36). Manohar.

Newman, K. J. (1959). Pakistan's preventative autocracy and its causes. *Pacific Affairs, 32*(1), 18–33.

Oldenburg, P. (2017). Loyalty, disloyalty and semi-loyalty in Pakistan's hybrid regime. *Commonwealth and comparative politics, 55*(1), 11–23.

Paul, T. V. (2014). *The warrior state: Pakistan in the contemporary world*. Oxford University Press.

Potter, D. (1986). *India's political administrators*. Clarendon Press.

Rahman, T. (2004). *Denizens of alien worlds: Study of education, inequality and polarisation in Pakistan*. Oxford University Press.

Rais, R. B. (2017). *Imagining Pakistan: Modernism, state and the politics of Islamic revival*. Lexington Books.

Rizvi, H.-A. (1974). *Military and politics in Pakistan*. Progressive Publishers.

Rizvi, H.-A. (2000). *Military, state and society in Pakistan*. St Martin's Press.

Rudolph, L., & Rudolph, S. H. (1968). *The modernity of tradition: Political development in India*. Chicago University Press.

Rudolph, L., & Rudolph, S. H. (1987). *In pursuit of Lakshmi: The political economy of the Indian state*. University of Chicago Press.

Samad, Y. (1995). *A nation in turmoil: Nationalism and ethnicity in Pakistan, 1937–1958*. SAGE Publications.

Schmidt, J. R. (2009). Unravelling of Pakistan. *Survival, 51*(3), 29–56.

Sehmitter, P. A., & Karl, T. L. (1991). What democracy is and is not. *Journal of Democracy, 2*(3), 75–88.

Shafqat, S. (1997). *Civil–military relations in Pakistan: From Zulffikar Ali Bhutto to Benazir Bhutto*. Westview Press.

Shafqat, S. (2021). Pakistan in 2020: The opposition fights back. *Asian Survey*, *61*(1), 183–193.

Shafqat, S. (2019). Pakistan army: Sustaining hegemony and constructing democracy? *Journal of South Asian and Middle Eastern Studies*, *42*(2), 20–51.

Shah, A. (2014). *The army and democracy: Military politics in Pakistan*. Harvard University Press.

Shaikh, F. (2009). *Making sense of Pakistan*. Columbia University Press.

Sharma, R. S. (2005). *Indian feudalism*. Macmillan.

Sheth, D. L. (1999). Secularisation of caste and making of new middle class. *Economic & Political Weekly*, *35*(34–35), 2502–2510.

Shils, E. (1965). *Political development in the new states*. Mouton.

Siddiqa, A. (2007). *Military INC: Inside Pakistan's military economy*. Pluto Press.

Siddiqa, A. (2014). Return of nationalism. *The Express Tribune*, 25 December. https://tribune.com.pk › story › return-of-nationalism

Stein, B. (1998). *A history of India*. Blackwell.

Swami, P. (2007). *India, Pakistan and the secret jihad: The covert war in Kashmir, 1947–2004*. Routledge.

Talbot, I. (1998). *Pakistan: A modern history*. Oxford University Press.

Talbot, I. (2000). *Inventing the nation: India and Pakistan*. Oxford University Press.

Vajpeyi, A. (2012). *Righteous republic: The political foundations of modern India*. Harvard University Press.

Varshney, A. (1999). *Democracy in the country side*. Cambridge University Press.

Varshney, A. (2000). Elite and mass politics in the context of economic reforms. In J. D. Sachs, A. Varshney & N. Bajpai (Eds.), *India in the era of reforms*. Oxford University Press.

Weber, M. (1958). *The religion of India: The sociology of Hinduism*. Free Press.

Weber, M. (2015). Politics as vocation. In T. Waters & D. Waters (Eds.), *Weber's rationalism and modern society* (pp. 129–198). Palgrave Macmillan.

Weidemann, D. (2007). Crisis of the state in Pakistan. In J. P. Neelsen & D. Malik (Eds.), *Crisis of state and nation: South Asian states between nation-building and fragmentation* (pp. 84–117). Manohar.

Weinbaum, M. G. (2011). Regime and system change. In S. P. Cohen (Ed.), *The future of Pakistan* (pp. 225–235). Oxford University Press.

Weiner, M. (1963). India's two political cultures. In *Political change in South Asia*. Firma K. L. Mukhopadhyay.

White, B. H. (2004). *India working*. Cambridge University Press.

Wilcox, W. A. (1965). Pakistan's coup d'etat of 1958. *Pacific Affairs*, *38*(2), 142–163.

Wittfogel, K. A. (1957). *Oriental despotism*. Yale University Press.

Young, R. (2016). *Postcolonialism: An historical introduction*. Wiley Blackwell.

Zafar, S. M. (2001). Constitutional development. In H. Malik (Ed.), *Pakistan: Founders aspirations and today's realities*. Oxford University Press.

Zaheer, H. (1998). *The Rawalpindi conspiracy case 1951*. Oxford University Press.

Zaidi, A. S. (2005). State, military and social transition: Improbable future of democracy in Pakistan. *Economic & Political Weekly, 40*(49), 5173–5181.

Zaidi, A. S. (2007). Is Pakistan a democracy? *Seminar, 576*(August), 13–27.

Ziring, L. (1982). South Asian tangles and triangles. In L. Ziring (Ed.), *The subcontinent in world politics: India, its neighbours and the great powers*. Praeger.

Ziring, L. (2003). *Pakistan: At the cross current of history*. One World.

Nuclear Nationalisms and Quest for Ontological Security

3

South Asia, which has had a chequered history of conflict and cooperation, is presently under multiple levels of stress of a subcontinental nuclear war, multi-ethnic strifes and the perils of left-wing insurgency and the resultant violence. So it is imperative to investigate the type of means of establishing lasting peace and stability in the region. This assumes added importance in the light of the fact that the countries of South Asia have failed to properly institutionalize cooperation and concretize peace, despite several endeavours.

In the case of South Asia, the issues jeopardizing peace in the region are deeply rooted in the internal space of the polities, but their virulence has a spill-over effect outside their boundaries. For instance, contestations of identity that produces fierce ethno-cultural conflicts, divergent notions of nationhood that may lead to geopolitical disputes like those of Jammu and Kashmir, and the struggle for power and strategic dominance largely engendered by a greed-stricken paranoid bureaucratic/military/political complex emanate from within and induce external conflicts. Hence, it may be argued that the sources of apocalyptical conflicts in South Asia have been endemic and mirror the fragility of intra-regional security architecture. So the region is imbued with several subterranean molecular impulses which have proved to be intractable and have factored deeply in pulverizing peace and stability in the region.

India–Pakistan animosity that possesses all the qualities mentioned above is an archetypal manifestation of the nature of South Asian conflicts. It has overdetermined all other considerations when we get down to make an analysis of the causes for the enfeeblement of the regional security architecture of South Asia. A deeper look into India–Pakistan hostilities also provides a pertinent explanation as to the reasons for the predominance of subcontinental dynamics over South Asian regional affairs. If we problematize South Asian security from the perspective of the security dynamics of the Indian subcontinent, May 1998 emerges out as a watershed in this regard. This is mainly because at this juncture, both subcontinental adversaries lifted the shroud of ambiguity that had cloaked their nuclear postures, after which the entire regional security architecture has come under the constant threat of massive destabilization. The key inducement to this effect is the unremitting adversarial relationship between the two States, owing to which a continuing fear of nuclear clash has got structured deeply into the architecture of subcontinental security. A perennial source to catalyse this is the unending cross-border terrorism and the resultant tension over their borders. Terrorism when fused with Jihad is a lethal combination and the emergence of radical Islamist movements has been a major challenge to the regional security architecture of South Asia. Though Muslims like others have multiple identities based upon, race, class, tribe, language and territory, the overemphasis on their Muslimness by the extremist practitioners of Islam puts them on a collision course with the State and other communities (Warikoo, 2006, p. 30).

One of the worst forms of such a trend is the anti-modernist religious extremism nurtured by the Taliban in Afghanistan which is a Frankenstein monster that emanated out of the United States' negative intellectual exercise. This transnational menace has penetrated deep into wider global spaces, largely due to the efforts of non-State agencies such as Al-Qaeda. However, Pakistan has emerged as the key nursing ground for fomenting transborder Islamist extremism and due to this, the nuclearization of the subcontinent has tended to intensify the security predicament of South Asia in several ways. First, the existence of terror infrastructures in a nuclearized Pakistan augments the threat of nuclear backlash by it in the event of any stringent operations to dismantle the same. This is because in Pakistan; the Inter-Services Intelligence (ISI), the army and the Islamist extremists have been interwoven into a vicious ensemble with surreptitious patronage rendered by US' defence and intelligence agencies and this nexus has been emboldened after Pakistan's overt acquisition of nuclear weapons, thus further excruciating the accomplishment of the said task. Above all, the United States' increasing influence in shaping key strands of Pakistan's security in the wake of the US-led post-9/11 war on terrorism, has been a compound effect in this regard.

Further, owing to these interlocked propositions and the increasing illegitimate nuclear commerce nurtured from Pakistan, the chances of terrorists laying their hands on weapons of mass destruction has escalated to manifold proportions. Hence, the rapidity with which the pervasive impact of Islamic extremism and the nuclear competition underway in the subcontinent prognosticates towards a perilous denouement. Thus, the advent of nuclear weapons competition, covertly in the 1980s and early 1990s, and overtly after 1998, coupled with violence, terrorism and religious hatred, seems to have destabilized the entire region. This scenario also seems to have mocked the notions of deterrence theorists that the existence of nuclear weapons qualitatively contributes to dissolving conflictual situations.

The region after coming under the vicious orbit of nuclear weapons is beleaguered by the fears of an inadvertent escalation of any conflict to the nuclear threshold, unauthorized use of nuclear weapons, access to weapons by the terrorists and nuclear accidents. So, the nuclearization of South Asia has not only been a detrimental factor for the regional security architecture of South Asia, but the prospects of finding an amicable solution to long-standing disputes of the region have also become complex. All this has happened primarily because peace talks, confidence-building measures, the intervention of multilateral institutions and initiatives towards constructive engagement have proved to be a parody in South Asia, under the constant threat of nuclear weapons and terrorism.

INDIA, PAKISTAN AND THE NATURE OF
THE REGIONAL SECURITY ARCHITECTURE

To make sense of the nature of the regional security architecture, we can take into account the ways in which South Asia as a region has been conceptualized by Barry Buzan and Ole Waever. For Buzan and Waever, in South Asia, the transformation from colonialism to an autonomous region happened by the simultaneous liberation of its States in a temporary parallel. Hence, the space between the transition from colonialism to an independent region was very limited in South Asia. Besides, the region was also characterized by inter-State rivalry, with States being involved in war with each other. Buzan and Waever explain this by problematizing the region in terms of the polarity theory. In accordance with this, the inter-State rivalry in South Asia has been between the two subcontinental adversaries that are India and Pakistan and hence, in the vocabulary of the regional security complex theory, the region denotes a space having a bipolar competition among the two regional powers (Buzan & Waever, 2003, p. 37). Thus, as the Cold War was defining an intense bipolar security structure at the global level, South Asia was structuring itself into a region that was characterized by conflicts that were founded upon mutual threat perceptions. This was apparent in the episodes of conflict between India and Pakistan.

At the bottom of this lies the partition of the Indian subcontinent in 1947. With the subcontinent getting cleaved into two hostile neighbours, foundations were laid for a tumultuous phase of regional conflicts in South Asia that has tended to be unremitting. Owing to this, the inherent fragility of South Asian regional security architecture has largely been fostered by the fierce bilateral rivalry between India and Pakistan. The region's security environment has largely been regulated by the temperature of relations between these two subcontinental adversaries. Primarily because both are embroiled in an antagonistic relationship for the last more than seven decades, the effect of which has been the nuclearization of the regional security environment.

Underpinning such an enduring trajectory of animosity has been the India-centred explanation of the State's security problematique of Pakistan. The irredentist claims over the territory of Jammu and Kashmir have been foundational to such an explanation which has factored deeply in determining the course of Pakistan's security and foreign policy in the Indian subcontinent, since the inception of the new State. Hence, due to the overdeterministic accentuation upon irredentism while moulding its security and foreign policy, Pakistan has evolved into a revisionist State that constantly endeavours at gaining escalation dominance over India through overt or covert military means. As a product of this, India has been coercively enmeshed into the quagmire of the Pakistani State's security problematique.

Such a regional security environment has compelled India to situate Pakistan as the key variable in determining the nature of its own State's security problematique. This problem got compounded as India also inherited several problems of democratization and State construction, as a consequence of the burden of the shared colonial legacy (Bajpai, 1998, p. 160). It confronted serious dilemmas of negotiating the internal challenges of governance and development that continued to get perplexed, due to the consistent security challenge handed down to the country by Pakistan which is an irredentist State (Paul, 2014, pp. 3–5).

Hence, India has coerced to fashion the contours of its State's security problematique, in accordance with the geostrategic challenge posed by Pakistan. Owing to the constant strategic provocation of Pakistan that emanated out of its clarion declaration of India as its primary enemy, it emerged as the central concern in the context of India's national security. As Pakistan concentrated its entire military and strategic might to advance a security contest with India by considering it as an existential threat, the latter was compelled to raise its own defence preparedness. In this way, India's national security imagery largely began to be shaped by the conception of Pakistan as an impending security menace.

What has been crucial is that even though India achieved a considerable degree of stability in maintaining the process of political development, it has always been a status quoist State. As a marked contrast to this, Pakistan has consistently attempted to emerge as a revisionist State, in spite of experiencing a precarious course of political development in the entire history of its existence. Implying that Pakistan constantly endeavoured at transforming the political cartography of the subcontinent, instituted in 1947 through the process of partition and the creation of it as an independent State. India on its part, persistently sought to maintain and consolidate the subcontinent's fixity of political territoriality, by adhering to the principle of nontransgression of the arrangements of 1947 by which it not only had derived liberation from colonial rule but its territory also got divided for the purpose of creating the new State of Pakistan.

Overall the end result has been that due to the policy of irredentism and the political paranoia for competition with India pursued unrelentingly by Pakistan, both States have ended up getting locked in a protracted trail of conflict since the day of their inception. Such a stalemate does not seem to defuse and the territory of Jammu and Kashmir has emerged as the key battleground of high politics between the two countries. This kind of situation continues, despite four wars and several attempts at peacebuilding. To further complicate the quagmire, the two subcontinental adversaries have got themselves embroiled in an aggressive nuclear arms race. On its part, the nuclearization of the Indo-Pak dyadic equations in 1998 has deepened South Asia's regional security dilemmas. This is because of the Pakistani involvement in a low-intensity conflict with India by way of using the instruments of supporting the insurgency in Jammu and Kashmir and State-sponsored cross-border terrorism deep inside its territory. Such a low-intensity warfare constantly haunts the region with the fear of both the States reaching the threshold of a nuclear war which may have fatal effects upon human security and the ecology in the region. Besides, the probable threat of terrorists operating in the region, gaining access to the nuclear arsenal has constantly bedevilled the security establishments across South Asia.

Hence, owing to all this, the Pakistan factor has assumed enormous significance in India's foreign policy calculus. An ontologically conflictual relation with it, parochialized India's national security paradigm to the subcontinent and the nuclearization of the security of both has intensified India's national security dilemmas. Thus, tumultuous neighbourhood coupled with disputed borders has been a major concern for India's policymakers. Although the discourse relating to security studies has undergone drastic changes in the case of India, the winds of this change seems to have not touched it. During the period of the Cold War, the term security was defined by Western intellectuals and practitioners of Statecraft as national security and threatening others (Dalby, 1988, p. 415). In this sense, the military-dominated conception of national security that engrossed the entire discourse of security studies during the Cold War, required the construction of the notion of a potential threat to identity and political stability of the polity (Chaturvedi, 1998, p. 702). In the post-Cold War era, however, competing visions of security have been articulated, and the conventional discourses have been subjected to interdisciplinary scrutiny (Agnew & Corbridge, 1993, p. 267). But irrespective of systemic global transformations, India's national security concerns have remained monolithic in character. That means, Pakistan factor has dominated the shaping of the country's national security paradigm since independence and it continues to do so even today.

Regional security threats, thus, have largely determined India's national security paradigm and also brought the nuclear dimension to its security considerations (Tellis, 2001, p. 12). This phenomenon then, brings to the fore, the significance of understanding Pakistan as a key factor in shaping India's national security policy. It has not only been the main security obligation that has preoccupied the thinking and imagination of the policymakers in India but has existed as the greatest threat to its external and internal security (Budania, 2001, p. 5).

Hence, the omnibus presence of the Pakistan factor in India's strategic calculus and foreign policy perception cannot be rebuffed. Although both in theory and in the view of the successive governments, India's security and defence policies have been depicted as holistic and security-specific. However, in practice, the excessive role of the Pakistan factor in their evolution has made them look very much Pakistan-centric (Budania, 2001, p. 5).

Thus, there seem to exist a policy parochialism in India which results in the paralytic nature of its security and foreign policy. It is also plagued by what Stephen Cohen called 'die realism–idealism conundrum' (2001, p. 308). Cohen's illustration also helps us to inter-rogate the methodological difficulty that India–Pakistan relations poses to international relations scholars to unpack the transient character of their interactable bilateral relations (McLeod, 2008, p. 5). In this regard, Varun Sahni has argued that Indian security policy appears to be characterized by its shortcomings, no matter whatever the issue area. The Indian security policy is unable to achieve what it sets out to do? It has always operated in the context of structural constraints that have restricted its efficacy. The shortcomings of India's security policy in a multiplicity of issue-areas have less to do with the well-known inadequacies in the policymaking process and much more to do with the context in which the policy has to operate (Sahni, 2008, p. 211).

NUCLEARIZATION OF SOUTH ASIA

De-colonialization of the Indian subcontinent was accompanied by the emergence of India and Pakistan as two neighbours. However, the traumatic days of partition left behind deep scars on both sides (Burke & Ziring, 1990, p. 4). The colonial callousness and imperial manoeuvrings further intensified the quagmire (Blinkenberg, 1999, p. 46). This belligerence became more adverse after Pakistan joined the US-sponsored military bloc in 1953. This helped Pakistan to receive massive military assistance from the United States. Compulsions of national security forced India to upgrade its defence capability in order to counter this Pakistani ascendancy. All this led to an arms race between the two that subsequently transformed into a competition for acquiring nuclear weapons capability.

Further, the threat from nuclear China factored deeply in India's security considerations and largely determined the alterations in its nuclear policy. India's policy of nuclear abstinence underwent a defini-tive change after the first Chinese nuclear test in 1964. This shift in India's nuclear policy to nuclear ambiguity began with its own nuclear test in 1974, which was a watershed in India's nuclear decision-making (Poulose, 1996, p. 44). The reasons for the 1974 nuclear tests are varied in character. First, domestic political factors such as the urge to shore up Indira Gandhi's and Congress party's slipping popularity, coincided with the maturing of the technological progress formed a strong impetus to the 1974 nuclear tests (Bidwai & Vanaik, 2000, pp. 218–220). The trauma of defeat at the hands of China in 1962 persistently beleaguered the Indian political class and hence national security threats were naturally inflated after the nuclearization of China. Here lie the roots of India's quest for acquiring nuclear weapons capability which induced the tests.

Viewed from this perspective, it may be stated that security, rather than international status, was the driving force behind India's nuclear programme (Singh, 1998, pp. 9–10, 24–25). Domestic pressures and ideological forces also played a significant role in this regard. The influence of the strategic enclave of scientists and key policymakers, and Nehruvian State's and Indian elite's desires for symbols and accoutrements of modernity and power, are some other incitements to this effect (Abraham, 1998, p. 19). However, the weak, indecisive and regionally limited policies resulted in retarding of the further development of a nuclear programme which resulted in a 24-year gap between the two tests (Karnad, 2002, p. 41).

Even post 1998, the problem remained the same. The inadequacies of India's nuclear doctrine, uncertainty over the issue of command and control, improper development of the technology to mate the nuclear weapons with delivery systems like the ballistic missiles, form some strategic bottlenecks in this regard (Kampani, 2014, pp. 384–389). Such a predicament was explicit during the Kargil crisis and 2001–2002 military standoff with Pakistan when India's decision-makers found out the country's weaknesses to mobilize its nuclear forces (Bommakanti & Desai, 2021). Worst of all, the Pakistan-centric character of India's nuclear weapons programme is yet another problem. In fact, India's nuclear programme right from its inception was largely shaped by global forces and to a considerable extent, the presence of a nuclear China played its own part.

However, of late, India's nuclear programme has tapered down to merely reflecting concerns over security against a nuclear-armed Pakistan. Mainly because India existed without any wars with a nuclear powered China, but has been constantly engaged in a conflictual relationship with Pakistan. In any case, this long peace with China may not remain in perpetuity. The realist aspirations of China, with an unsettled border dispute with India, may always be a security threat to South Asia. In this regard, the ambiguity over India's second-strike capability vis-à-vis China raises serious concerns for subcontinental security in particular and South Asian security at large. Such concerns tend to deepen as the prospects of a joint Sino-Pak venture in a nuclear standoff against India have been constantly increasing (Bommakanti & Desai, 2021).

On the other hand, India's quest for nuclear weapons capability emerged as a major challenge for the Pakistani strategists, significantly because India haunted the psyche of the Pakistani ruling elite in the same manner as China did for India. India's military engagement with Pakistan in 1971 and the resultant dismemberment of East Pakistan had a catalytic impact in this regard. Hence, acquiring military parity with India became the sole national objective for Pakistan. This paranoiac urge for parity and the megalomaniacal fantasies of the Pakistani political class pressed it towards exploring avenues for attaining nuclear weapons capability. The acquisition of nuclear weapons became the epitome of national pride.

Zulfikar Ali Bhutto, the progenitor of Pakistan's nuclear program, jingoistically proclaimed 'If India developed an atomic bomb, we too will develop one. Even if we have to eat grass, leaves or to remain hungry because there is no conventional alternative to the atomic bomb' (Bhutto, 1969, p. 21). Bhutto also justified the need for a nuclear deterrent against India by framing it in terms of the metaphor of Pakistan's weapon in the service of Islamic civilization (Shaikh, 2002, p. 39). Bhutto situated his passionate defence of nuclear weaponization in the framework of Pakistan's foundational ideology that is rooted in the Islamic identity.

This became apparent when he designated nuclear weapons as an Islamic bomb (Das, 2009, p. 401). Bhutto has stated thus, 'the Christian, Jewish and Hindu civilizations have this capability too … only the Islamic civilization was without it … but this was about to change' (Bhutto, 1969, p. 151). Hence, immediately after the 1971 defeat, Bhutto government in Pakistan took the decision in pursuance of developing nuclear weapons in January 1972 (Subrahmanyam, 1990, p. 126). Consequently, a covert nuclear competition began between the two subcontinental rivals that ultimately culminated in their overt nuclearization in 1998.

NUCLEAR WEAPONS TESTING BY INDIA AND PAKISTAN

India's postcolonial history has witnessed one of the most polemic national debates that centred on the country's nuclear policy. The broad national opinion was, of course, averse to nuclear weaponization. However, there still existed several hawks in the sociopolitical circles who contested this general opinion. They campaigned for nuclear weaponization on the basis of India's nuclear neighbourhood and the international turmoil generated by Cold War intrigues. The Jana Sangh was the most vocal pro-bomb political party. It argued that India's prestige and national security depended on nuclear weapons (Perkovich, 1999, p. 151). Anyhow, the moderate opinion prevailed over that of the hawks and restraint became the mantra of India's nuclear policy. It was marked by the twin objectives of using nuclear energy for peaceful purposes while keeping the weapons option open. Even the 1974 nuclear test was indicative of this binary objective. Nevertheless, this dualism thrust the country's nuclear policy into a state of ambiguity. This ambiguity, however, ended in 1998, when India conducted the Pokhran II nuclear tests. However, this happened, only at the cost of India losing its conventional military superiority over that of Pakistan.

As regards the Pokhran II nuclear weapons tests, it emerged as a path-breaking event in India's contemporary political history. It not only transmogrified the country's foreign policy by adding the nuclear dimension but also induced enormous interest in the domestic sphere regarding issues concerning foreign policy and national security. Since May 1998, India's electoral politics and parliamentary debates have been deeply engrossed in issues concerning national security and foreign policy and nuclear issues have been a major aspect in this regard. Unlike earlier precedence of electoral battles and interparty parlance that were dominated by mere mundane issues relating to the common man, the post-May 1998 scenario has been entirely different. Issues—like those of nuclear deterrence, weaponizing of nuclear capability, South Asian security, the country's energy security and the acquisition of global nuclear status for India—have also acquired considerable space in the domestic political sphere. The politico-strategic equations between India and Pakistan have also been visualized in the domestic sphere from the nuclear dimension since May 1998. Above all, the special session of the Parliament that took place on 21 and 22 July 2008 has been a landmark event in India's parliamentary history, as it was convened to discuss the confidence vote purely on a foreign policy issue and this epoch-making development has also been fountained by the nuclear issue. All these developments indicate to a considerable extent a metamorphosis that seems to have been engendered by the overt acquisition of nuclear weapons capability by the two subcontinental adversaries (Kumar, 2011).

The Pokhran II nuclear testing of 1998 itself was the first major policy decision of the nascent Bharatiya Janta Party (BJP)-led coalition government that was related to national security. Not only that, it was an epoch-making decision in the history of India as it trumpeted the overt acquisition of nuclear weapons capability by the country. The motives for the tests were candidly spelt out in the statements from official quarters. The government was unambiguous in articulating that the aim of this nuclear test was to portray India's credentials as a nuclear weapons power. It was also made amply clear that the tests were conducted under the compulsions of the prevailing nuclear environment. The government vindicated the tests by stating that they were not directed against any country and were meant to provide a credible option to counter the geostrategic threats in the region (*The Hindu*, 1998). The then national security advisor, to the Prime Minister, Brijesh Mishra, had indicated, 'The Government is deeply concerned as were the previous Governments, about the nuclear environment in India's neighbourhood. These tests provide reassurances to the people of India that their national security interests are paramount and will be promoted and protected' (Mishra, 1998).

Thus, the prime motive driving India towards an open declaration of nuclear weapons capacity has been the requirement of strategic might to fashion the regional security dynamics and hegemonize the regional security system by annihilating any potential threat to its regional strategic supremacy. Historically viewed, India's nuclear weapons programme has been factored deeply in diverse circumstances. First, domestic determinants like the influence of personalities, such as Bhabha and Nehru, have been as important as that of external security threats. Apart from the domestic State structures and politics, there is also a non-neorealist second image explanation to the issue. In this sense, the nuclear programme has also been attributed to psychological factors such as the paranoia of racist colonialism and fantasy of obtaining major power status (Perkovich, 1999, pp. 444–445).

India's policy of maintaining deliberate nuclear ambiguity was large because of the benign security environment of the region that it confronted in the early years (Tellis, 2001, p. 12). So, although the origin of the nuclear programme was non-military, it acquired a military dimension owing to the changing regional and global security systems. This shift marked a departure from the earlier strategic stance, wherein the first nuclear test of 1974 was declared to have been carried out specifically for peaceful purposes. As regards Pokhran II, however, the strategic aspect was candidly accented by the government at the very outset and the logic of security predicament in the neighbourhood was employed to impart rationality to the decision. In view of this, the most pressing concerns that led to the 1998 nuclear tests may be regarded as follows. First, it was in one respect, a reaction to the indefinite extension of the Nuclear Nonproliferation Treaty and the growing pressures of the United States on India to sign the Comprehensive Test Ban Treaty, the CTBT, that would have closed India's nuclear option. It was also to a considerable extent, the product of the philosophy of the BJP (Kapur, 2001, pp. 213–214).

Based on this it may be stated that India's nuclear behaviour pattern in the recent past has thus been governed by a combination of three factors. Security against China and Pakistan, a search for international status, and acting as a strong domestic determinant have been the electoral commitments of the BJP (Ganguly & Hagerty, 2005, pp. 120–124). In addition to this, the clandestine nuclear programme of Pakistan and its growing nuclear and missile collaboration with China in the 1980s and 1990s is yet another influence towards a definitive transition in India's nuclear programme. Apropos Pokhran II, the Ghauri missile test by Pakistan on 6 April 1998 has been seen as an impelling force. Besides this, oppositional nationalism that is a combination of the fear of the enemy and pride in one's nation tends to construct the national identity and makes strong leaders seek symbols of power. This conceptualization of oppositional nationalism suitably represents BJP's ideology and in this vein, a comparison between Gaullist nationalism and the French programme and BJP's Hindu nationalism and the Pokhran II nuclear tests could be drawn (Hyman, 2002, pp. 139–160).

On its part, the underlying motives for Pakistan's reaction to India's nuclear tests 'Shakti' are deeply rooted in the historical complexities produced at the time of partition. Its anxieties over India's superiority in terms of regional political geometry and India's brazen affirmations of its desires for the creation of larger space for accomplishing its global ambitions heightened Pakistan's anxieties (Rizvi, 1986a). Rizvi argues that three factors contribute to the national insecurity as a state of mind in Pakistan. A narrow and weakly defined purpose in terms of an Islamic State, the absence of a consensus regarding the evolution of national institutions and the heterogamous nature of the State (Rizvi, 1986b). Additionally, a bitter history of wars has contributed significantly in intensifying its security dilemma and signified the question as to how the perceived Indian threat should be countered.

To confront this dilemma, a twin-edged approach of fighting a low-intensity conflict by fomenting cross-border terrorism to spread terror on the Indian soil, with the acquisition of nuclear weapons capability acting as a suitable foil to this policy was adopted. Since the 1980s, Pakistan successfully used the nuclear brinkmanship through their covert nuclear capabilities to deter the chances of India using its conventional capacities to gain supremacy during the brasstacks crisis and at the time of the outbreak of militancy in Jammu and Kashmir in 1989–1990. This then braced the conviction of the Pakistani policy-makers that the best antidote to desensitize India's combat capacity is by acquiring nuclear weapons. So, the aim of Pakistan was to acquire a strategic parity with India based upon the concept of essential equivalence. The notion of essential equivalence did not mean quantitative equality of all nuclear forces between the two countries, but being essentially equal to the other (Nitze, 1979, pp. 48–49). Thus, the prime mover of Pakistan's nuclear programme and the tests of May 1998 was the urge to acquire a deterrent capability vis-à-vis India. Hence, faced with the concentration of military power in a region, the weaker States seek to balance their powerful neighbour (Sahni, 2008, p. 211).

NUCLEAR DETERRENCE, CONFLICT MANAGEMENT AND THE PROBLEMATIQUE OF PEACE-BUILDING IN SOUTH ASIA

There prevails an old and time-tested presumption that 'nuclear weapons cannot be an effective tool of foreign policy, to deal with everyday problems and challenges' (Spanier, 1989, p. 112). If we look in terms of two nuclear-powered adversaries, the fear of an all-out war is mutual (Kissinger, 1957, p. 15). Hence, nuclear deterrence rather than nuclear conflict should naturally characterize the relationship between two nuclear-powered adversaries. This was exactly the case between the two Cold War rivals, the United States and the Soviet Union (USSR). However, the nuclear situation in South Asia is unique and marks a clear departure from the superpower rivalry at the time of the Cold War, hence, the classic deterrence theory is insufficient to explain the Indo-Pak nuclear situation (Sridharan, 2007, pp. 9–10).

India and Pakistan are two nuclear-powered adversaries, whose tumultuous history after their overt acquisition of nuclear weapons capacity in 1998, has tended to contravene the classical theorizing on nuclear deterrence. Both countries have proved to be recurrently incapable of reducing the intensity of the conflictual nature of sub-continental politics. This phenomenon is paradoxical when we see it in the context of nuclear deterrence and upon Cold War politics. It is now well accepted among historians and scholars of international relations that the emergence of nuclear deterrence between the Soviet

Union and the United States largely contributed to the reduction of tension between them (Kumar, 2010).

However, India and Pakistan, unlike the United States and the Soviet Union, were once the same country, they have a common border and very short missile flight times limiting reaction time to almost nothing. Add to this a history of wars and the territorial dispute in Jammu and Kashmir marked by a separatist rebellion and a low-intensity war against India supported by Pakistan. This entire situation in turn is nested in a US-dominated global order, with a post-9/11 US military presence in Afghanistan and with nuclear powered China bordering both India and Pakistan, but which has historically been a clandestine supporter of the development of Pakistani nuclear and missile capabilities (Sridharan, 2007, p. 10).

Thus, when we attempt to understand the problems of peace and the nature of conflicts in a nuclearized security environment, the instance of Cold War confrontation between the United States and Soviet Union, and post-Cold War subcontinental hostilities between India and Pakistan present themselves as two antithetical propositions. If one generated the belief that nuclear weapons deter two adversaries from fighting with one another, the other contested the foundations of this cognition and has tended to reflect antithetical notions to this belief. The theories of nuclear deterrence that emerged during the height of the Cold War, basically aimed at arguing that there occurred a reduction of tension between the two Cold War adversaries, mainly due to the presence of nuclear weapons on both sides. However, there has been a plethora of historical instances of deterrence failures in which non-nuclear States and movements attacked nuclear States, often succeeding in their political objectives. In this regard, the failure of deterrence may occur due to structural causes like the lack of offence-defence distinction, strategic aspect of the stability-instability paradox, cognitive factors such as misperception and miscommunication, and organizational components like military-organizational pathologies (Bajpai, 1999, p. 251).

Hence, nuclear deterrence is not a monolithic conception and varied patterns of its manifestation may be witnessed. The subcontinental nuclear situation is one such unique instance and is far apart from that of the Cold War deterrence situation of the United States and the Soviet Union. It totally contradicts the notion of nuclear deterrence as there has been no substantial diminution of conflict in the region after the overt acquisition of nuclear weapons by India and Pakistan. Rather, the prospects of the continuation of conflict have been enhanced, hence creating an epistemological challenge to deterrence theorists. More significantly, the domestic environment in the polities of the subcontinent largely differs from that of the Cold War rivals which in itself contributes to the asymmetric notions of nuclear deterrence.

Yet another dimension is that deterrence theories developed during the period of the Cold War are embedded in the framework of the realist and neorealist theory of international relations which in turn is structured in accordance with the Western notions of Westphalian system of States. Wherein, the international system is characterized by anarchy generated by the struggle for power among the States, with the impact of the nature and structure of those polities' internal spheres upon their international relations is considered to be inconsequential. In this regard, the basic inadequacy of the deterrence theories and the realist and neorealist theories is their Eurocentricism that limits their capacity to render a comprehensive explanation to the nature of the international sub-systems formed by different regions. Their meta-interpretations of the world order, based upon the dominant politico-historical discourses shaped by Western experiences, fail to explain the diversities that characterize the regional sub-structures. These regional diversities are carved out of distinct notions of nationhood, the multiplicity of ethno-cultural leanings and distinct geo-demographic patterns that impart exclusivity in determining the identity of different regions.

THE NUCLEAR DIMENSION IN INDO-PAK CONFLICT

Since the 1970s, the prognosis of the potential nuclearization of India–Pakistan conflict was manifest. This manifestation appeared first in Pakistan's defeat in the war of 1971 and the subsequent germination of a hidden motive for countering India's conventional military superiority with nuclear weapons. India's nuclear test of 1974 acted as a catalyst to this effect and its ramifications were visible during the 1980s, when the covert presence of nuclear weapons in the subcontinent created serious tensions between the two countries. The testing of nuclear weapons in 1998 brought all this into the open and resulted in the explicit nuclearization of the long-standing bilateral conflict. Thus, in the subcontinent, the post-1998 security scenario has been marked by a crisis-prone brittle nuclear deterrence situation which has experienced strains intermittently due to the continuing low-intensity war on Indo-Pak borders, bolstered by terrorism and violence perpetrated by Pakistan based non-State actors. So, the stability of the deterrence situation in a tumultuous security scenario is imperative for conflict resolution in South Asia.

There are five crises situations to be reckoned with when we examine the impact of nuclearization upon India–Pakistan adversarial relationship and they must be categorized into two broad streams. The instances in the 1980s fall under the phase in which the two subcontinental rivals possessed a de facto nuclear status and after 1998, the condition of conflict transformed drastically, as both brazenly unveiled their nuclear weapons capabilities. However, all the five crises situations: the crisis over the fear of an Indian attack over the Cahuta nuclear complex in Pakistan of 1984, the 1986–1987 operation Brasstacks crisis, the May 1990 tension in the Kashmir valley and the resultant frictions between the two countries, the Kargil crisis and the 2001–2002 border mobilization after the December 13 terror attack on the Indian Parliament fall in a single line and must be viewed as a montage. Specifically, in so far as the impact of covert or overt presence of nuclear weapons constituting the quintessential component underlying all these crises situations is concerned (Kumar, 2014a, pp. 83–99).

However, one factor separating the covert and overt phases of the subcontinental nuclear scenario is that during the 1980s, the covert presence of nuclear weapons was considered to be a deterring phenomenon in averting three crises, that of 1983–1984, 1986–1987 and 1989–1990. These crises situations occurred in different strategic environments and diverse international situations. If in the 1980s, the backdrop was the Cold War, in the 1990s, it was the immediate post-Cold War scenario. The India–Pakistan crises since 2001 have been situated in the post-9/11 international environment (Chari et al., 2007, p. 9) against an emerging nuclearized security environment in South Asia, but each one stopped short of getting precipitated into a full-blown conflict. It is at this juncture that scholars, strategists and policymakers on both sides of the subcontinental divide, became optimist of the prevalence of a stable deterrence situation in the region. First, in 1983–1984, there were persistent reports that India intended to attack Pakistan's nuclear weapons production facilities and Pakistan threatened to retaliate with a similar attack on Indian facilities (Nightly News, 1994). In 1986–1987, there occurred a crisis when India conducted its biggest military exercise named Operation Brasstacks near the borders of Pakistan. The latter fearing that this was a preparation for an attack on it launched a defensive operation named Operation Sledgehammer. In reaction, India launched its Operation Trident and the situation reached the threshold of a massive conflict which was fortunately averted without any further damage. It is at the height of this crisis that Pakistan made an apparent admission that it had acquired nuclear weapons capability.

Finally, the crisis in the Kashmir valley that transpired in the spring of 1990, was the offshoot of Pakistan's biggest military exercise 'Zarb-i-Momin' in late 1989. Due to this, insurgency which was being spawned from the camps located in Pakistan precipitated to unprecedented proportions in the Kashmir valley. Responding to this, India threatened to carry out cross-border attacks in Pakistan to dismantle the terror infrastructures. Considering this as an act of hostility, Pakistan threatened to weaponize its nuclear capability to confront any Indian attack. Fears of escalation to the nuclear threshold brought in the active diplomatic engagement of the United States and the Soviet Union in order to dilute the crisis situation. By the time the United States sent the deputy National Security Adviser, Robert Gates, to visit India and Pakistan, the crisis had almost reached the stage of resolution (see Hersh, 1993; Krepon & Faruquee, 1994). These crises were not played out with a ready nuclear arsenal, but all three crises were about nuclear weapons. It was the threat of preventing the construction of nuclear facilities by the opponent in 1983–1984, there was the threat to build nuclear weapons in 1986–1987 and in 1989–1990, it was the threat of nuclear weapons being used in future. In these crises situations, war supposedly did not occur because of the tacit recognition on both sides regarding the surreptitious presence of nuclear weapons capabilities with the opponent (Kumar, 2014b, pp. 83–99).

This kind of opaque nuclear situation has been described in different ways as non-weaponized deterrence, wherein deterrence is derived by the power of each to construct nuclear weapons quickly (Perkovich, 1999, p. 86). Or recessed deterrence, which is a situation in which the countries have the capability to build and deliver nuclear weapons, but that capability is not exercised (Singh, 1993, p. 66; Tellis, 2001). It is also called existential deterrence which argues that any aggressor would be deterred from attacking if it feared a similar kind of retaliation. And in this way, nuclear weapons rather than encouraging wars helps to secure peace (Bundy, 1984, pp. 8–9). But the post-1998 subcontinental situation entirely metamorphasized and the perceived stability of nuclear deterrence was pushed into shambles. The explicit nuclearization of subcontinental security coerced the entire region into the short fuse of a nuclear conflict (Kumar, 2014b). This scenario was demonstrated first during the Kargil crisis.

KARGIL CRISIS

Right from the time of partition, the two subcontinental adversaries have got themselves embroiled in four wars and twice for at least, they were at the brink of war. Despite several attempts to break the stalemate, both appear to be locked in a seemingly perpetual and unremitting conflict (Ganguly, 2001, p. 1). Kashmir issue still remains to be an imbroglio impeding the process of normalization of their relations. The most recent discomfiture, manifested in the massive mobilization of troops along their borders during 2001 and 2002, is archetypal of a macabre situation. The perpetual advocacy of an irredentist policy by Pakistan has fundamentally resulted in the continuity of conflict in the subcontinent. One of its disturbing expressions occurred in 1999 when the Kargil crisis broke out.

It marked a clear departure from the earlier three Indo-Pakistani conflicts. This is because the conflict transpired at a juncture when the subcontinent had just barged into a nuclearized security environment. Since the beginning, many experts on nuclear issues in India had been contemplating that Pakistan may use the nuclear status as better bargaining clout in advancing its goals in Jammu and Kashmir (Ganguly, 1995, p. 328). The Kargil crisis seems to be the first example of such prognostications. The conflict ridiculed the nuclear deterrence framework and was symptomatic of the overt declaration of nuclear capabilities (Kumar, 2010, pp. 35–50).

Yet another feature of the Kargil crisis was that the intrusions came as an utter surprise for the Indian army and even the intelligence officials had been unable to anticipate this Pakistani offensive. The complacency on the part of India's military and intelligence machinery mainly resulted due to a substantial decline in the insurgency in Kashmir. The Indian government in the post-insurgency era had successfully conducted elections for the State Assembly and the Parliament and the turnout during these elections was also satisfying (Ganguly, 2001, p. 121). Hence, by the late 1990s, although patches of insurgent activities continued to cause devastation in the valley, still a considerable degree of normalcy had been restored. All this engendered a callous approach on the part of India's intelligence brigade which subsequently encouraged the calibrated strategic initiative that the Pakistani establishment took in Kargil. The Pakistani misadventure in Kargil also aimed at igniting the rapidly eroding insurgency in Kashmir (Ganguly, 2001, p. 120).

Hence, fashioning the strategic initiative in Kargil in accordance with the newly transpired nuclear equation that favoured it, Pakistan acted more as a revisionist state, which fancied chances of gaining a vantage point over a rather status quoist state, that is, India. Pakistan's objective clearly was to use the nuclear capability as a shield to occupy territory in a limited conventional thrust and acquire a bargaining chip in its conflict with India over Kashmir (Kumar, 2007, p. 246). Thus, the newly emerging nuclear relationship and the resultant embodiment of Pakistan made it perceive that it could make territorial gains in Kargil. To put it simply, Pakistan was convinced that India would be deterred and would not engage in a full-scale conflict or resort to a limited operation, because of the fear of escalation. Another reason for the conviction among Islamabad's military brass that the Kargil operation would not bring an immediate escalation to the nuclear level, emanated out of India's unilateral no-first-use declaration (Sidhu, 2007, p. 216).

During the Kargil crisis, it may be argued that the theory of comparative advantage worked in favour of Pakistan in so far as its endeavour of testing the limits of the Indo-Pak nuclear dyadic equation was concerned. The nuclear deterrence factor has been operating in Indo-Pak relations since 1987 (Subrahmanyam, 2000, p. 11) but the brazen venture in Kargil indicated how this deterrence situation has emerged as a relatively advantageous position for Pakistan. India's inability to stem the rising tide of insurgency that intensified in Kashmir since 1989 and to launch an aggressive conventional attack in the Kargil crisis, as it had done in 1965 and 1971, signifies the better bargaining advantages that Pakistan gained after the overt nuclearization of subcontinental security (Basrur, 2006, pp. 73–74; Narang, 2014, p. 297).

THE 2001–2002 CRISIS

The nuclear dimension was most apparent during the 2001–2002 military impasse that resulted out of the terror attack on the Indian Parliament by Pakistan-based militant outfits. On 13 December 2001, Pakistan-sponsored cross-border terrorism assumed alarming proportions, when one of the most firmly shielded structures in India—the Parliament House Complex—became the target of terrorist attacks. The then Union Home Minister Mr L. K. Advani designated the attack on the Parliament as the 'most audacious and alarming episode in the history of Pakistan-sponsored terrorism in India' (Hagerty 2020, p. 18). The incident brought the two subcontinental adversaries to the brink of a full-scale war (Kapur, 2007, p. 134) that was imminent with portents of an apocalyptical nuclear conflict (Hagerty, 2012, pp. 223–224; Swami, 2009, p. 144). This event was preceded by a successful terror strike on Jammu and Kashmir assembly house in Srinagar in October 2001 which was perpetrated by Jaish-e-Mohammad

(Hagerty, 2020, p. 17). Although the attack on the Indian Parliament house complex was masterminded by Jaish-e-Mohammad, Lashkar-e-Tayyiba also played a significant role in accomplishing the incident (Tankel, 2011, p. 112).

The breach of such high-security zones set off alarm bells not only for the government but also for the entire natioOn. The events ushered in one of the most perilous security situations in the chequered history of India–Pakistan relations. The situation got further deteriorated by the sinister acts of militants when the family quarters of army personnel were attacked at Kaluchak of Jammu and Kashmir by the Lashkar-e-Tayyiba in May 2002 (Gokhale, 2017, pp. 1–52). Owing to these developments, the then Indian Prime Minister A. B. Vajpayee went to the extent of declaring that the war on terror had now reached a definitive stage. With Pakistan exhibiting a sense of reticence towards Indian admonitions regarding its involvement in the trail of terrorist attacks, the latter took recourse to military brinkmanship. The result was consternating. Both India and Pakistan ordered the largest mobilization of their armies in 15 years and a total of nearly one million troops on the border were stationed (Milewiski, 2002, p. 123). With this impending conflict, the invalidity of the nuclear deterrence framework in Indo-Pak dyadic equations again resurfaced. From this perspective it may be noted that if nuclear deterrence actually worked in the context of the subcontinental conflicts, instability on the Indo-Pak borders would not have intermittently escalated to perilous proportions, making the region constantly vulnerable to threats of a nuclear exchange (Kumar, 2002, cited in Kumar, 2007, p. 247)

This has happened mainly because the overt acquisition of nuclear capability by India and Pakistan seems to have brought contrasting ramifications for the State behaviour of the two subcontinental adversaries. On the one hand, it appears to have enfeebled India's capacity to initiate even a limited conventional military offensive and on the other hand, it seems to have emboldened Pakistan in the pursuit of more hawkish strategic and foreign policy against India (Kumar, 2010, pp. 35–50). Such an incapacity of India that rendered it to contend with a relatively disadvantageous bargaining position after 1998 was clearly evident in the military standoff of 2001–2002. In spite of mobilizing nearly a million troops on the Line of Control (LOC), India was not successful in achieving any conventional military advantage over Pakistan (Ganguly & Hagerty, 2005, p. 180).

In June 2002, at the height of the eyeball-to-eyeball confrontation, President Pervez Musharraf claimed the inability of India to attack Pakistan or to conduct a so-called limited war. It amply testifies that Pakistan's conventional and nuclear capability together deterred the aggression by India (Kumar, 2010, 2011). Underpinning such a weaker bargaining position was the deterrence that was established by the acquisition of nuclear weapons by the two subcontinental rivals (Basrur, 2008, p. 62; Rajagopalan, 2005, p. 204).

All this was symptomatic of the combustive security situation of South Asia during 2002. In addition to this, the United States strategic presence in the region, as a part of its war on terrorism increased the complication of the already perplexed dyadic nuclear relationship between India and Pakistan (Sidhu, 2007, p. 209). It also led to scepticisms that Washington might provide Pakistan with technology to ensure the safety of nuclear weapons which in turn might give Islamabad enough confidence to field its nuclear arsenal with greater self-assurance (Hoagland, 2002). So the two instances of conflicts, the Kargil crisis and the 2001–2002 pandemonium make it clear that nuclear weapons can deter only a nuclear war and not a conventional or sub-conventional war (Kumar, 2007, p. 256). Anyhow propitiously for South Asia in particular and even the world in general, the 2001–2002 explosive situation did not aggravate any full-blown conflict. Serious diplomatic initiatives, by the United States, were instrumental to a considerable extent in averting the crisis.

This conjuncture also demonstrated that the nature of crises in the subcontinent had dramatically transformed. In marked contrast to the earlier instances of conflict where India exhibited capability to affect a decisive end to the subcontinental conflicts, the post-Pokhran strategic scenario has been entirely different (Kumar, 2011, pp. 63–80). The nature of subcontinental conflict has got complicated to such an extent that it required outside intervention to fuse the simmering tensions. The 2001–2002 crisis has been one such instance that was averted primarily by the intervention of the United States. Thus, the occurrence of five major crisis situations within the span of 20 years clearly indicated towards a fundamental structural problem. As for crisis stability, South Asia's strategists are divided on the issue. Some boost as to how stable the relations are, a view held by many Indians and a few Pakistanis. Contrastingly, few Indians and many Pakistanis argue that the situation has become very dangerous. Besides, it has also been demonstrated that India Pakistan crisis does not move linearly. The level of tensions is nonlinear, moving up and down or remaining up constantly (Chari et al., 2007, p. 197).

NUCLEARIZATION AND THE DYNAMICS OF SUBCONTINENTAL SECURITY

According to P. R. Chari et al.,

> South Asia presents itself as a useful test-bed for theorizing about the transition from crisis to conventional and nuclear conflict and about escalation control. The crises prone India Pakistan relations seem to have followed the cold war model of deep and persistent conflict, nuclearisation and limited war. Despite the apparent danger that India Pakistan crisis might cross the nuclear threshold, the idea that limited wars can be fought within the framework of nuclear deterrence has gained currency in India. (Chari et al., 2007, p. 10)

Out of the five instances of conflict or the situation reaching the threshold of conflict, that may be taken into cognizance here, the first three wars: the 1947–1948 Kashmir war, the second Kashmir war of 1965 and the war of 1971 resulting out of the crisis in East Pakistan, it is apparent that in all of them, India had a definite edge over Pakistan. Especially, the war of 1971 decisively established India's conventional military superiority and by this also braced India's position as a regional hegemon. As a paradox, the overt nuclearization of 1998 was the first source for the creation of splinters in India's hegemony in South Asia as it brought the two subcontinental adversaries on an equal footing. Hence, the latter two instances of conflict, the Kargil crisis and the 2001–2002 instability that merely proved to be a brilliant military exercise devoid of any concrete results. Both cases highlight

India's inability to cross the LOC and affect a military victory which could be deemed anything near parallel to those that occurred prior to 1998. Hence in these two recent examples, one of limited war and another averted at the threshold of conflict, India and Pakistan were placed in a position of parity (Kumar, 2011, pp. 63–80).

Further, India's inability to make a decisive attempt at dislodging the terrorist infrastructure across the LOC even after animated public wrath in the aftermath of the 26/11 Mumbai ordeal seems to be yet another manifestation of the strategic balance that has been created between the two subcontinental adversaries. It is also symptomatic of the decline of India's hegemony in South Asia. In 2008, the Lashkar-e-Tayyiba struck at India's megalopolis and the financial capital Mumbai (formerly Bombay), targeting luxury hotels such as the iconic Taj Palace Towers, the Oberoi Trident and the Leopold Cafe (Rabasa et al., 2009, p. 4; Riedel, 2013, p. 5). The target sites also included a busy central railway station, the Chhatrapati Shivaji Terminus (formerly known as the Victoria Terminus which is a UNESCO heritage site) and the Nariman House or the Chabad House which is a Jewish outreach centre (McDonald, 2017, pp. 189–207; Menon, 2016, pp. 60–81). However, unlike 2001–2002, India did not involve itself in military brinkmanship and hot pursuit. Such a scenario again established to a considerable extent the benefits of the stability–instability paradox for Pakistan.

In this regard, a number of scholars and experts in India argue that overt acquisition of nuclear weapons by India and Pakistan has created a kind of stability–instability paradox which has proved to be favourable for Pakistan. Rajagopalan (2005, p. 47) argues that the stability–instability paradox has benefitted Pakistani interests to walk on the edge of war. So due to this, the penalties of the stability–instability paradox have been borne disproportionately by India, as it has facilitated Pakistan's support for militancy across the Kashmir divide (Krepon, 2003, p. 18). In view of this, Varun Sahni has cogently argued that the impact of the nuclearization of South Asia on India and Pakistan has been asymmetric as regards their respective capabilities to use force against each other is concerned. While it has given unlimited freedom to Pakistan for using force against India, it has placed serious constraints on India to do the same against it. So, in this regard, the weaker State seems to have largely benefitted by this strategic parity as it has gained greater confidence to follow an offensive policy against the stronger State, simultaneously restricting the availability of policy options and manoeuvrability for the stronger State to counter such ascendancy of the weaker State (Sahni, 2007, p. 194).

In this regard, Varun Sahni has argued that

Apart from the focus on the illusions lurking within India's nascent nuclear deterrence policy, dangerous instabilities currently exist in the India–Pakistan nuclear equilibrium. In the India–Pakistan context, the gap between asymmetric warfare and a nuclear exchange could be uncomfortably small. (Sahni, 2008, p. 216)

Continuing his argument, Sahni has further contended that the reason for this is obvious enough: in order to counter Pakistan's asymmetric warfare, the temptation for India to initiate a sub-conventional war remains strong. The problem is that sub-conventional war which the Indian policy community has labelled as a limited war under nuclear condition (not to be confused with limited nuclear war), has the distinct potential of escalating into a full-blown conventional war. If that were to happen, Pakistan's avowed (albeit) unwritten doctrine of first use/early use may lead to nuclear weapon use by Pakistan, followed by a devastating second strike by India (Sahni, 2008, p. 216). These arguments attempt to indicate how disadvantageous for India the post-May 1998 strategic scenario of the subcontinent has been, mainly due to the decline in its capability to obtain a decisive military victory over its nuclear neighbour. Sahni has noted in this regard that 'although India supposedly has escalation dominance, it has been unable to respond to Pakistan's asymmetric challenge by upping the ante' (Sahni 2007, p. 213). He argues that India's clearly a situation of contested dominance in the South Asian region. Any approach to understanding the nature of South Asian regional security must take into account this structural constraint (Sahni 2007, p. 213).

Such a scenario has emerged even as India is an emerging power. This is a status that triangulates between a great power status possessing system-shaping capabilities and intentions to do it and a middle power status that lacks the same. However, the size, resources and role of middle powers make them crucial actors for the dynamics of global and regional power calculus. Emerging powers like India are middle powers that are rapidly acquiring system-shaping capabilities and have also displayed their intentions towards catapulting to the great power status. In other words, India is not a great power, but 'it has the potential to emerge as one' (Walker, 2006, p. 23). For powers like India, the region of their location becomes their sway of influence (Sahni, 2011, p. 58).

However, India has lacked the capability to shape regional dynamics, despite its enormous hard power exercised through tangible resources consisting of stable political institutions, a strong economy and superior defence capacity. In addition to this, India also has demonstrated a wider growth trajectory in terms of its soft power capabilities, especially manifest in the fields of popular culture, health, education, and the consistency and the deeper dissemination of the values of its liberal democracy. However, India has not been able to fully utilize its soft power potential which is exercised indirectly by setting up an agenda to which other neighbours in the region follow without being coerced to do so. Due to India's inability to exercise co-optive power behaviour, it has failed to strengthen its claims to be an emerging power in the region. All this has also considerably undermined its upward mobility in the global geo-economic calculus.

The key reasons for such a state of affairs have been India's entanglement in cartographic disputes with neighbours pertaining to borders, river water sharing and migration. Although, contemporary international relations have moved beyond State-centric connotations and are now manifest in the postmodern structures characterized by multilateral governance and soft borders. Socio-economic and cultural issues form the crucial component of such a trajectory of international relations. Now, its contours do not represent a monadic focus on the State and exhibit a dyadic interplay between the State and other multiple forces. But in spite of this multilayered fabric of international relations, South Asia still is entrenched in the trappings of the modern Westphalian system in terms of the issues of sovereignty and territorial integrity. Securitizing of physical threats to territoriality and war-making for the defence of the same still constitute part of the core agenda of the region's States. The interests of South Asian States like India in this count have been primarily defined in terms of cartographic fundamentalism which is guided by the cardinal principle of safeguarding sovereignty and fixity of political territoriality. In such a scenario, the choices and policy options for India have also been factored deeply by the neorealist paradigm. The entire gamut of the subcontinent's history in the post-9/11 epoch, apparently demonstrates this phenomenon.

Signifying this is the persistent challenge of sub-conventional war in South Asia, manifest in the saga of Pakistan-sponsored militancy. The episodic representation of this has been visible at regular intervals in the region. After the Pakistan-sponsored terror struck at India's financial capital, the terrorists belonging to the Jaish-e-Mohammad struck at the Pathankot airbase of the Western command of the Indian Air Force in Punjab in 2016. The Jaish-e-Mohammad struck again in September 2016 at the Uri army camp in Jammu and Kashmir (Gokhale, 2017, pp. 1–52). The recent instance in the trail of terror paranoia perpetrated by the Jaish-e-Mohammad was the attack on the paramilitary troops of India's Central Reserve Police Force in February 2019 (Yusuf, 2019, p. 6). A suicide bomber drove a car full of explosives into a convoy of vehicles, detonating the improvised explosive device killing 40 soldiers at Pulwama in Jammu and Kashmir (Hagerty, 2020, pp. VII–VIII).

Such an enduring trail of terror theatrics indicated the advantages that a nuclearized Pakistan achieved in the form of its ability to sustain asymmetric warfare with India. Overall, the entry of nuclear weapons into the subcontinent, ostensibly for national security, has not made South Asia more stable and conflict less likely. The Kargil conflict and the year-long border confrontation of 2001–2002 have proven to be exceptions to the accepted wisdom that nuclear weapons stabilize relations, strengthen deterrence and discourage both conventional and nuclear conflict. Nuclear deterrence thus has been irrelevant in so far as mitigating or preventing tensions and instabilities in the region is concerned (Chari et al., 2007, p. 199). All these observations also answer the fundamental epistemic question as to why there was a persistent criticism of Pokhran II, by the opposition parties in India, even as post-Pokhran sanctions lasted barely three and a half years and hardly had any effect on the Indian economy (Rajamohan, 2003, p. 25). So the key question for discontent in India's domestic sphere over Pokhran II should not be sought in the larger international theatre but must be visualized from the prism of the transformed complexion of subcontinental dynamics. The strategic parity that was created between the two asymmetric adversaries and the stability-instability paradox demonstrated by the occurrence of two instances of crisis within a short span of time, braced the convictions of the opposition and compounded the criticisms against the BJP-led government in India. The intensity of criticism heightened when the then BJP-led government failed to put even a minimum degree of restraint upon the unremitting spate of cross-border terrorism, despite the emblem of Indian democracy 'the Parliament house complex' being targeted by the terrorists. Regardless of the massive military build-up along the border in 2002, an episode like that of Kaluchak of May 2002 made a mockery of India's policy of military brinkmanship and hence hardened the anti-government criticisms.

CONCLUSION

The effects of the tempest that was actuated by the post-partition pogrom and large-scale demographic shifts are intermittently being experienced in the form of destructive wars thanks to the unending politico-strategic rivalry between India and Pakistan. The standardization of this kind of security instability reached ominous proportions after the paranoid strategic competition between the two subcontinental rivals, assumed the nuclear dimension. In this context, it may be argued that the nuclearization of India–Pakistan dyadic equations added a critical dimension to the nature of conflicts in South Asia. Crossing of the nuclear Rubicon by the two subcontinental adversaries embroiled the region into a quagmire of uncertainties that pushed the prospects of establishing lasting peace into shambles and became symbiotic of a dire existential crisis. The mirror images of such probable security instabilities were witnessed during the Kargil crisis and the 2001–2002 military impasse between India and Pakistan. Such turmoil always keep the region at the edge of potential mass destruction and hamper the socio-economic development of the region because the populous seems to be continually angst for a safe and peaceful survival.

In any case, history should be a lesson for the two subcontinental adversaries to understand the fact that the nuclear arms race would only be an unavailing endeavour in so far as the protection and promotion of national interests through force is concerned. The deterrence situation of the Cold War explicitly displayed as to how nuclear weapons served as potential instruments that deterred direct and all-out conflicts between the two superpowers. The presence of nuclear weapons did not facilitate either side for a forceful assertion of the spheres of their national interests. Rather, nuclearization enhanced the misperceptions and lack of trust on the two sides, hence vitiating their relations. The subcontinental experience during the phase of nuclear weaponization on its part demonstrated that the deep-rooted antagonistic relations between India and Pakistan remained untrammelled. As long as the nuclear status of the subcontinental rivals remained covert, it was assumed that a deterrence situation prevailed in the region which successfully averted three crises situations in the 1980s. The moment this status got explicit, the fragility of this deterrence situation became apparent, with two crises situations almost reaching the threshold of a nuclear confrontation. This epitomizes the limited explanatory capability of classical deterrence theories in imaging nuclear relationships such as that of India and Pakistan.

Hence, the deterrence theories are deficient in accomplishing the purpose of exploring modes of conflict resolution in South Asia. This is also largely due to the fact that unlike the United States and the Soviet Union, the power asymmetry between India and Pakistan is very much manifest which itself factors deeply in accentuating eccentric security situations, mainly due to the deeper, psycho-cultural antecedents, affecting animosity. Hence, it is essential to view the subcontinental conflict not merely from the perspective of its nuclearization rather as the conflict in the region predates its nuclearization, the means for conflict resolution must be explored from a larger politico-historical, socio-economic and psycho-cultural spectrum. Anyhow, in military sphere, the process of institutionalizing confidence-building measures

(CBMs) and managing deterrence between two antagonists can lead to the institutionalization of co-operative security management that stabilizes deterrence and leads to some sort of détente (Morgan, 2003, p. 4). This process to a considerable extent holds the key for conflict resolution and stabilization of peace in South Asia.

REFERENCES

Abraham, I. (1998). *The making of the Indian atomic bomb: Science, secrecy and the postcolonial state*. Orient Longman.

Agnew, J., & Corbridge, S. (1993). The new geopolitics: The dynamics of geo-political disorder. In R. J. Johnston & P. J. Taylor (Eds.), *A world in crisis? Geographical perspectives*. Blackwell.

Bajpai, K. (1998). India: Modified structuralism. In M. Alagappa (Ed.), *Asian security practice: Material and ideational influences* (pp. 157–197). Stanford University Press.

Bajpai, K. (1999). The fallacy of an Indian deterrent. In A. Mattoo (Ed.), *India's nuclear deterrent: Pokhran II and beyond* (pp. 250–290). Haranand Publishers.

Basrur, R. M. (2006). *Minimum deterrence and India's nuclear security*. Stanford University Press.

Basrur, R. M. (2008). *South Asia's cold war: Nuclear weapons and conflict in comparative perspective*. Routledge.

Bhutto, Z. A. (1969). *The myth of independence*. Oxford University Press.

Bidwai, P., & Vanaik, A. (2000). *South Asia on a short fuse: Nuclear politics and the future of global disarmament*. Oxford University Press.

Blinkenberg, L. (1999). *India–Pakistan: The history of unsolved conflicts*. Odense University Press.

Bommakanti, K., & Desai, S. (2021). *China's nuclear ambiguity and its implications for India* [ORF Occasional Paper No. 309, April 2021]. Observer Research Foundation. https://www.orfonline.org›research›chinas-nuclear-a

Budania, R. (2001). *India's national security dilemma: The Pakistan factor and India's policy response*. Indus.

Bundy, M. (1984). Existential deterrence and its consequences. In D. MacLean (Ed.), *The security gamble: Deterrence dilemmas in the nuclear age*. Rowman and Allenheld.

Burke, S. M., & Ziring, L. (1990). *Pakistan's foreign policy: An historical analysis*. Oxford University Press.

Buzan, B., & Waever, O. (2003). *Regions and powers: The structure of international security*. Cambridge University Press.

Chari, P. R., Cheema, P. I., & Cohen S. P. (2007). *Four crises and a peace process: American engagement in South Asia*. Brookings Institute Press.

Chaturvedi, S. (1998). Common security? Geopolitics, development, South Asia and the Indian ocean. *Third World Quarterly, 19*(4), 701–724.

Cohen, S. P. (2001). *India: An emerging power*. Brookings Institute Press.

Dalby, S. (1988). Geo-political discourse: Soviet union as the other. *Alternatives, 13*, 415–442.

Das, R. (2009). The prism of strategic culture and South Asian nuclearisation. *Contemporary Politics, 15*(4), 395–411.

Ganguly, S. (1995). Indo-Pakistani nuclear issues: Stability/instability paradox. *The Study of Conflict and Terrorism, 18*(4), 325–338.

Ganguly, S. (2001). *Conflict unending: India–Pakistan tensions since 1947*. Oxford University Press.

Ganguly, S., & Hegerty. D. T. (2005). *Fearful symmetry: India–Pakistan crisis in the shadow of nuclear weapons*. Oxford University Press.

Gokhale, N. A. (2017). *Securing India the Modi way: Pathankot surgical strikes and more*. Bloomsbury.

Hagerty, D. T. (1998). *The consequences of nuclear proliferation: Lessons from South Asia*. MIT Press.

Hagerty, D. T. (2012). Nuclear holdouts: India, Israel and Pakistan. In T. Ogilvie-White & D. Santoro (Eds.), *Slaying the nuclear dragon: Disarmament dynamics in the twenty-first century*. University of Georgia Press.

Hersh, S. (1993). On the nuclear edge. *The New Yorker. 99*(March), 56–73.

Hoagland, J. (2002). India looks with a new favour on a natural ally. *International Herald Tribune*, 22 January.

Hyman, J. (2002). Why do states acquire nuclear weapons? In D. R. Sardesai & Raju G. C. Thomas (Eds.), *Nuclear India in the 21st century* (pp. 139–160). Palgrave Macmillan.

Kampani, G. (2014). Is the nuclear tiger changing its stripes? *The Nonproliferation Review, 21*(3–4), 383–398.

Kapur, A. (2001). *Pokhran and beyond: India's nuclear behaviour*. Oxford University Press.

Kapur, P. S. (2007). *Dangerous deterrent: Nuclear weapons proliferation and conflict in South Asia*. Stanford University Press.

Karnad, B. (2002). *Nuclear weapons and India's security: The realist foundations of strategy*. Macmillan India.

Kissinger, H. (1957). *Nuclear weapons and foreign policy*. Harper and Brothers.

Krepon, M. (2003). *The stability-instability paradox, misperception and escalation control in South Asia*. The Henry L. Stimson Center.

Krepon, M., & Faruquee, M. (Eds.). (1994). *Conflict prevention and confidence building measures in South Asia: The 1990 crisis* [Occasional Paper No. 17]. Henry L. Stimson Center.

Kumar, A. (2002). Nuclear deterrence: A waning motif. *Deccan Herald*, 22 August.

Kumar, A. (2007). Theories of deterrence and nuclear deterrence in the subcontinent. In E. Sridharan (Ed.), *The India Pakistan nuclear relationship: Theories of deterrence and international relations* (pp. 239–265). Routledge.

Kumar H. M., Sanjeev. (2010). Internal dynamics of sub-continental security: Indo Pak tensions and the political response. *India Quarterly, 66*(1), 35–50.

Kumar H. M., Sanjeev. (2011). The Pakistan factor in India's domestic politics. *South Asian Survey*, 18(1), 63–80.

Kumar H. M., Sanjeev. (2014a). Nuclear weaponisation and the nature of conflict in South Asia. *Turkish Journal of Politics*, 5(2), 83–99.

Kumar H. M., Sanjeev. (2014b). Reconceptualising deterrence: Nudging toward rationality in Middle Eastern rivalries (Review Article), *E-International Relations* (3 March). http://www.eir.info/2014/03/03/review-reconceptualising-deterrence/

McDonald, M. (2017). *Defeat is an orphan: How Pakistan lost the great South Asian war*. Hurst.

McLeod, D. (2008). *India and Pakistan: Friends, rivals or enemies?* Ashgate Publishing Company.

Menon, S. (2016). *Choices: Inside the making of India's foreign policy*. Brookings Institution Press.

Milewiski, P. (2002). Pakistan India and the events of September 11. *Polish Quarterly of International Affairs*, Winter, 123–128.

Mishra, B. (1998, May 16). Press statement by national security adviser. *The Hindu*.

Morgan, P. M. (2003). *Deterrence now*. Cambridge University Press.

Narang, V. (2014). *Nuclear strategy in the modern era: Regional powers and international conflict*. Princeton University Press.

Nightly News. (1994). In S. Kumar, *Reconceptualising deterrence: Nudging toward rationality in Middle Eastern rivalries* (Review Article), *E-International Relations* (3 March). https://www.e-ir.info/2014/03/03/review-reconceptualising-deterrence/

Nitze, P. H. (1979). Assuring strategic stability in an era of Détente. In W. Hanrieder (Ed.), *Arms control and security: Current issues*. Westview Press.

Paul, T. V. (2014). *The warrior state: Pakistan in the contemporary world*. Oxford University Press.

Perkovich, G. (1999). *India's nuclear bomb: Impact on global proliferation*. Oxford University Press.

Poulose, T. T. (1996). India's nuclear option and national security. In P. R. Chari, P. I. Cheema, & I. Uzzaman (Eds.), *Nuclear non-proliferation in India and Pakistan: South Asian perspectives* (pp. 44–59). Manohar.

Rabasa, A., Blackwill, R. D., Chalk, P., Cragin, K., Fair, C. C., Jackson, B. A., Jenkins, B. M., Jones, S. G, Shestak, N., & Tellis A. J. (2009). *The lessons of Mumbai*. Rand Corporation.

Rajagopalan, R. (2005). *Second strike: Arguments about nuclear war in South Asia*. Penguin.

Rajamohan, C. (2003). *Crossing the Rubicon: Shaping of India's new foreign policy*. Penguin.

Riedel, B. (2013). *Avoiding Armageddon: America, India and Pakistan to the brink and back*. Brookings Institution Press.

Rizvi, G. (1986a). The rivalry between India and Pakistan. In B. Buzan & G. Rizvi (Eds.), *South Asian Security and the great powers*. Macmillan.

Rizvi, G. (1986b). Pakistan: The domestic determinants of security. In B. Buzan & G. Rizvi (Eds.), *South Asian security and the great powers*. Macmillan.

Sahni, V. (2007). The stability-instability paradox: A less than perfect explanation. In E. Sridharan (Ed.), *The India–Pakistan nuclear relationship: Theories of deterrence and international relations* (pp. 185–207). Routledge.

Sahni, V. (2008). The agent-structure problem and India's external security policy. In N. C. Behera (Ed.), *International relations of South Asia: Search for an alternative paradigm* (pp. 210–234). SAGE Publications.

Sahni, V. (2011). Regional dynamics of emerging powers: Power/control or leadership/consent? In E. Sridharan (Ed.), *International relations theory and South Asia: Security, political economy, domestic politics, identities and images* (pp. 56–107). Oxford University Press.

Shaikh, F. (2002). Pakistan's nuclear bomb: Beyond the non-proliferation regime. *International Affairs, 78*(1), 29–48.

Sidhu, W. P. S. (2007). Operation Vijay and Operation Parakram: The victory of theory? In E. Sridharan (Ed.), *India–Pakistan nuclear relationship: Theories of deterrence and international relations* (pp. 208–238). Routledge.

Singh, J. (1993). Prospects for nuclear proliferation. In S. Sur (Ed.), *Nuclear deterrence: Problems and perspectives in the 1990s.* United Nations Institute for Disarmament Research.

Singh, J. (Ed.). (1998). *Nuclear India.* Knowledge World.

Spanier, J. (1989). *American foreign policy since World War Second.* Tata McGraw-Hill.

Subrahmanyam, K. (1990). *Security in a changing world.* B. R. Publication Corporation.

Subrahmanyam, K. (2000, May 15). Underestimating India: Project a credible nuclear deterrent. *The Times of India.*

Swami, P. (2009). A war to end a war: The causes and outcomes of the 2001–2002 India–Pakistan crisis. In S. Ganguly & S. Paul Kapur (Eds.), *Nuclear proliferation in South Asia: Crisis behaviour and the bomb.* Routledge.

Tankel, S. (2011). *Storming the world stage: The story of the Lashkar-e-Tayyaba.* Columbia University Press.

Tellis, A. (2001). *India's emerging nuclear posture: From recessed deterrent to ready arsenal.* Santa Monica.

Tellis, A. J., Fair Christine, C., & Jamison, M. J. (Eds.). (2001). *Limited war conflict under the nuclear umbrella: Indian and Pakistani lessons from the Kargil crisis.* Rand.

The Hindu. (1998, May 14). Nuclear Test not Directed Towards Any Country. *The Hindu*, p. 1.

Yusuf, M. W. (2019). The Pulwama crisis. *Arms Control Today, 49*(4), 6–9.

Walker, M. (2006). India's path to greatness. *The Wilson Quarterly, 30*(3), 22–30.

Warikoo, K. (2006). Islamic extremism: A challenge to South Asia. *Strategic Analysis, 30*(1), 30–45.

Sub-conventional War and the Problematique of Liberal Peace

The conceptual interweaving of the notions of politics, morality and the legitimate exercise of power has largely shaped the modes through which one attempts to understand the structural–functional linkages between the sovereign state and systemic contours of international relations. The epistemological focus of international relations theory in this regard has been largely centred around concerns relating to the maintenance of order, welfare, law and justice at the systemic level. However, at the bottom of these concerns exists an intellectual divide among the epistemic community of international relations scholarship pertaining to the 'modes' of undertaking such tasks. At one end of the spectrum, it is argued that order, welfare, law and justice can be maintained by practising certain universal ethical principles as above the sovereign authority of a state. On the other end, scholars hold that any systemic concerns cannot be addressed based on any higher moral law that transgresses the sovereign authority of the state. Such an epistemological divide is rooted in the divergent philosophical positions of Samuel von Pufendorf and Immanuel Kant (Devetak, 2007, pp. 151–174).

Pufendorf and Kant attempted to address the issue of the dialogue between politics, morality and law in terms of the dyadic relationship that exists between the exercise of state's sovereignty and the normative exemplars determining the systemic interaction among the states. Pufendorf and Kant tackled it from the vantage point of two distinct axiological positions: On the one hand, Pufendorf argued in favour of the state's absolute autonomy in exercising its sovereignty and not submitting to any higher moral norms while engaging with the international system. On the other hand, Kant defends the authority of the moral law and contends that de-ontological ethics provide higher normative authority in shaping the systemic interaction, as compared to that of a state's absolute sovereignty. These antithetical positions express themselves currently in the rivalry between notions of the realist paradigm of statism grounded in the post-enlightenment logic of instrumental rationality, and the idealist 'cosmopolitanism' rooted in the conception of metaphysical transcendentalism (Devetak, 2007, pp. 151–154).

One prominent aspect of the dialectical contest between the realist conceptions of Statism and the idealist notions of cosmopolitanism is found in the debate pertaining to the linkages between democracy and war. The classic statement on this debate has been that of the German philosopher Immanuel Kant, who established an inverse relationship between democracy and war in his famous pamphlet on 'perpetual peace'. The neo-Kantian articulations of the cosmopolitan notion of the negative linkages between democracy and war are found in the defenders of the 'democratic peace thesis'. This chapter engages in a critique of the Kantian epistemological conception of universal moral law or, what contemporary international relations theory designates as 'cosmopolitan idealism', as it is mediated through the 'democratic peace thesis' advanced by the liberal theory of international relations. This idea of 'cosmopolitanism' is shaped by the critique of the anthropocentric logic of post-enlightenment reason and is embedded in the notion of abstract metaphysical reason. The critique of the democratic peace thesis has been undertaken in this chapter by mapping the problematique of State security in South Asia. This has been done here by deconstructing the protracted trajectory of conflict between the two nuclear-powered adversaries; India and Pakistan. The analysis itself in this chapter has been undertaken according significance to the historical turn in the discipline of international relations.

WHAT HAVE THE LIBERALS OFFERED US?

Theories of international relations have long focused on a particular set of phenomena: the role of States and their tendency to engage in recurring conflict-prone behaviour. The most significant contribution in this regard emerged from within the Western academy, a kind of contribution that exhibited a definitive tilt towards Western values and vantage-points (Bleiker, 2008, p. 313). As a manifestation of this, the liberal theory of international relations represented by Michael Doyle and Francis Fukuyama advocates an idealist cosmopolitan peace model as an antidote to the anarchical character of international relations. Such a model, designated as the democratic peace hypothesis, was propounded during the high noon of cultural and ideological contest of Cold War bipolarity in international relations. The democratic peace thesis contends that democratic polities seldom fight against each other because the mutual existence of democracy itself becomes a moral check on countries to restrain themselves from engaging in the use of force in resolving conflicts. Through this propositional assertion, the defenders of the liberal peace model offered an idealist formulation to chart the pathways for ordering the international. This liberal assertion has also been the result of their unilinear assumption that perpetual peace is an achievable proposition. It also stems out of their strong conviction that the existence of linkage between the domestic milieu and the international environment is incontrovertible. Such a concept of special peace between democracies has been a potent idea in international relations since the 1970s when scholars began to reinterpret the philosophical speculations of Immanuel Kant on the notion of perpetual peace (Hayes, 2009, pp. 979–978).

The democratic peace hypothesis deals with the Manichean dichotomy between order and anarchy based on the foundations of the notion of shared values of liberalism and democracy. For the liberal theory of international relations, interdependence among actors is the key to negating the condition of anarchy in international relations. Such interdependence is determined by a configuration of distinct preferences that states pursue in international relations. In the international context, state behaviour is underpinned by the ways in which states attempt at realizing their preferences, which in turn is shaped by the preferences of other states. In this context, the preferences of the states and the relationship among them are interdependent (Moravcsik, 1997, p. 520). Looking at such a kind of interdependence, it may be stated that the notion of distinct preferences and the mutually accepted norm of respecting the preferences of others can emerge as a common consciousness of shared values among similar political formations. Such a consciousness becomes a strong underpinning for determining the nature of international order.

However, it is affirmed here that the liberal school of international relations has emanated as the intellectual product of the Western academy and hence suffer from Western solecism. Taking into account the argument of Darby (2006, p. 6) that 'the conceptualization of global politics is mainly geared towards understanding and by extension also promoting, the interests of the powerful', it is contended here that most of the theories of international relations, seeking to interpret State behaviour and the international system seem to have been laced with a tinge of Western capitalist culture. And as Marx and Engels (1968, p. 127) have indicated, the bourgeoisie attempts to create a world after its own image, the tendentious character of these theories cannot be repudiated. Hence, the liberal framework of international relations and its most contested product, the democratic peace hypothesis, also appear to be modelled in accordance with the requirements of the developed West.

Confronted by a contest of normative choices from the Soviet-led socialist world, the US-led capitalist world attempted at crafting the epistemology of international relations theory in a manner to support its Cold War grand strategies for responding to such a competition. These endeavours were situated in the world order imageries that were weaved in terms of the Manichean dichotomy between order (good) and anarchy (bad). The goal of devising modes for ordering the international that was anarchical due to such a competition constituted the language of the technical discourse of the discipline of international relations. Such discourse was getting conditioned in the hegemonic Cold War vocabulary and was directed towards becoming a prescriptive enterprise for supporting the policies of US ventures.

Diverse theoretical formulations were proposed to enunciate the capitalist modes of ordering the international. The classical realism of Hans Morgenthau advocated the foundational principles of foreign policy-making; the structural realism of Kenneth Waltz offered an explanation to the ontology of systemic anarchy in international relations and its influence on state behaviour. As regards neorealism or structural realism, it is based upon the materialist epistemology of bounded territoriality and distribution of power in its interpretation of the structure of international relations. It treats States as unitary rational and functionally undifferentiated actors, with differences only in the distribution of their capabilities. It argues that the international system moulds the States and defines the possibilities of conflict and cooperation. Thus, for structural realism, international security concerns are overtly Statist, having apparent military connotations.

During the Cold War, the concept of security mainly denoted the State's security which meant that in the discourse of security studies, the State was the major referent object. In the understanding of security in international politics, State was the major component (Williams, 2008, p. 7). Stephen P. Walt largely emphasized the military dimension of security and hence for him, the threat of war and the requirement of military preparedness to mitigate the same were crucial for security in international politics. Thus, State's security was the most important component of security studies for Stephen Walt (1991, p. 213).

As regards the liberal paradigm, two distinct propositions emerged as a critique of the realist formulations of the modes of ordering the international. Robert Keohane and Joseph Nye provided a framework for institutionalized cooperation to deal with an anarchical international system through the theory of neoliberal institutionalism. It emerged as a reaction to the structuralist ontology of the anarchy problematique that was offered by the neorealism of Kenneth Waltz.

The neorealist emphasis on defining the international system in terms of the State being the sole actor, facing existential strains in an anarchical world, was countered by the neoliberal institutionalists' argument that supranational institutions had gained primacy over the State by virtue of globalization. The proper functioning of these institutions and strict adherence to rules, for them, would facilitate in mitigating the anarchical character of the international order and stabilize democracy and peace. This meant that cooperation in world politics, leading to mutual benefit among States, can be enhanced through the construction and support of multilateral institutions. In pursuance of this, neoliberal institutionalism provides one basis of authority conceived in terms of the fusion of power and legitimate social purpose. The social purpose of institutional liberalism is to promote beneficial effects on human security, human welfare and human liberty as a result of a more peaceful, prosperous and free world. Institutional liberalism justifies the use of power for constructing institutions on the basis of this conception of social purpose (Keohane, 2012, p. 125).

The key proponents of these ideas are the theorists of the anarchy problematique that include Robert O. Keohane and Joseph Nye. They understand cooperation as an instrumentalist relationship and focus on situations of interdependent decision-making that involves conflicting as well as complimentary interests among States. They understand that cooperation means that one or more States take decisions in such a manner that the resulting outcomes are likely to serve the interests of other States. To cooperate in international politics, in this view, means to make decisions and embark on courses of action that are advantageous for other actors (Ashley, 1988, p. 236). In this regard for Axelrod and Keohane, 'cooperation occurs when States adjust their behaviour to the actual or anticipated preferences of other actors' (Axelrod & Keohane, 1985, p. 226).

Apart from this, through the concepts of complex interdependence, agenda-setting, regimes and international organization, Robert Keohane and Joseph Nye (1989) developed a critique of the stationary and anarchical character of the international structure advocated by the neorealists. For them, 'complex interdependence involves multiple channels of communication between societies involving multiple actors and not just States, multiple issues arranged without any hierarchy and the irrelevance of the threat of force' (Keohane & Nye, 1989, pp. 23–25). For Keohane and Nye,

> In the post World War II period countries have become more and more intertwined economically. The exponential growth of the size and number of transnational organisations has blurred State boundaries, rendering

the realist assumption of the centrality of the State questionable. Realists contend that State is the dominant actor in world politics and they achieve their goals in international relations through military force and violence. (Keohane & Nye, 1989, pp. 23–25)

To counter this, Keohane and Nye provide an ideal type of complex interdependence based on cooperation rather than conflict. For them, nonsecurity issues such as international monetary relations and global environmental concerns have become more important (Keohane & Nye, 1989, pp. 23–25).

As regards the notion of power in international relations, the neoliberal institutionalists focus on factors such as technology, education and economic growth as against geography, population and raw material (Nie, 1990, p. 179). This change has led to the categorization of power into hard and soft power. Hard power for Nye 'entails inducements (carrot or threats) and is exercised with the help of tangible resources such as economic and military strength' (Nie, 1990, p. 183). Contrary to this for Nye,

> There is also an indirect exercise of power, which involves setting an agenda that others follow without any coercion. This is called co-optive power behaviour. It is based on ideas and political agenda that shape the preferences of others. The sources of co-optive power behaviour come from intangible resources such as culture, ideology and institutions. This dimension of power is regarded as soft power. (Nie, 1990, p. 183)

Thus, soft power facilitates co-optive power behaviour and hard power leads to command power behaviour.

However, this notion of power of neoliberal institutionalism is critiqued by Robert Cox who has elaborated the nature of soft power by using the Gramscian conception of hegemony. Through this, he indicates how countries dominate the world order without the use of force. He refers to British and American domination, facilitated by the institutionalization of a liberal economic order (Cox, 1987, p. 41). In any case, neoliberal institutionalism also fails to provide viable solutions to the social challenges posed by globalization. It merely offers a market-based framework for conducting contemporary world politics as it speaks of linking State power with capitalism. Hence, it falls short of explaining how States engaged in conflicts driven by cartographic fundamentalism can build peace through economic cooperation. Above all, neoliberal institutionalism also operates within the neorealist framework as it accepts the neorealist contention that institutions can function effectively within the given structures of power and interest.

Besides, the neoliberal institutionalists merely succeeded in substituting the realist notion of an anarchical international order wherein, States compete for survival without any hierarchal authority for protection with their own belief in a pattern of world politics, governed by an open market competition, guided by liberal institutions, adhering to a set of rules. Thus, neoliberal institutionalists tended to follow the framework of an international structure of the neorealist model. This replica model envisaged a world order wherein the capabilities of the States as the substructures of the broader international structure become important for their survival in a competitive environment in which the structure itself is governed by the ordering principles of the market. In view of this, neoliberal institutionalism as a critique of the structuralist/materialist reductionism of the neorealists proves to be an empty signifier (Grieco, 1988, pp. 485–507).

On the other hand, Michael Doyle came up with the democratic peace thesis as an ideal prescription of liberal cosmopolitanism for determining the modes of ordering an anarchical international system. Apart from manufacturing the syntactic and semantic formulation of the Cold War vocabulary, the dominant theoretical discourses such as the liberal theory of international relations also emerged as an ideal heuristic tool to explain the place of liberal values in a post-Cold War setting. In this endeavour, Francis Fukuyama's invocation of the democratic peace thesis manifested in his celebration of the victory of liberal capitalism as an ideal form of political economy in a world led by the United States, attempted at reframing the discourse on order/anarchy in terms of the divide between the values of the liberal world (order) and that of the non-liberal world (anarchy). Designated as 'the end of history', Fukuyama's propositions were contemplated to visualize a world order that was made possible by the globalization of capital with the US vision spearheading the entire process of such a systemic transformation (Ruggie, 1998, p. 73). In any case, this theoretical formulation of the democratic peace hypothesis is entrenched in the epistemological imperialism of the West and an exclusionary idea of the history of international relations that largely considered the Westphalian settlement as the epistemological starting point to explain the nature of the international order. It means that the contours of the modes of ordering the international that these discourses have offered as being universal tends to represent a set of ethno-centric theoretical constructs that have been developed upon the Euro-centric foundations of the epistemology of international relations.

THE PHILOSOPHICAL FOUNDATIONS OF THE DEMOCRATIC PEACE THESIS

The roots of the democratic peace hypothesis may be traced to the liberal theory of international relations (Smith, 1992, p. 89). The foundations of contemporary liberal internationalism were established in the 18th and 19th centuries, by the liberals who proposed certain necessary conditions for the construction of peaceful world order. In a nutshell, these conditions include the proposition that the prospects for containing war between States largely depend on their preference for democracy as against aristocracy, free trade rather than autarky, and prioritizing of collective security over that of the balance of power system (Burchill, 2001, p. 32). This liberal framework for peace gained currency as the democratic peace hypothesis.

The German philosopher Immanuel Kant provided a prelude to the liberal peace model or the democratic peace hypothesis. He stated thus: 'the establishment of republican form of governments in which rulers were accountable and individual rights were respected, would lead to peaceful international relations because the ultimate consent for war would rest with the citizens of the State' (Kant, 1970, p. 100). The neo-Kantian romance for invoking this classical statement of liberal cosmopolitan Idealism got inspired by the ingenious goal of providing an intellectual defence and moral high ground for the values of the liberal capitalist world that was led by the United States. The neo-Kantian reflections upon the liberal peace model have been presented by Francis Fukuyama and Michael Doyle. Michael Doyle (1986, p. 1152) contends that liberal states are uniquely willing to eschew the use of force in their relations with one another. The central argument of the liberal peace model lies in its contention that democracies tend to refrain while making consequential use of force against each other (Biddle & Long, 2004, p. 525). Similarly, according to Francis Fukuyama, liberal states are more stable internally and more peaceful in their international relations (Fukuyama, 1992, p. 19).

The defenders of the democratic peace hypothesis argue that the mere presence of democratic regimes in the polities itself is a sufficient cheque to inhibit States from resorting to conflictual means while dealing with contentious international issues. Hence, for the protagonists of the liberal world order, the idea of the inter-State conflict itself would become taboo, in an ideal situation wherein all States in the international political system became democracies. Fukuyama thus stated, the spread of legitimate domestic political orders will eventually bring an end to international conflict. This is because, a world made up of liberal democracies should have less incentive for war, since all nations would reciprocally recognize one another's legitimacy (Fukuyama, 1992, p. 21). Doyle has also presented his views in a similar spirit. He opined thus, liberal democracies have a unique ability and willingness to establish peaceful relations between themselves. This pacification of foreign relations among liberal States is said to be the direct product of their shared legitimate political orders based on democratic principles and institutions. The reciprocal recognition of these common principles; a commitment to the rule of law, individual rights and equality before the law, representative government based on popular consent means that liberal democracies evince little interest in conflict with each other and have no grounds to contest each other's legitimacy and hence have constructed a separate peace (Doyle, 1986, p. 1153)

The post-Cold War refashioning of the democratic peace thesis was highly optimistic about the establishment of such a separate peace among the industrialized states of the newly emerging world order (Cummings, 1991, p. 1999). This optimism was widely advertised in Francis Fukuyama's notion of 'the end of history'. For Fukuyama, the end of history meant the celebration of the triumph of the West and Western ideas, marked by the total exhaustion of viable systematic alternatives to Western liberalism (Fukuyama, 1992, p. 7). For him, the modes of ordering the post-Cold War international relations rested upon the wider dissemination of liberal values that was made possible by the emergence of a post-dialectic world wherein liberal capitalism triumphed over all other antithetical formations of ideology and social theory (Therborn, 2007, p. 63–64). It was represented by the demise of communism that was the only impediment to achieving the Kantian dream of perpetual peace. Kant advocated a pacific federation of states based on the notion of cosmopolitan rights wherein the federation aimed to preserve and secure the freedom of each state. Since the federation itself would not aspire for power like a state, this international arrangement would ensure perpetual peace to become an objective reality (Kant, 1970, p. 104).

The victory of liberalism after the age of bipolarity, for Fukuyama, emerged as an appropriate circumstance for the objectification of this Kantian philosophical abstraction that would symbolize the fruition of the global liberal civilization. This systemic transformation for Fukuyama not only created new pathways for the reclamation of American power in a post-hegemonic era but also created a favourable spatio-temporal topography for the flourishing of long peace, which would emerge as a product of the complex interdependence of interests and preferences among the democracies of the world. Such an order according to the liberal theory of international relations was characterized by three features. They included penetrated hegemony wherein the United States assumed a renewed global leadership; semi-sovereignty that allowed rigid cartographies to become malleable to facilitate such penetration; and the co-binding of states on the basis of commonly shared liberal values (Deudney & Ikenberrry, 1999, pp. 179–196). These features of liberal international order as it is argued by the proponents of the democratic peace thesis would make separate peace an achievable proposition among democracies.

Situating on this epistemic assessment, we seek to place the arguments of the democratic peace thesis in the perspective of three broad trajectories of analysis. First, the analysis of the impact that structural-functional dimension of the State working in Pakistan asserts upon the condition of democracy in the country. This is essential because the democratic peace theory does not take the regime type within a polity into consideration while contemplating its thesis. It rather has cosmopolitan imagery of the character of democracies, driven by an essentialist formulation on the universal ethical goodness of its nature as a regime type. To evolve such a critique, we need to take into consideration the determinants that have contributed to the weakness of the democratic architecture in Pakistan, which tends to disqualify it for being tested as an ideal case for the study of the democratic peace theory.

Second, the chapter also locates its critique in the context of the failure of nuclear deterrence theory in the Indian subcontinent. This is essential because the democratic peace theory is founded upon a cosmopolitan imagery of world order that holds the system as the unit of analysis. This limits its capability to examine the idiosyncrasies of regional or sub-regional formations. Hence, the understanding of the failure of the nuclear deterrence theory in the Indian subcontinent emerges as a supportive analysis in the process of critiquing the democratic peace theory. By adding the nuclear dimension, the validity of the democratic peace theory in a specific regional or sub-regional context can be tested.

The third pertains to the problematizing of the nature of war. In so far as the democratic peace thesis is concerned, it largely deals with the conception of war that is purely defined in its conventional sense. It meant that for the democratic peace thesis, an open militarized conflict involving the security forces of the two countries becomes the empirical source for testing its hypothesis. However, here we attempt at transcending this conventional definition of war and bring in conflict types that are designated as either asymmetric conflicts, proxy war or sub-conventional conflicts. Such an emendation becomes an imperative when we endeavour at understanding the problematique of regional security in South Asia. Although, the region has experienced three conventional-type wars involving India and Pakistan. However, after 1971, the nature of war in South Asia has drastically transformed, with Pakistan launching an asymmetric war against India with the help of militant proxies.

It becomes essential to problematize asymmetric wars for the purpose of mapping the working of the democratic peace thesis because like conventional wars, the South Asian experience has demonstrated that the security forces of India and Pakistan have been deeply engaged in the proxy war. Thus, like conventional wars, a State is coerced to engage in an asymmetric war, in terms of strategy, resources and leadership. Hence, considering this phenomenon, we have selected the year 1989 for the purpose of this study. First, because at this juncture the Pakistan-sponsored proxy war in Jammu and Kashmir reached the fruition point. Second, it was precisely during this period that the long military rule under General Zia had ended in Pakistan and the country had witnessed democratic transition, with an elected government under Benazir Bhutto assuming office.

We further argue that the democratic peace thesis proposed by the liberal theory of international relations prefers to imagine the functioning of international relations in terms of a limited spatio-temporal context that is largely Euro-American in character. Such an ontological and epistemic vantage point of the West implies that South Asia does not emerge as a suitable test site for understanding the thesis. Such a phenomenon would be interrogated here by examining the sub-continental security predicament between the two nuclear-powered adversaries—India and Pakistan. This would be done by deconstructing the protracted asymmetric conflict that is ongoing between the two countries by situating it in the epistemological framework of the historical turn in international relations (Hobden, 1998; Puchala, 2003; Smith, 1999; Teschke, 2003; Vaughan-Williams, 2005).

The epistemology of the historical turn considers history itself as an autonomous theoretical perspective in international relations. It is practised by adhering to a sophisticated philosophy of history, which is theoretically very enriching. History for this epistemology occupies a large space in the analysis of contemporary developments (Roberts, 2006, p. 703). The historical turn in international relations makes a case for re-historicizing the concepts and theories that we employ to problematize the phenomenon of the international which would result in a greater epistemological value for the purpose of theorizing in international relations (Vaughan-Williams, 2005). By doing this, it calls upon the scholars of international relations to engage in a constructive dialogue with the historians (Buzan & Little, 2000; Elman & Elman, 2001).

In order to understand the method of doing history in the spatiotemporal trajectory of the democratic peace theory, this chapter adopts the interpretation of the phenomenon of historical writing that was given by Hayden White. For White, history writing can be compared to the act of narration that is adopted commonly in literature (White, 1973, pp. 281–314). History according to this methodological perspective is not merely a chronology of events (White, 1975, p. 275). Rather, history as a field of epistemology becomes meaningful, only when it uses the method of narration (White, 1980, pp. 5–28).

THE COSMOPOLITAN IMAGERY OF LIBERAL PEACE AND THE SECURITY PROBLEMATIQUE OF IDIOSYNCRATIC SPATIALITIES

As Carl Schmitt writes, the political world is a pluriverse and not a universe, meaning that the political entity cannot be universal in a manner to encompass the entire world (Schmitt, 1996, p. 53). Each political formation as a collectivity offers itself as a distinct category to be examined with the help of different methods. Universalizing the dominant tropes of enquiry that manifest in the form of paradigms and meta-theories, often tend to be misleading. The same may be the case if we attempt at making an over-deterministic accentuation of the liberal theory of international relations as a universal model, for the purpose of charting the contours of ordering an anarchical international system. This kind of over-deterministic accentuation merely turns out to be hegemonic assertions of concepts and arguments that are directed towards constructing relations of inclusion and exclusion, visibility and invisibility, particularity and generality (Calhoun, 1995, p. 187). Such relations get structured in terms of a sense of linear history, ethno-centric tropes of knowledge and a teleological acclamation of the idea of time and space.

On the foundations of this framework, an analysis of the democratic peace thesis and its significance in the context of South Asian dynamics becomes imperative. It has been argued here that the democratic peace theory seems to be an inadequate explanatory mode for the purpose of deconstructing the security problematique in South Asia. To examine this, we need to take a particular historical period and bring out specific indicators that can provide credence to such a statement. In pursuance of this, we have to discuss three factors that signify the symptom of the ineffectiveness of the democratic peace thesis in the Indian subcontinent. First, an examination of the regime type in Pakistan during the chosen period must be done. Second, the idiosyncratic character of the insecurity predicament of this sub-region of South Asia must also be analysed. Third, the nature of war must also be problematized. It is essential to understand the regime type in Pakistan for the purpose of demonstrating whether it fits into the model of the democratic political structure that has been idealized by the democratic peace thesis. Similarly, the kind of security environment that became the spatio-temporal context, in which the democratic peace thesis has been contemplated, must also be compared and contrasted with that of the scenario in the Indian subcontinent. Finally, the conception of war that the democratic peace thesis has considered for examination must be refashioned, by considering the subcontinental security predicament that has been engendered by the Pakistan-sponsored asymmetric war.

Based on these three indicators, we attempt at advancing a critique of the democratic peace thesis. To do this at the outset, the theoretical significance of history in the study of international relations must be foregrounded. Although a deep sense of historical consciousness strongly underpinned the epistemic conviction of the major theoretical discourses in international relations. The value of history as an autonomous theoretical instrument for the purpose of mapping the broad contours of the phenomenon of the international surfaced only with the advent of the historical or the narrative turn in international relations (Roberts, 2006, pp. 703–714). If we take the example of the different variants of realism which has proved to be the most dominant paradigm international relations theory (Walt, 1998), the ways in which successive variants problematize history in their epistemic formulations becomes apparent (Carr, 1939; Gilpin, 1983; Morgenthau, 1967). In any case, despite an abundant use of history as a narrative and as a philosophy, history did not find a serious theoretical space in the discipline of international relations. It is evident in the gross negligence by the dominant theoretical discourses in international relations of the methodological significance of various manifestations of the past for understanding the present (Bell, 2001, p. 116). The structural realism of Kenneth Waltz signifies this phenomenon, which attempts to build a system's theory of International relations in an ahistorical way (Cox, 1986, p. 211).

However, the normative turn in international relations (Shapcott, 2000) with all the criticisms levelled against positivism, a priori assumptions, rationalism and empiricism, foregrounded the significance of history for international relations theory (Hobden & Hobson, 2002). It was a response to the over-determinism of positivism and rationalism in the making of international relations theory (Isacoff, 2002; Kratochwil, 2006; Vaughan-Williams, 2005). Such a transition was also a product of the need felt among the social scientists for moving beyond objectivism and relativism (Bernstein, 1983). Considering the importance of history for the purpose of theorizing the phenomenon of the international we must look at historical instances that have challenged the propositions made by the liberal theory of international relations.

CONTESTING THE DEMOCRATIC PEACE THESIS THROUGH ASYMMETRIC WARFARE

If South Asian dynamics are to be visualized from the liberal contention manifest in the democratic peace thesis, we would be induced to comport with the canard that fully democratized South Asia would be less vulnerable to intra-regional conflicts. This is because the sellers of the democratic peace hypothesis seem to have merely proffered a perennial cliché, by building a moral case for democracy. In order so to coerce a consensual cord, regarding the mythical notion that the idea of war among democratic States itself is a rhetoric. By building the 'doctrine of harmony of interests' among the democratic regimes, the privileged order (the dominant world powers) seek to invoke this as an ingenious moral device in order to justify and maintain their own dominant position (Carr, 1939, p. 102). Hence, the liberal utopian model of peace; the democratic peace hypothesis has merely been yet another instrument crafted by the Western bourgeoisie in pursuance of the accentuation of its own global domination. Hence, once industrial capitalism and the manifestation of its class configuration became the recognized structure of the society, the doctrine of the harmony of interests (international peace as a mutual interest of symmetric political formations that is democracies) became the ideology of a dominant group which attempted to maintain its predominance by asserting the identity of its interests with those of the community as a whole (Carr, 1939, p. 58).

Thus, through the dexterous affirmation of the ethical imperativeness of international peace ensured by capitalist-friendly domestic political formations (democracies) all around, the Western capitalist elites merely sought to translate their own domestic predominance into a position of pre-eminence for their countries in the international arena. So just as for the capitalist ruling class in the domestic sphere, peace without class war guaranteed its own security and predominance, in the same way, the normative conceptions of liberal internationalism characterized by democracy and universal peace are also nothing more than tools for perpetuating the domination of some privileged class of powerful States in global politics (Carr, 1939, p. 104). Thus, a sedulous use of liberal idioms such as 'long peace', 'separate peace', 'cosmopolitan democracy' and 'perpetual peace' are all directed towards providing an intellectual backing for the capitalist attempts at maintaining its own global domination.

Hence, the spatio-temporal dynamics of democratic peace hypothesis must be comprehended by dissecting historical evidence that has pointed towards an entirely countervailing syndrome. Evidence that has reflected the instance of two democratic States indulging in open conflict, or the case of reaching the threshold of conflict, must be identified. In South Asia, the asymmetric war that Pakistan has launched against India in Jammu and Kashmir since 1989 can be considered as one instance in this regard. The sub-conventional war in Kashmir that was launched when Pakistan had experienced the phase of democratic transition after a long period of military rule has contested the viability of the democratic peace thesis in South Asia. Further, this asymmetric war endures, despite Pakistan's spectacular move towards democratic transition since 2008. In this entire period, the nature of the Pakistani State's offensive has not changed, irrespective of the type of regime that it possessed. In this sense, we must examine the trajectory of war and peace in the context of the period from 1989 to 1999 and the period since 2008 till date which are the years in which Pakistan has had democratically elected governments.

To make sense of this, it is crucial to take note of the events of 1971. The catastrophic defeat of 1971 profoundly impacted the strategic thinking in Pakistan. The realization regarding the inviable path of achieving its irredentist goals in Kashmir with conventional means of warfare, not only catalysed Pakistan's strategic moves towards waging an asymmetric war against India with the help of militant proxies but the urge to acquire nuclear weapons was also considerably boosted after the Bangladesh debacle. The territorial jeopardy of 1971, hence, had convinced the security establishment in Pakistan that India's conventional military superiority had to be fought with alternative means such as proxy war and the building up of capacity for nuclear deterrence. Considering this, Pakistan initiated a rigorous programme of nuclear weaponization in 1972, as a reaction to the immense loss that it had suffered in 1971 (Kapur, 2007, pp. 72–73). The aim behind this was to pursue its irredentist national goals, without being bogged down by the threat of Bangladesh type conventional counter-offensive by India (Kapur, 2007, pp. 32–63). This led to the development of a symbiotic relationship between nuclear weapons and militant strategy in Pakistan's security policy (Kapur, 2017, p. 70).

This happened as the acquisition of nuclear weapons capability, covertly in the 1980s and overtly after 1998, significantly bolstered Pakistan's endeavours at sustaining asymmetric warfare with India (Narang, 2014, pp. 15–17). The possession of nuclear weapons capacity encouraged Pakistan towards a tendency for risk-seeking behaviour and facilitated the army and the ISI to continue a sub-conventional warfare with India (Fair, 2014, p. 169). Many experts on nuclear issues had been contemplating that Pakistan may use the nuclear status as better bargaining clout in advancing its goals in Jammu and Kashmir (Ganguly, 1995, p. 328). The enduring asymmetric conflict that has been sustained for almost four decades by the army and the ISI of Pakistan, mediated by the jihadi groups operating from the country's soil has been an attempt in such a game of bargain.

Beginning in 1989, the asymmetric war launched by Pakistan against India, got intensified with the Mumbai terror attack in November 2008. The genesis of this can be seen when the coalitional interdependence between the army, ISI, the Islamists and the jihadi militants got a big push with Zia's State-sponsored Islamization drive in the domestic politics of Pakistan. In addition to this under Zia, the military conflict with India was ardently advocated as a jihad. All this created a fertile ground for the spread of militant jihadi networks which are non-State actors such as the Hizbul-Mujahideen (allied to the Jamaat-e-Islami) (Rana, 2004, pp. 436–438), Harkat-ul-Mujahedin also known as the Harkat-ul-Ansar (allied with the Jamiat Ulema-e-Islam), Lashkar-e-Tayyiba renamed as Jama'at-ud-Dawa (allied with the Daw'at-ul-Irshad; Abou-Zahab & Roy, 2004, pp. 32–44), the Harkat-ul-jihad al-Islami (Rana, 2004, pp. 263–274) and the Jaish-e-Mohammad. This dense network of jihadi groups became the backbone of Pakistan's asymmetric war that was waged by the army and ISI against India (Hussain, 2008, pp. 24–25).

The Soviet occupation of Afghanistan also came as an opportunity for Pakistan in the context of its rivalry with India. In return for the support rendered to the United States in the Afghan jihad, Pakistan's nuclear programme got protection from the former. This largely contributed towards the bolstering of Pakistan's pursuit of the sub-conventional war in Kashmir in the 1990s (Swami, 2007, p. 4). For Pakistan, its rivalry with India pivoted upon the Kashmir issue, largely dictated the contours of its strategy in Afghanistan (Rashid, 2010, p. 186). The Afghan conflict allowed Pakistan to present itself as the champion of the first international Islamic brigade and to mobilize potential allies for its conflict with India (Pande, 2011, pp. 59–87). For General Zia, the Afghan crisis was an opportunity to bolster the jihad in Kashmir (Riedel, 2011, p. 26). This is because the Afghan jihad allowed the Zia-ul-Haq–led Pakistan government to considerably divert the resources generated from the United States and the oil-rich Gulf monarchies such as Saudi Arabia to fund the insurgency in Kashmir (Wirsing, 1991, p. 56).

The US preoccupation with the Afghan war facilitated Pakistan to devote considerable attention towards preparation for launching the proxy war in Kashmir. The United States negligence of sensitive issues such as Pakistan's nuclear programme and its bad human rights records profoundly encouraged Zia to carry forward the preparations for a proxy war in Kashmir completely unhindered (Coll, 2004, pp. 60 & 74; Kux, 2001, pp. 252–253 & 274). As the global eye was entirely focused on Afghanistan in the 1980s, Pakistan advanced its clandestine endeavours towards building up the insurgency groups such as the Jammu Kashmir Liberation Front (JKLF) for the eventual jihad against India. As part of this, Pakistan not only helped JKLF by way of arms supplies and training but also published and disseminated the jihadi materials for the militant organization (Jamal, 2009, pp. 109–112 & 126–128). The success in the Afghan jihad further emboldened the Pakistan-based jihadi groups, aided by the army and the ISI, not only to deepen their presence in Kashmir (Ziring, 2009, pp. 64 & 74) but also to pervasively spread their activities across India (Rashid, 2012, p. 56). Since then, the Pakistan-based jihadi groups have been able to orchestrate targeted attacks on prime locations in Jammu and Kashmir in particular and India at large.

The insurgency in Kashmir that commenced in 1989 redefined the strategic equations in the Indian subcontinent. It happened as Pakistan began to balance India's conventional military superiority by initiating an asymmetric war which it constantly endeavoured to maintain at the level of a low-intensity conflict. In material terms for Pakistan, such a covert war was beneficial because it operationalized the conflict with the help of sub-conventional modes such as the jihadi proxies. The major feature of this insurgency was that the moral foundations of the liberation struggle in Kashmir hence was framed in terms of the vocabulary of Islam, rather than defining it in terms of Kashmiri nationalism. Thus, according to Navnita Behera, the meaning of freedom for the protagonists of the liberation struggle in Kashmir was to be defined in the following manner: 'Azadi ka matlab kya? la ilahi il-allah'. [What is the meaning of freedom? There is no god but god] (Behera, 2000, p. 173). The notion of Azadi was also conjoined with the idea of an Islamic State (nizam-e-mustafa; Swami, 2007, p. 183). In the formulation and execution of such a project of jihad, the triad of the army/Islamists/militant jihadi groups of Pakistan have played a significant role (Jamal, 2009, pp. 128–130).

The low-intensity conflict was escalated by Pakistan to a higher level in 1999 at Kargil. The Kargil crisis itself signified the deadly impasse that has been engendered between India and Pakistan since 1947. Such a deadlock has been the product of the animosity between the two postcolonial rival States of the Indian subcontinent which is deeply structured within the trajectory of the Kashmir dispute (Ganguly, 2016, p. 3). The dispute had already embroiled the two subcontinental neighbours in three wars, with the war of 1971 leading to the breakup of Pakistan. Such a debacle had considerably weakened Pakistan that led to some sort of reduction in tensions between the two subcontinental rivals (Thomas, 2004, pp. 317–318). However, after a period of long peace, Pakistan initiated a low-intensity war by aiding the insurgency in Kashmir from 1989 which reached the fruition point during the Kargil crisis (Ganguly, 2016, pp. 8–10).

At the time of the Kargil crisis, both India and Pakistan had democratic governments, (with India having a caretaker government), but still, a democratic State Pakistan decided to venture into an armed conflict with another democratic State, that is, India. It indicated how the army can easily bypass the civilian rulers to execute their strategic designs. This exactly happened during the Kargil crisis when Pakistani Prime Minister Nawaz Sharif was taken completely by surprise as he received the information regarding the Pakistan army's decision to send in intruders into the Indian territory (Singh, 2001, p. 35). Pakistan's politically degenerate institutional environment tends to obfuscate any scope for consultation between the civilian and military authorities on crucial matters of national security (Wirsing, 2003, p. 47). In this kind of situation, the army has enjoyed complete autonomy in matters of shaping the national security strategy.

The military top brass is constantly engaged in planning the strategy to execute the war machine of Pakistan, irrespective of the nature of the government that is leading the country. Even the Kargil crisis was not an abruptly launched project but it was being dexterously planned since 1996 by the Pakistan army (Jones, 2002, pp. 92–93). Rather, the atrophy in the quality of civil–military relations in Pakistan and the rapidly eroding sharpness of the insurgency in Kashmir acted as a catalyst in accentuating the move of the army towards war in Kargil.

Besides, the Kargil crisis also demonstrated the better bargaining power of Pakistan which allowed the military to make brazen provocations regarding the use of the nuclear options in the event of an emergent existential threat from India when conventional alternatives failed to protect the sovereignty and territorial integrity of the country. This is evident by the fact that India had initiated a plan for conventional strikes across the LOC to dislodge terrorist infrastructure in 2002 (Gupta, 2002, p. 7), which failed to materialize. This happened due to Pakistan's brazen proclamation regarding its intention to use nuclear weapons. In June 2002, Pakistan's ambassador to the United Nations, Munir Akram, cautioned that Pakistan could resort to the use of nuclear weapons even in a conventional conflict if it considers the losses to be unacceptable (Jayaraman, 2002, cited in Sidhu, 2007, p. 227). Such provocations, which were made both during the covert and the overt phases of the nuclearization, largely played upon the psyche of Indian policymakers, by enhancing their dilemmas pertaining to the availability of strategic choices to deal with the Pakistani sub-conventional offensive (Hagerty, 1998, p. 163).

This was also evident in the aftermath of the Mumbai terror attacks wherein India was not able to respond with a conventional military response (Tellis, 2017, p. 36). Overall, the limited conflict in Kargil and the sustained low-intensity conflict in Jammu and Kashmir that is signified by recent instances like those occurring at Uri and Pulwama, indicated that the ugly stability created by the nuclear deterrence has quelled any chances of total war in South Asia (Narang, 2009–2010, p. 64). Sumit Ganguly argues in this context that the events in South Asia since the 1980s demonstrated that the stability/instability paradox was working in the region. Indicative of this, Pakistan was successful in guarding against an Indian retaliation and pursue a sub-conventional warfare by using the threat of its nuclear weapons (Ganguly, 1995, pp. 325–334).

The offensive in Kargil is a manifestation of the advantages of the stability/instability paradox for Pakistan in the context of South Asian security. In this regard, the Kargil Review Committee has made a cogent observation that the stability/instability paradox does play a role in India–Pakistan relations. Additionally, the perceived mutual deterrence might have also influenced the prolonged proxy war in Jammu and Kashmir by disabling India from using its assumed conventional military superiority (Kargil Review Committee report, 2000, p. 183). In any case, whatever may be the strategic dimension of the Kargil crisis, its crucial fallout was that it resulted in the negation of the central proposition of the democratic peace hypothesis that if there are two democratic regimes standing at loggerheads they tend to eschew the use of force against each other. In the case of the Kargil crisis, the ethical yoke of democracy did not restrain Pakistan from aspiring to achieve a strategic advantage over India. That too, in a situation when only a few months ago, both had reached the zenith of constructive engagement by signing the Lahore Declaration. As Machiavelli (1674) argued, 'the democratic republics may also favor wars in situations in which they deem as winnable because they expect to share in the spoils of victory'. As Carr (1939, p. 103) has noted, 'Ethics is the function of politics and morality is the product of power,' the normative consideration of a democratically constructed peace accord proved to be unavailing in containing a power-mongering military establishment, assisted by a weak democratic political class of Pakistan in crushing the righteousness of bilateral peace. Due to this, the post-Kargil Indo-Pak relations slipped from a summit of optimism to a nadir of agony. This meant that even the establishment of democratic regimes would not invariably lead to the reduction of tension between two traditional adversaries, like India and Pakistan. This is primarily because the aspirations for dominance of a democratic state, plagued by the domineering influence of powerful agents, like the Pakistani army, would always thwart any peace deal and regional stability thus becomes an ephemeral phenomenon.

In this regard, if we look at the major part of the history of the low-intensity conflict between India and Pakistan, the latter has been under democratically elected governments except for the period of the rule of General Musharraf. Such a scenario signified that the democratic peace thesis did not work in the context of subcontinental security. Such an aberration can be understood by looking at the regime type that Pakistan actually had during this period which has been discussed in the previous chapter. It has already been discussed that owing to the deep-seated trajectories of political decay and the legitimation crisis, the democratic experiment in Pakistan has been an unsuccessful endeavour. Hence, Pakistan does not qualify to be recognized as the classic model of the Western liberal democratic prototype that is essential for the democratic peace thesis to function successfully. This is mainly because of the larger-than-life role of the army in the political sphere of the country. Hence due to such an intrusive role, the army in Pakistan has had a definitive say in the moulding of the country's security policy. It is precisely because of this that the sub-conventional warfare against India launched by Pakistan has been sustained unhindered, even during the times of democratic transition.

Rather, the greatest irony in the history of subcontinental security has been that whenever there have been democratic governments in Pakistan, the urge for war on the part of the military State tended to intensify. This has been the case because the democratically elected leaders have demonstrated a penchant towards warmongering. This was signified when Prime Minister Benazir Bhutto reiterated her father Zulfikar Ali Bhutto's clarion calls for a thousand-year fight with India on Kashmir (Gupta, 1990). Ms Bhutto made this declaration at the cusp of the genesis of the insurgency in Kashmir. Such brazen provocations encourage the army in Pakistan to pursue its revisionist agenda through the means of asymmetric warfare. Further, the Mumbai terror attacks, which was another episode in the asymmetric warfare of Pakistan it has carried out with the help of militant proxies, also occurred when Pakistan had moved into a course of democratic transition.

Pakistan had returned back to democracy after almost nine years of military rule under Musharraf and the Mumbai incident manifested as the biggest challenge encountered by the civilian government. This is because the attacks happened barely within six months of the assumption of the office by the government under Asif Ali Zardari (Shafqat, 2019, p. 41). This again indicated the inability of the civilian governments to exercise any control over the activities of the army. It demonstrated that the security establishment continued to monopolize Pakistan's security policy, with the processes of consultation completely being neglected. As the events unfolded, India alleged Pakistan of sponsoring the attacks and in response, President Zardari announced to send the Director General of the ISI to India for facilitating the investigations. However, General Kayani immediately vetoed the decision of Zardari and the proposed visit never happened (Ganguly, 2010). This event once again accentuated the hegemonic role of the army in the politics of Pakistan. It reflected how the army exercises totalitarian control over Pakistan's security and foreign policy.

Such a state of affairs signifies why Pakistan does not suit the appropriate model of democracy that has been idealized by the democratic peace thesis, as a universal ethical exemplar. On this count, the democratic peace thesis reflects a deep sense of ethno-centricism as its epistemological foundations tend to emanate out of the experiences of the developed capitalist democracies of Europe and America.

Hence, as the nature of the democratic structure in Pakistan does not match the postulated framework of the same given by the democratic peace thesis, we cannot apply its principles to explain the conditions of conflict and peace in South Asia. The democratic peace thesis contemplates the formation of a security community that is based on the shared democratic values among States. However, Pakistan possesses all the attributes of a non-democratic regime, even if it demonstrates the facade of a working democracy. In this sense, Pakistan does not share with India the same values of democratic politics, which has been nurtured by the latter throughout the time span of its postcolonial history. Hence, the Indian subcontinent has not emerged as a security community, but Pakistan has constantly attempted at portraying India as its biggest external threat. All this explains why Pakistan ventured to wage asymmetric war against India with the help of the jihadi proxies, despite having a democratically elected regime. Since Pakistan does not cherish the values of democracy, despite being a functioning democracy, it does not tend to share the values of a separate peace with India.

Hence, the structure of the democratic regime, surreptitiously controlled by an army that is animated by the weaponized nuclear capability, lies at the bottom of the nature of the warring State in Pakistan. As Pakistan has been unable to institutionalize the command and control of nuclear arsenal in the hands of the civilian authority, the army has always fancied the chances of putting India on the backfoot through the use of nuclear brinkmanship. Such an attempt has been at the heart of the protracted low-intensity war that Pakistan has launched against India. It is this very triadic linkage between the illiberal character of the democratic regime in Pakistan, the urge of the military State to achieve its revisionist goals through asymmetric warfare and the failure of nuclear deterrence in South Asia that enables us to understand the workability of the democratic peace thesis in the context of the Indian subcontinent.

Thus, it has been argued that what makes democracies peaceful towards one another is something more subjective which perhaps results from the fact that one democratic State perceives other democratic States as sharing its values whether they do in reality or not. (Barkawi & Laffey, 2001, p. 10) In this sense, it has also been argued that what should qualify one State as a democracy should be tied to the historical epoch in which the State is considered (Belle & Douglas, 2000, p. 14). This is because the features in virtue of which a State is counted as a democracy, vary across time and space (Chernoff, 2008, p. 91).

THE POVERTY OF LIBERAL PEACE?

The besmirched epoch of the subcontinent's history became a witness to an unprecedented instance where the democratic mandate was ripped apart by calculated employment of brute force by the State itself. It resulted in one democratic State waging a war with another State whose people had voted for democracy but the democratic process was held for ransom by a tiny class of power-paranoid rapacious politicians. The fierce civil war of 1971 in Pakistan was ignited when democracy was aborted in its embryonic stage. The juggernaut of language dichotomy thus ushered in the most decisive inter-State conflicts in South Asian history, that is, the Indo-Pak war of 1971. This war which could unequivocally be dubbed as a war fought on the grave of democracy, not only demonstrated the frailty of democratic institutions in the region but also exhibited the weakness of the democratic peace hypothesis, only to be reaffirmed after 1989 when the protracted asymmetric conflict began between India and Pakistan.

The Indo-Pak war of 1971 and the genesis of sub-conventional war in 1989 that intermittently intensified in the form of the Kargil crisis of 1999, thus illustrated that the existence of democratic mandate in the domestic sphere does not even commend a minuscule influence in deterring the conflict-prone behaviour of the States. It also demonstrated the infelicity of applying the democratic peace hypothesis for understanding subcontinental dynamics as democracy's penchant for indulgence in conflict has been no less than the other regime types (Gleditsch & Hegre, 1997, p. 284). Pakistan's enduring proxy war against India clearly demonstrates such a conjuncture in international relations. This conjuncture also contradicts the theory that democracies and nuclear-weapon States are reluctant to go to war against each other (Chari et al., 2007, p. 3). Here, it may be stated that it is not the axiological power of democratic norms that have inhibited India and Pakistan from going to an all-out war. Rather, it is the fear of the conflict crossing beyond the nuclear Rubicon that has deterred the two subcontinental rivals from escalating the conflict to a higher level.

Thus, the democratic peace thesis merely remains as an observation that is still searching for theory. Although there is a vast literature on democratic peace theory, the literature fails to actually explain how democratic peace exists (Hayes, 2009, p. 979). In this regard, it has been argued that the dominant mechanisms in the literature of political structure and political norms are the monadic mechanisms attempting to explain the dyadic phenomenon. The mechanistic ambiguity of democratic peace leaves the theory open to legitimate counterarguments based on the critiques of correlation (Ward et al., 2007, p. 583) or reverse causality (Thompson, 1996, p. 141). The lack of clear mechanistic understanding also makes it difficult for scholars and policymakers to integrate democratic peace into a coherent foreign policy to enable democracies to take advantage of the phenomenon (Hayes, 2009, p. 979).

Such an issue of correlation and reverse causality becomes evident when we problematize the crisis situations such as the enduring asymmetric war between India and Pakistan. It happens when we begin to deconstruct the genealogy and archaeology of the democratic architecture in the specific context of spatio-temporal topography of both countries. While doing this, the lacuna between procedural, substantive and deliberative notions of democracy becomes apparent. A comparative analysis of the democratic experiences of India and Pakistan, with a relative analysis of the norms, processes and institutions that are in place in both countries, would indicate this phenomenon. On this count, it may be stated that mere possession of institutionalized formation of procedural democracy becomes insignificant for achieving the liberal romance of perpetual peace. It means that if the institutions lack the substantiveness for the purpose of proper operationalization of political processes and if the notion of popular sovereignty is not exercised in terms of deliberative ethics, the functioning of democracy gets obfuscated. This would ultimately render the existence of a direct relationship between the values of domestic political formation with that of the norms of ordering the international, as it is affirmed by the liberal theory of international relations to become a negative phenomenon.

The mere presence of procedural democracy that does not recognize the need for substantiveness in political processes and the value of deliberative ethics for gaining popular consent, would ultimately result in the rupturing of the direct relationship between the domestic presence of democracy and the modes of ordering the international that are situated upon the foundations of liberal peace. This is exactly what has happened in the case of the subcontinent, wherein Pakistan represents the example of a perfect procedural democracy but is devoid of the normative exemplars of a successful democracy such as substantiveness and deliberative ethics. The absence of substantiveness is rendered due to the deep embodiment of its civilian institutions into the interests of the country's army and the ISI.

The policy processes in Pakistan are heavily influenced by the institutional hegemony of its deep state, which ultimately results in the absence of democratic norms in the making of the contours of its domestic politics. Owing to this, the norms of liberal institutionalism get considerably eroded and political processes are held for ransom in pursuit of the assertive class interests of the overdeveloped state, which emerged as the legacy of postcolonial transition. Similarly, as the military state dominates the civilian political processes, the deliberative ethics that is essential to objectify the notion of popular sovereignty also emerges to be an empty signifier. This is because the very idea of deliberative discourse becomes meaningless, as the extra-constitutional authority of the security and strategic establishment tends persistently to dominate the policy perception and responses of constitutionally ordained democratic regimes.

We can substantiate this by looking at two examples. First, in a recent instance, the Prime Minister of Pakistan Imran Khan took one of the most prominent diplomatic decisions of his government regarding the country's relations with India. It pertained to the opening of the border corridor at Kartarpur in Punjab which is a home to Sikh holy site for pilgrims from India. Despite claiming the civilian government's autonomy in the making of domestic and foreign policy, the initiative itself was contemplated under the stewardship of the Chief of Army Staff, General Qamar Javed Bajwa. General Bajwa offered to open the corridor in his bid towards ending Pakistan's diplomatic isolation, by being conciliatory towards India, in a meeting with India's cricketer-turned-politician Mr Navjot Singh Sidhu. The meeting between General Bajwa and Sidhu took place when Sidhu had visited Pakistan to attend the inauguration ceremony of Imran Khan's government (Shah, 2019, p. 140). Such an example denoted how the civilian elite was unable to take any decision pertaining to international relations, foreign policy and security strategy, without the tacit approval of the army (Dutt, 2018). The ability of Pakistan to sustain a sub-conventional low-intensity conflict with the help of the Mullah/military/militants triad indicates the profound control that the army exercises over the security policy of Pakistan, both at the domestic and the international levels (Fair, 2018, p. 25). Second, in the arena of domestic politics, the military also disapproved Imran Khan's handling of the coronavirus crisis and it was announced that the army would coordinate the State's response to the epidemic exigency (Hussain, 2020).

All this renders the notion of popular will, one of the most significant pillars of the making of the security and foreign policy of any state, to become an irrelevant factor. Hence, the influence of domestic political formations upon the ways in which the international is perceived by Pakistan gets deeply embedded in the interests and aspirations of its army and agencies of covert services rather than becoming an embodiment of popular will. Indicating that the liberal values of the domestic political formations do not play any role in the ways in which Pakistan approaches the notions of war and peace. Contrarily, the imagery of the condominium of the army and the ISI tends to determine the way in which the cost-benefit calculus of Pakistan's perceptions of war and peace is shaped. The implications of all this for Pakistan's imageries of order and anarchy is profound, because of the erasure of popular will and the penetration of the organizational class consciousness of the security and strategic establishment into the structural dynamics of its policy processes.

The notion of anarchy, in this sense, for Pakistan is defined in terms of the class interest of the army and the ISI, rather than popular will. It implies that the external security threat perception of Pakistan is largely determined by the ways in which its deep state actually intends to contemplate and presents it to the public. On this count, the ways in which the phenomenon of international, gets linked with the domestic sphere, becomes a prerogative of the security establishment in Pakistan. Due to this, the process of the construction of the external security threat in Pakistan does not rely on the wisdom of its democratically elected leaders. Rather, even if an external security threat is voiced by the high functionaries of the popular government in power, the tone and tenor of the same is mediated by the language of the security establishment. So, the notion of security and insecurity tends to be determined by the language of the interpretations of anarchy that is disseminated in accordance with the class interest of the military-intelligence complex.

If that is the case, the presence of democracy inside and in the polity of its adversary does not hold any ethical value to deter the state in Pakistan to initiate a conflict, on the basis of its own notions of anarchy. The anarchy problematique becomes advantageous for the security establishment to justify armed aggression in the name of self-help and survival of the state. The military means of negotiating with anarchy emerges to be the ultimate mode of ordering the international in the context of the imagery of Pakistan's military/intelligence complex. The revisionist stance that has been imposed upon the country's democracy by its deep state recognizes solutions that are part of the use of military force and hard balancing as the only means of ordering the international. Any mode involving soft balancing or institutionalized means of cooperation to negotiate anarchy does not commend significance for policies and strategies to deal with the world beyond its cartography, for the deep state in Pakistan.

CONCLUSION

As Fred Halliday puts it, facts in the academic discipline of international relations are not enough. We need certain preconceptions to determine which facts are important and which are not. This is because facts are myriad and do not speak for themselves (Halliday, 1994, p. 25). Similar to what Halliday states, we cannot just merely rely on datasets to prove or disprove as to whether anything is a fact or not. Rather, data always need interpretations and like facts that can be told in several ways, datasets that are collected through processes of quantification and verification can also be presented in multiple ways. More significantly, in many cases, the dichotomy between what is referred to as facts and the datasets that are offered to provide credence to the same may appear to be immense. On the basis of this, we must understand the heuristic value of the democratic peace thesis which is disseminated by its proponents with an affirmative claim for accuracy that is supported by empirical datasets.

Keeping this in perspective, it may be stated that although the subcontinental political experience with democratic institutions may be a fact for a lay observer of procedural democracy. However, the fact of its substantiveness in terms of determining the transformative reach of its domestic liberal values into the domain of the international becomes a debatable phenomenon. In the process of experimenting, the workability of the democratic peace thesis, the existence of the structures of democracy in the subcontinent can emerge as a kind of positive heuristics to determine the success of the experiment. However, mere reliance on such facts in the academic discipline of international relations as admonished by Halliday may render our analysis to be parochial. A mere positivist understanding of the working of democratic institutions, deeply grounded in a rationalist approach that is heavily dependent upon quantitative data, would not be sufficient to explain the multifaceted security predicament of the subcontinent and the multilayered policy responses of states in this subregional spatiality. Rather, a more nuanced explanation that is located in a post-positivist emphasis on norms would lead us to a better choice of heuristics for the purpose of experimentation, observation and verification.

The working of democracy in the sub-continental spatial topography and its implications for the domain of the international must therefore be mapped by subjecting our understanding to the framework of a more reflectivist or interpretivist perspective. Any understanding of the reasons for the failure of liberal peace in South Asia must question the objectivity of what is designated by the defenders of positivist and rationalist approaches as empirical which plainly discounts the value of a phenomenon that is unseen. In other words, the over-determinism of the Cartesian dualism between subject (the knower) and object (the known) which is done by the proponents of the rationalists and positivists must be challenged by recognizing that the objectivity of the subject is not always beyond doubt. We must take into cognizance the ethno-centric bias, epistemological leanings and methodological choices of the subject for the purpose of mapping the actual heuristic implications of any theoretical model in international relations. Hence, any such endeavour should transcend the ethno-centric modes of knowing, whose roots are always traced through adherence to a nonlinear notion of history that often culminates into acquiescence to historicist teleology. Thus, what is required is to engage ourselves in a treatment of history that is more pluralist in character. In addition to this, to understand the nature of conflicts in South Asia, we must go beyond Euro-American ethno-centric theoretical formulations and explore alternative models that suit the region's spatio-temporal context.

REFERENCES

Abou-Zahab, M., & Roy, O. (2004). *Islamist networks: The Afghan-Pakistan connection.* Columbia University Press.

Ashley, R. K. (1988). Untying the sovereign state: A double reading of the anarchy problematique. *Millennium: Journal of International Studies, 17*(2), 227–262.

Axelrod, R., & Keohane, R. O. (1985). Achieving cooperation under anarchy: Strategies and institutions. *World Politics, 38*(1), 226–254.

Barkawi, T., & Laffey, M. (2001). Introduction: The international relations of democracy, liberalism, and war. In T. Barkawi & M. Laffey (Eds.), *Democracy, liberalism and war: Rethinking the democratic peace debate* (pp. 7–41). Lynne Reinner Publications.

Behera, N. C. (2000). *State, identity and violence: Jammu, Kashmir and Ladakh.* Manohar.

Belle, V., & Douglas, A. (2000). *Press, freedom and global politics.* Praegar Publishers.

Biddle, S., & Long, S. (2004). Democracy and military effectiveness: A deeper look. *Journal of Conflict Resolution, 48*(4), 525–546.

Bleiker, R. (2008). Traversing Patagonia: New writings on postcolonial international relations. *Political Theory, 36*(2), 313–320.

Burchill, S. (2001). Liberalism. In S. Burchill, A. Linklater, R. Devetak, J. Donnelly, M. Paterson, C. R.-S., & J. True (Eds.), *Theories of international relations.* Palgrave.

Buzan, B., & Little, R. (2000). *International systems and world history: Remaking the study of international relations.* Oxford University Press.

Calhoun, C. (1995). *Critical social theory: Culture, history and the challenge of difference.* Wiley-Blackwell.

Carr, E. H. (1939–1981). *The twenty years crisis 1919–1939: An introduction to the study of international relations*, Reprint. Macmillan.

Chari, P. R., Cheema, P. I., & Cohen, S. P. (2007). *Four crises and a peace process: American engagement in South Asia.* Brookings Institute Press.

Chernoff, F. (2008). International relations, paleontology, and scientific progress: Parallels between democratic peace studies and the meteor impact extinction hypothesis. *International Studies Perspectives, 9*(1), 90–98.

Coll, S. (2004). *Ghost wars: The secret history of the CIA, Afghanistan and Bin Laden, from the Soviet invasion to September 10, 2001.* Penguin.

Cox, R. W. (1986). Social forces, states and world orders: Beyond international relations theory. In R. O. Keohane (Ed.), *Neorealism and its critiques* (pp. 204–254). Columbia University Press.

Cox, R. W. (1987). *Production, power and world order*. Columbia University Press.

Cummings, B. (1991). Trilateralism and the new world order. *World Policy Journal*, 8(2), 195–222.

Darby, P. (2006). *Postcolonising the international: Working to change the way we are*. University of Hawaii Press.

Deudney, D., & Ikenberry, J. (1999). The nature and sources of a liberal international order? *Review of International Studies*, 25(2), 179–196.

Devetak, R. (2007). Between Kant and Pufendorf: Humanitarian intervention, statist anti-cosmopolitanism and critical international theory. *Review of International studies*, 33(1), 151–174.

Doyle, M. (1986). Liberalism and world politics. *American Political Science Review*, 80(4), 1151–1161.

Dutt, B. (2018). Imran Khan is close to Pakistan's army: Here's why that's good for India. *Washington Post*, 4 December. https://www.washingtonpost.com›2018/12/04›imran

Elman, C., & Elman, M. F. (Eds.). (2001). *Bridges and boundaries: Historians, political scientists and the study of international relations*. MIT Press.

Fair, C. (2014). Fighting to the end: The Pakistan army's way of war. Oxford University Press.

Fair, C. (2018). *In their own words: Understanding the Lashkar-i-Tayyaba*. Oxford University Press.

Fukuyama, F. (1992). *The end of history and the last man*. Free Press.

Ganguly, S. (1995). Indo-Pakistani nuclear issues: Stability/instability paradox. *The Study of Conflict and Terrorism*, 18(4), 325–338.

Ganguly, S. (2010). General Kayani: A Musharraf in the making? *The Times of India*, 20 March. https://timesofindia.indiatimes.com›...›Pakistan News

Ganguly, S. (2016). *Deadly impasse: Indo-Pakistani relations at the dawn of a new century*. Cambridge University Press.

Gilpin, R. (1983). *War and change in world politics*. Cambridge University Press.

Gleditsch, N. P., & Hegre, H. (1997). Peace and democracy: Three levels of analysis. *Journal of Conflict Resolution*, 41(2), 283–310.

Grieco, J. (1988). Anarchy and the limits of cooperation: A realist critique of the new liberal institutionalism. *International Organization*, 42(3), 485–507.

Gupta, S. (1990). Playing with fire. *India Today*, 31 May. https://www.indiatoday.in›Magazine›Cover Story

Gupta, S. (2002). When India came close to war. *India Today*, 23 December, 7–12.

Hagerty, D. T. (1998). *The consequences of nuclear proliferation: Lessons from South Asia*. MIT Press.

Halliday, F. (1994). *Rethinking International Relations*. Macmillan.

Hayes, J. (2009). Identity and securitisation in the democratic peace: The United States and the divergence of responses to India's and Iran's nuclear programs. *International Studies Quarterly*, 53(4), 977–999.

Hobden, S. (1998). *Historical sociology and international relations: Breaking down boundaries*. Routledge.

Hobden, S., & Hobson, J. M. (Eds.). (2002). *Historical sociology of international relations*. Cambridge University Press.

Hussain, T. (2020). Pakistan's Imran Khan loses control of coronavirus fight to the military, amid corruption scandal. *South China Morning Post*, 9 April. https://www.scmp.com›This Week in Asia›Politics

Hussain, Z. (2008). *Frontline Pakistan: Path to catastrophe and the killing of Benazir Bhutto*. I. B. Tauris and Co.

Isacoff, J. (2002). On the historical imagination of international relations: The case for a deweyan reconstruction. *Millennium: Journal of International Studies*, 31(3), 603–626.

Jamal, A. (2009). *Shadow war: The untold story of jihad in Kashmir*. Melville House.

Jayaraman, T. (2002, 8–21 June). Nuclear crisis in South Asia. *Frontline*, 19(12). http://www.frontlineonnet.com/fl1912/19121230.htm

Jones, O. B. (2002). *Pakistan: Eye of the storm*. Yale University Press.

Kant, I. (1970). *Immanuel Kant's wrightings* (H. Nisbet, Trans.). H. Reiss (Ed.). Cambridge University Press.

Kapur, P. S. (2007). *Dangerous deterrent: Nuclear weapons proliferation and conflict in South Asia*. Stanford University Press.

Kapur, P. S. (2017). *Jihad as grand strategy: Islamist militancy, national security and the Pakistani state*. Oxford University Press.

Kargil Review Committee Report. (2000). *From surprise to reckoning*. SAGE Publications.

Keohane, R. O. (2012). Twenty years of institutional liberalism. *International Relations*, 26(2), 125–138.

Keohane, R. O., & Nye, J. (1989). *Power and interdependence: World politics in transition* (2nd ed.). Pearson Education.

Kratochwil, F. V. (2006). History, action and identity: Revisiting the 'second' debate and assessing its impact for social theory. *European Journal of International Relations*, 12(1), 5–29.

Kux, D. (2001). *The United States and Pakistan 1947–2000: Disenchanted allies*. Johns Hopkins University Press.

Machiavelli, N. (1674). *Machiavelli's discourses upon the first decade of T. Livius* (E Dacres, Trans.) Charles Harper and John Amery.

Moravcsik, A. (1997). Taking preferences seriously: A liberal theory of international politics. *International Organization*, 51(4), 513–553.

Morgenthau, H. J. (1967). *Politics among nations*. Knopf.

Narang, V. (2009–2010). Posturing for peace? Pakistan's nuclear posture and South Asian stability. *International Security*, 34(3), 38–78.

Narang, V. (2014). *Nuclear strategy in the modern era: Regional powers and international conflict*. Princeton University Press.

Nie, J., Jr. (1990). The changing nature of world power. *Political Science Quarterly, 105*(2), 177–192.

Pande, A. (2011). *Explaining Pakistan's foreign policy: Escaping India.* Routledge.

Puchala, D. (2003). *History and theory in international relations.* Routledge.

Rana, M. A. (2004). *A to Z of jehadi organisations in Pakistan.* Mashal Books.

Rashid, A. (2010). *Taliban: Militant Islam, oil and fundamentalism in Central Asia.* Yale University Press.

Rashid, A. (2012). *Pakistan on the brink: The future of Pakistan, Afghanistan and the West.* Allen Lane.

Riedel, B. (2011). *Deadly embrace: Pakistan, America and the future of the global jihad.* Brookings Institution Press.

Roberts, G. (2006). History, theory and the narrative turn in IR. *Review of International Studies, 32*(4), 703–714.

Ruggie, J. G. (1998). *Constructing the world polity: Essays on international institutionalization.* Routledge.

Schmitt, C. (1996). *The concept of the political.* University of Chicago Press.

Shafqat, S. (2019). Pakistan army: Sustaining hegemony and constructing democracy? *Journal of South Asian and Middle Eastern Studies, 42*(2), 20–51.

Shah, A. (2019). Pakistan: Voting under military tutelage. *Journal of Democracy, 30*(1), 128–142.

Shapcott, R. (2000). Solidarism and after: Global governance, international security and the normative 'turn' in international relations. *Pacifica Review, 12*(1), 147–165.

Sidhu, W. P. S. (2007). Operation Vijay and Operation Parakram: The victory of theory? In E. Sridharan (Ed.), *India Pakistan nuclear relationship: Theories of deterrence and international relations* (pp. 208–238). Routledge.

Singh, A. (2001). *A ridge too far: War in the Kargil heights 1999.* Moti Bagh Palace.

Smith, M. J. (1992). Liberalism and international reform. In T. Nardin & D. Mapple (Eds.), *Traditions of international ethics* (pp. 87–122). Cambridge University Press.

Smith, T. W. (1999). *History and international relations.* Routledge.

Swami, P. (2007). *India, Pakistan and the secret jihad: The covert war in Kashmir, 1947–2004.* Routledge.

Tellis, A. J. (2017). *Are India Pakistan peace talks worth a damn?* Carnegie Endowment for International Peace.

Teschke, B. (2003). *The myth of 1648: Class, geopolitics and the making of modern international relations.* Verso.

Therborn, G. (2007). After dialectics: Radical social theory in a post-communist world. *New Left Review, 43*(43), 63–114.

Thomas, R. G. C. (2004). The South Asian security balance in a western dominant world. In T. V. Paul, J. Wirtz, & M. Fortman (Eds.), *Balance of power: Theory and practice in the 21st century.* Stanford University Press.

Thompson, W. R. (1996). Democracy and peace: Putting the horse before the cart. *International Organisation, 50*(1), 141–174.

Vaughan-Williams, N. (2005). International relations and the 'problem of history'. *Millennium: Journal of International Studies, 34*(1), 115–136.

Walt, S. M. (1991). The renaissance of security studies. *International Studies Quarterly, 35*(2), 211–239.

Walt, S. M. (1998). International relations: One world many theories. *Foreign Policy, 110*, 29–32 and 34–46.

Ward, M. D., Siverson, R. M., & Cao, X. (2007). Disputes, democracies and dependencies: A reexamination of the Kantian peace. *American Journal of Political Science, 51*(3), 583–601.

White, H. (1973). Interpretation in history. *New Literary History, 4*(2), 281–314.

White, H. (1975). *Metahistory: Historical imagination in nineteenth-century Europe.* Johns Hopkins University Press.

White, H. (1980). The value of narrativity in the representation of reality. *Critical Enquiry, 7*(1), 5–27.

Williams, P. D. (2008). Security studies: An introduction. In P. D. Williams (Ed.), *Security studies: An introduction.* Routledge.

Wirsing, R. G. (1991). *Pakistan's security under Zia, 1977–1988: The policy imperatives of a peripheral Asian state.* St Martin's Press.

Wirsing, R. G. (2003). *Kashmir in the shadow of war: Regional rivalries in a nuclear age.* M. A. Sharpe.

Ziring, L. (2009). Unravelling the Afghanistan–Pakistan riddle. *Asian Affairs: An American Review, 36*(2), 59–77.

Conclusion

The notion of world order has been subjected to a multilayered and complex interpretation. The debate over its nature has intensified and the discipline of international relations seems to be divided on the issue of defining concepts such as multipolarity, hegemony, imperialism and supra-national. These concepts, in a way, have taken a back seat, and the nature of world order is now being broadly understood through phenomena such as multilateral governance, complex interdependence, agenda-setting and the replacement of the notion of hard power with soft power. Thus, in the scenario of a globalizing international circumstance, the very notion of world order itself has not remained as a monolithic phenomenon, with the course of international relations witnessing kaleidoscopic transformations. This has led in the discipline of international relations, to the rise of the 'neo/neo debate', wherein an inconclusive triangular argument is on among the neorealists, the neoliberals and the neo-Marxists regarding the nature of the contemporary world order. The persistent debate has also led Stephen Walt to describe this state of affairs as 'one world many theories' (Walt, 1998, pp. 29–32 and 34–46).

On account of this, serious questions have been posed in the discipline of international relations as to whether there has been the end of international relations theory after the third and the fourth debate? In answering this, Tim Dunne et al. (2013, p. 405) have optimistically predicted that international relations theory may demonstrate a resilient existence as it is theory-led, theory-literate and theory-concerned (Dunne et al., 2013, p. 405). Further, scholars like Christian Reus-Smit have challenged the argument that meta-theories are out of fashion.

He has argued that we can at best bracket meta-theoretical enquiry but cannot completely free our work from meta-theoretical assumptions. Reus-Smit further argues that the main objective of international relations is the generation of practical knowledge and empirical theoretical insights alone cannot provide such knowledge. It has to be integrated with normative forms of reasoning that focuses on meta-theoretical reflections and an expansive and ambitious eclecticism (Reus-Smit, 2013, p. 589). Andrew Bennett on his part indicates that the organization of the discipline of international relations around the major paradigms or 'Isms' prominently, neorealism, neoliberalism, constructivism, Marxism and feminism has been based on a flawed reading of the philosophy of science and has run its course. Hence, the study of international relations must be grounded in structured pluralism consisting of major paradigms (Bennett, 2013, pp. 459–460). Finally, John Mearsheimer and Stephen Walt accentuate the continuing significance of theory for the discipline of international relations, as against simplistic hypothesis testing (Mearsheimer & Walt, 2013, p. 427). Apart from this inter-paradigm debate, the second level of concern that has been expressed pertaining to the discipline of international relations is the post-positivist critique of international relations as a science (Lapid, 1989). One of the most prominent offshoots of this critique has been the questioning of the very notion of international relations as the State-centric discipline. With this, serious questions are also being raised regarding the validity of the State-centred theories that define the nature of world order.

Based on this epistemological assessment of the notion of world order and international relations, this book has raised the fundamental epistemic question, as to What is the most viable solution for the contemporary conundrum that South Asia is undergoing currently? The liberal scholars in international relations have advocated an option through their widely debated conception of democratic peace hypothesis. But the crucial question that arises again here is: Whether is it a credible vehicle to navigate us through the dense conundrum of South Asian dynamics so that we could discover the proverbial path for achieving peace and stability? In the light of this question, a critique of the democratic peace hypothesis has been proposed in this book which is situated in the obscure and scabrous politico-cultural terrain of South Asia.

Here, it has been argued that the democratic peace hypothesis seems to be an inadequate tool, in so far as its applicability as an explanatory mode to explore ways of establishing regional peace and stability in South Asia is concerned. Historical evidence point to a totally contrasting syndrome to what the democratic peace hypothesis actually argues. Instances of two democratic regimes indulging in open conflict or getting locked in a situation of conflict have occurred repeatedly in the region. The example of India and Pakistan engaging in armed conflicts in times of both having democracies underscores this phenomenon. It has also been argued here that the infirmity of democratic regimes of South Asian States has factored deeply in precipitating an unstable security environment in the region.

Owing to this, the idea of South Asia has existed as a complex phenomenon that has consistently been subjected to a multilayered and multifaceted interpretation. These interpretations often have tended to emerge as mere paralogistic explanations that are located in borrowed epistemes which are devoid of any native intellectual traditions. Such a conundrum has been the product of the intricate interplay between sameness embedded in the communion of histories and dissimilarities expressed in terms of divergent nation-building project and strategies towards State-construction practised by the polities of South Asia. This has engendered a Daedalian sociocultural and political mosaic in the region. It has considerably jeopardized the coherence of the region and has brought enforced reflexivity and fluidity to its identity. This reflexivity and fluidity are evident in the attempts of the region's polities to grapple with the dilemma of engaging with the processes of modernity and democratization and simultaneously attempting at preserving their indigenous cultural identity.

The dilemma has not only resulted in the region getting enmeshed in a twilight zone between modernity and traditionality but also has led to the fractured process of regional integration. Owing to all this, the very concept of South Asia has surfaced as a complex phenomenon that is subjected to diverse interpretations. It has emerged as a subject of in-depth scholarly interventions by historians, sociologists, anthropologists, political scientists and scholars of international relations. Mainly because the idea of South Asia has been evolving in a contentious trajectory wherein, not only its cartographic identity but its cultural identity and the legitimacy of its nation states has perpetually been in question.

Considering the experience of South Asia pertaining to political decay and legitimation crisis, it has been argued in this book that the roots of the notions of political decay and legitimation crisis can be traced to the imported morals of modernity in the region. Historically speaking, such a process of importation was done by the immigrant political institutions that were brought in by the colonial metropolis in the region, leading to the creation of an artificially constructed identity of modern South Asia, which was crafted by an arbitrary formulation of national cartographies. Owing to such a colonial construction, this modern idea of South Asia witnessed a considerable erosion of its ancient civilizational values such as tolerance, accommodation and eclecticism because of which the region had evolved into a space that not only possessed a wide variety of sociocultural diversities but also was marked by certain common features that imparted a sense of collective recognition to it.

All this compels us to ruminate over two imponderables that the South Asians have been left to negotiate with. First, whether the debate over the very process of decolonization and the persistent condition of post-coloniality has actually reached a point of fruition? Or second, is it the case that the debate still rages and tends to over-determine the political consciousness and cultural imagery of the postcolonial self in South Asia? It is these very imponderables mentioned here that lie at the bottom of what we call the postcolonial predicament in South Asia. Such a condition of postcoloniality fits into the theoretical models of political decay and the legitimation crisis which manifests in the multilayered forms of the crisis of governability, the conundrum of democratization, the unresolved exigencies of conflict resolution, and the hampering of the developmental trajectory of the polities in South Asia.

DEMOCRATIZATION IN SOUTH ASIA: SUSPENDED BETWEEN THE COLONIAL AND POSTCOLONIAL

For any serious attempt at understanding the social phenomenon, it is imperative to locate its examination in the framework of history (Mills, 1959, p. 145). Taking cognizance of such a cogent observation of Mills, it has been argued here that at the level of the State's substructure, the psychology of colonialism has left a deep imprint upon the processes of State-making and State-construction in the countries of the region. These processes have been characterized by instability which is caused due to the rebelling stakeholders of power who are competing with the existing regimes. The causal impulse to this has been the institutional approach that resulted in the adventitious imposition of Western style of metropolitan Governance done by the outgoing colonizers in liaison with the existing powerful local groups, leading to the complete marginalization of the weak and powerless groups in these polities. This marginalization led to the structured domination of the powerful groups in all sectors of society.

Due to this, these processes emerged as a top-down pyramidic approach, with the democratic consciousness remaining considerably oblivious of the political processes governing their lives. A lack of a bottom-up approach thus drastically hampered the democratization processes in South Asian States and also left wide spaces open for intra-State intergroup conflicts. All this, seem to be signifying the syndrome of what has been designated as the postcolonial predicament in South Asia. Underpinning this, seem to be a kind of a project of modernity, democratization and development that is rather dilettantish in character, carried out by the States of South Asia. Such a project appears to be mediated by flirtatious employment of received forms of metropolitan governance that has been handed down by British imperialism through the mechanisms of colonial governmentality (Kaviraj, 2010, p. 212). In any case, the postcolonial predicament of South Asia cannot be explained through a mere singular monovalent emphasis on the role of imported values of European enlightenment. Rather, the predicament deepened, owing to the modes of transculturation[1] and worlding[2] by which the native wisdom in South Asia reacted to such importations in their engagement with the imperial metropolis in the contact zone.[3] This is because the native postcolonial wisdom, tended to engage in the act of appropriating[4] the post-enlightenment values imported from the imperial metropolis, for the purpose of deconstructing their own past legacy, present condition and future prospects. Implying that the decolonized periphery began to interpret the trajectory of its postcolonial condition with the help of the prism of the values handed down to them by the colonizing metropolis.[5]

In this regard, Dipesh Chakrabarty has argued that the ideas of the modern State, popular sovereignty, democracy, civil society, public

[1] The term 'transculturation' in the vocabulary of the colonial discourse theory refers to the transfer of culture in a reductive fashion to the colony. The idea of such transfers is imagined purely in terms of the interests of the imperial metropolis. Although transculturation involves a reciprocal interaction of cultures such reciprocity is always laden with asymmetric relations of domination and subordination. This has a profound sense of eurocentrism as Europe tends to imagine itself as the critical determinant in structuring the cultural life of the colonized periphery. In this regard, the concept of transculturation raises the question as to how the modes of metropolitan representation are received and appropriated by the periphery (Pratt, 1992, pp. 4–6 & 228).

[2] Worlding is a term coined by the postcolonial critic Gayatri Spivak to describe the modes by which the eurocentric formulations of the imperial metropolis construct the imaginary of the colonized space as a part of the world. Describing the process as worlding of the world on uninscribed earth, Spivak indicates that worlding implies that the imperial discourse is inscribed by the colonizer on the colonized space with the purpose of constructing the identity of the colonized in the framework of the imperial vocabulary (Spivak, 1985, pp. 128 & 133).

[3] The term 'contact zone' was developed by M. L. Pratt to signify those social spaces where disparate cultures tend to interact with each other. These interactions for Pratt often tended to occur in an asymmetrical relationship of domination and subordination like the one that exists between the colonizer and the colonized (Pratt, 1992, p. 4).

[4] In the vocabulary of the colonial discourse theory, metropolis refers to the relationship that the colonizing centre has with the colonized periphery. In other words, the metropolis is the parent State of the colony (Ashcroft et al., 2000, p. 122).

[5] The term 'appropriation' is used in the technical discourse of postcolonial criticism to describe the ways in which postcolonial societies take over aspects of imperial culture, language, the metropolitan institutions and modes of thought to interpret their own sociocultural identities. The colonized engages in such acts of appropriation, for the purpose of gaining cosmopolitan appeal for the native sociocultural and political formations (Ashcroft et al., 2002).

sphere, the individual distinction between the public/private spheres, human rights, rule of law, social justice, citizenship, political authority and scientific rationality, all carry the imprint of the imported post-enlightenment values of Europe. Although these concepts are foundationally situated at the cusp of the making of what has been designated as political modernity in South Asia that is characterized by the rule of modern institutions of the State, bureaucracy and capitalist enterprise but the genealogy of these concepts and categories can be traced to the intellectual and even theological traditions of Europe (Chakrabarty, 2000, p. 4). Even the concepts of nation and nationalism that underpinned the movement for self-determination of the colonized periphery, and defined the trajectory of their postcolonial project of modernity encompassing the formation of institutions of governmentality, also bore the influence of the cultural import from the imperial metropolis. This is because the genealogy of these concepts is rooted in the spatio-temporal history of capitalism, a genealogy that did not form part of the history of postcolonial societies (Chatterjee, 1999, pp. 132–133).

As a result of such an act of appropriation, the indigenous sociocultural and political formations remained neither native nor cosmopolitan. Signifying that the location of the native sociocultural and political formation and the sense of history associated with the same in the context of the received post-enlightenment values of the imperial metropolis rendered them to remain as a mere parodies of what they actually meant to be. These formations, hence, manifested as temporally anachronistic, spatially anomalous and incompatible with the native tradition. Overall, the framing of the native sociocultural and political formations in the colonially transmitted vocabulary of the imperial metropolis resulted in those formations becoming a misnomer and they became a mere travesty of what they actually ought to be representing. Hence, the act of appropriating the cultural logic of post-enlightenment Europe by the colonized, proved to be a catachresis.[6] In the discourse of the postcolonial criticism of Homi K. Bhabha,

---

[6] Gayatri Chakrovorty Spivak uses the word 'catachresis' to signify a process of appropriation, whereby the colonized applies a particular term to a thing that it does not properly denote. When the colonized take and reinscribe something that was

such an act of appropriation, emerged to be what he designated as mimicry.[7] Hence, the very state of the postcolonial predicament in South Asia appears to be a product of the process of structuration that happened with an active engagement of the colonizing metropolis and the colonized periphery. Owing to this the postcolonial States exhibit the traits of the colonizer, as their cultures are deeply influenced by the metropolitan culture and ideology of their former colonizers (Majid, 2000, p. 23).

To make sense of this, this book has attempted to transcending the mere nonlinear historical explanations that associate the colonial metropolis with all the problems of postcolonial South Asia. Rather, the book endeavoured at exploring how the values and structures of colonial governmentality were actually received by the native intelligentsia who began to command the postcolonial political spatialities. In this way, an attempt has been made to conceptualize the intersectionalities between the colonial and postcolonial periods of South Asia by according agency to both the colonizing metropolitan elite and the colonized native intelligentsia in the process of the structuration that led to the emergence of the postcolonial predicament in South Asia. Herein, it becomes pertinent to bring in the conception of historian E. H. Carr, for whom history is a dialogue between the past, the present and the future (Carr, 1987, p. 30). Situating ourselves on the plank of this notion of history, it may be stated that the contemporary dynamics of postcolonial States tend to get inextricably linked to their colonial past, owing to colonialism's transhistorical ontology. Based on

---

traditionally an element of imperial culture, it becomes what she designates as catachresis. Catachresis occurs, when the concepts such as parliamentary democracy and nation that emerged out of a specific ontic and epistemic context of Europe are adopted by postcolonial societies. In the process of such adoptions, those concepts end up not literally representing the correct narrative of their actual genealogy (Spivak, 1991, p. 70).

[7] The term 'mimicry' in the language of the postcolonial criticism of Homi Bhabha referred to the act of the colonized to adopt the sociocultural values, civic virtues, political morality and institutional values of the colonizer. Such a mimicry for Bhabha was threatening for the colonized because copying the attitudes, behaviour, manners and values amounted to a kind of menacing mockery. It was a mockery as although colonized copied the colonizer, but as a result of this, the former began to appear as a disfigured replica of the latter (Bhabha, 1984, p. 127).

this, it has been argued in this book that due to the omnibus presence of a collective memory characterized by the dominating influence of hegemonic structures of colonialism, the countries of postcolonial South Asia have been compelled to navigate through turbulent waters in their endeavour to accomplish the task of State-making, State-construction and economic modernization.

HISTORY, VIOLENCE AND THE DEMOCRATIC EXPERIMENT IN SOUTH ASIA

For Sugata Bose and Ayesha Jalal,

> The failure of postcolonial States to assure equal citizenship rights and to deliver on the promise of a redistributive justice has brought to these enti-ties into some disrepute. As the general concept of the modern centralized nation-State has been drawn deeper into a crisis of legitimacy, a raging battle has begun between State-sponsored and anti-State nationalism. (Bose & Jalal, 2004, p. 204)

This phenomenon becomes apparent in South Asia, as the region has witnessed a trail of violence engendered by ethnic nationalism and religio-civilizational confrontations. An apparent manifestation of this is the partition of the Indian subcontinent and the subsequent horrendous maelstrom, owing to which, in the post-partition epoch, history itself has become both an epistemic and the ideological dis-course which seems to lie at the bottom of violent political conflicts.

Further, the specific conditions under which new States achieved their independence have till date proven to be a grave burden, making South Asia continue as a conflict zone. This burden itself incarnates in the form of a crisis of the State, which, in turn, seems to be the product of the lengthy process of the development of colonial rule (Weidemann, 2007, p. 84). Thus, it becomes very difficult to de-emphasize history when we attempt to deconstruct the origins of the contemporary developments in South Asia. Our epistemological initiative in this regard has been deeply underpinned by the heuristic conviction that the phenomenon of international in South Asia is pro-foundly influenced by the contours of the domestic spatialities within the countries of the region. This influence is so deep and pervasive that it has had a significant influence upon the inter-State contest over sovereignty and fixity of political territoriality (Brass, 2010, p. 22). Situating ourselves on the plank of such an assessment of the trajectory of political development in South Asia, we have attempted at understanding the linkages between history, violence and the nature of democracy in the region.

This leads us to the critical question of defining a democracy which appears to be a convoluted one, 'as it agglomerates a range of institutional and other features with separate effects on decision-making' (Ferejohn & Rosenbluth, 2008, p. 31). So merely having an elected government does not imply that a State is a democracy. The actual question to be pondered is whether the governments that appear as democracies are really democratic? and are their decisions actually formulated in accordance to the popular will and not dictated by the whims and fancies of a particular section of the society? The answers to these questions may be found only by an understanding of the actual nature of the democratic architecture in the subcontinent, so as to delineate the reasons for the unremitting ethno-religious conflicts in the region. The imperative in this regard for democracy is the need for an egalitarian society that is munificent in recognizing the equal status of all groups of people, irrespective of any anthropologically imposed superficial distinctions and free from any threats of a particular section of the society acquiring such leverage so that they become armed to dominate or hegemonize the entire society. This also implies that a democratic State without a democratic society will only be a parody. Or, in other words, a liberal democratic State would merely be a tapestry that would perform the role of masquerading the discrepancies of an undemocratic society.

Clipped to this is the crucial question, that is, whether democratic governments purely function according to the popular will without being perturbed by any dominant section of the society? This question has to be taken into account as the physiognomy for visualizing the state of democracy in India and Pakistan. The first and foremost issue here is whether democratic mechanisms in the subcontinent are truly democratic, or they exhibit pretentious gestures of being so.

To widen the scope of this argument, we can invoke the telling phrase of Marx and Engels (1968, p. 57) to describe the nature of democratic States in the region. They thus, designate 'the modern State as nothing more than a committee for managing the affairs of the bourgeoisie'. Viewing things from the prism of the framework of this statement, the democratic States in South Asia, maybe reckoned merely as having acted as bazaars that have facilitated a tiny class of power paranoid merchants to establish their monopoly by entirely marginalizing the weaker sections of the society. This is because in a way, democracy has emerged as an institutional device to exercise power in bourgeois society. As democracy like other sociopolitical structures is born not only out of social antagonisms manifesting and recreating forever the distinction between the rulers and the ruled but also defends, cements and advances a social order based on exploita-tion (Neelsen & Malik, 2007, pp. 27–28). It may be the predominance of the Punjabi community in Pakistan, a dominant Sinhala fringe in Sri Lanka, a conservative Islamic group in the Maldives and the hegemonic Brahmin dominated Hindu social order in India and Nepal, all have determined the illiberal nature of the democratic State in South Asia.

Thus, the nature of the democratic State in South Asia, tend to transgress national boundaries in one respect that is every country recognized as a liberal democracy, seem to possess illiberal features. On this front, all South Asian countries appear to cascade into a tightly knit ensemble, as all of them tend to assume upon themselves the mere role of a balancer of competing for elitist claims. So as the State became simply a mechanism for patronizing the hegemonic tenden-cies of dominant groups in the society, widespread discontent and clash of interests pushed the region into a spiral of conflicts. As aptly pointed out by Ayoob (1995, p. 17), the Third-World governing elites are preoccupied, if not obsessed by the concerns for their regimes. In addition to this, the incongruity among national elites of South Asia resulting from such causes as different stages of political development, conflicting nation-building strategies, differing attitudes and responses to cross-national ethnic and religious problems, presents a complex situation. It is further complicated by the conflicting strategic and diplomatic positions held by the different South Asian States with regard to both regional and global systems (Ghosh, 1989, p. 229).

The results have been obvious; the countries of the region have been ceaselessly grappling with pressing problems such as the enduring threat of left-wing insurgency in Nepal and India, the unbridled Talibanization and Islamic extremism in Pakistan, Bangladesh and Afghanistan, and the sinister designs of big powers such as the United States which has sought to fashion the politico-strategic equations of the region, in a manner that would suit its own neoimperialist grand strategy. All these problems have compounded together and held the region's peace and security to ransom. Thus, security threats in many parts of the Third World are mostly endogenous in character, rather than being of exogenous origin (Azar & Moon, 1998, p. 11). Here, what prominent South Asian observer Stephen Cohen wrote decades ago is of great contemporary relevance. According to him,

> The South Asian security system is an insecurity system and the trade off for each regional Government involves minimising insecurity, not maximising security. Insecurity, whether internal disorder or external conflict, has become a norm and one cannot say that the situation will change for the better in the foreseeable future. (Cohen, 1975, p. 783)

However, the most dominant aspect of the tumultuous character of the region has been the politico-strategic wrangle between the two subcontinental adversaries, that is, India and Pakistan. The end of Cold War has ushered in an era of hope. A hope of a better future with decreased global tensions and definite demilitarization. While the global trends are at reduced force levels, the trends in South Asia are developing in the opposite direction. The Line of Control, LOC, dividing the Indian and Pakistan-controlled Kashmir continues to simmer and has the potential to burst into flames (Durrani, 2000, p. 81). Apart from presenting a case for a vexed geopolitical and strategic issue, Indo-Pak adversarial relations are also a classic embodiment of the politico-strategic consequence of ethno-religious dichotomies. Much credit in this regard must be assigned to the political exploitation of these cleavages on both sides of the border that has led to the protracted nature of the subcontinental embranglement. The genesis of such tendencies may be traced to the days of the partition of the Indian subcontinent. The foundational aspect here was the inability of both the Hindu and Muslim leaders to resolve their differences which ultimately became intractable, ushering in the subcontinental schism. Today, even after seven decades, the hysteria of that division still haunts people on both sides of the cartographic divide.

Owing to this, the subcontinental experiences with war and democracy suggest that the liberal peace thesis does not hold adequate ground. The underlying causes for this have been the region's idiosyncratic politico-strategic, socio-economic and psycho-cultural dynamics. One key factor among such idiosyncrasies has been the flawed and pretentious democracy of Pakistan which possesses eccentricities marked by non-political and non-state actors that tend to dictate their own terms upon the democratic process. So, as Pakistan has depicted symptoms, admittedly of amateurish ventures in fabricating the architectures of democratic governance, the interpretation of the subcontinent's tryst with war and peace by invoking the democratic peace hypothesis would be nothing more than like compliance to a kind of systematically crafted sophistic.

Regarding the democratic peace hypothesis, it may be argued that it is a utopian conception and suffers from the confinement into a didactic logic that democracy is the ideal antinomy to conflict. In this sense, it is liberated from the limits of spatio-temporal dynamics and objective ecological factors. It represents a structured fantasy and not a dynamic component of history because it situates conflict in a synchronic context, completely oblivious of its diachronic element. It is also plagued by a sense of teleological reductionism, as it considers the Hegelian notion of the 'end of history', as an ultimate nonlinear historical factuality. Such a sense of teleological reductionism is evident in Fukuyama's celebration of the victory of the liberal capitalist world as the denouement of all forms of ideological struggles in the world.

These kinds of celebrations not only reflect a sense of denial regarding the effectiveness of non-democratic ideologies to penetrate into wider spaces but it also signify a delusional consonance among the States of the liberal world, regarding the perpetuity of the fruits of the victory of the ideology of capitalism. Hence, the democratic peace thesis has manifested as more of a capitalist shibboleth offered by the protagonists of the liberal order, in aspiration of preserving the dominance of the ruling class of a few powerful countries in world politics. Through the moral assertions of long peace, the liberals intend to create the entire world into a microcosm of capitalist rubric and hence immortalize their hegemony. Viewed in this sense, the liberal apologia for a separate peace in international relations has merely been like an intercession obliged towards obtaining a kind of uncontested dominance for the capitalist world. We can sum up by encapsulating this in the provocative phrase of the post-modern scholar Fredric Jameson; that a surrender to the democratic peace hypothesis would be no less than like a 'cognitive estrangement from the reality'.

REFERENCES

Ashcroft, B., Griffiths, G., & Tiffin, H. (2000). *Postcolonial studies: The key concepts* (2nd ed.). Routledge.

Ashcroft, B., Griffiths, G., & Tiffin, H. (2002). *The empire writes back: Theory and practice in postcolonial literatures.* Routledge.

Ayoob, M. (1995). *The Third World security predicament.* Lynne Rienner.

Azar, E. E., & Moon, C. (Eds.). (1988). *National security in the Third World: The management of internal and external threats.* Edward Elgar.

Bennett, A. (2013). The mother of all isms: Causal mechanisms and structured pluralism in international relations theory. *European Journal of International Relations, 19*(3), 459–481.

Bhabha, H. K. (1984). Of mimicry and man: The ambivalence of colonial discourse. *Discipleship,* 28, 125–133.

Bose, S., & Jalal, A. (2004). *Modern South Asia: History, culture, political economy.* Routledge.

Brass, P. R. (Ed.). (2010). Introduction. *Routledge handbook of South Asian politics* (pp. 1–24). Routledge.

Carr, E. H. (1987). *What is history? The George Macaulay Trevelyan lectures delivered in the University of Cambridge January–March 1961.* R. W. Davies (Ed.). Penguin Books.

Chakrabarty, D. (2000). *Provincialising Europe: Postcolonial thought and historical difference.* Princeton University Press.

Chatterjee, P. S. (1999). Andersonian utopia. *Diacritics, 29*(4), 128–134.

Cohen, S. P. (1975). Security issues in South Asia. *Asian Survey, 15*(3), 782–791.

Dunne, T., Hansen, L., & Wight, C. (2013). The end of international relations theory? *European Journal of International Relations, 19*(3), 405–425.

Durrani, M. A. (2000). *India and Pakistan: The costs of conflict and the benefits of peace.* Oxford University Press.

Ferejohn, J., & Rosenbluth, F. M. (2008). Warlike democracies. *Journal of Conflict Resolution*, 52(1), 31–56.

Ghosh, P. S. (1989). *Cooperation and conflict in South Asia*. Manohar.

Kaviraj, S. (2010). *The imaginary institution of India*. Permanent Black.

Lapid, Y. (1989). The third debate: On the prospects of international relations theory in a post-positivist era. *International Studies Quarterly*, 33(3), 235–254.

Majid, A. (2000). *Unveiling traditions: Postcolonial Islam in a polycentric world*. Duke University Press.

Marx, K., & Engels, F. (1968). Manifesto of the Communist Party. In *Selected works of Marx and Engels*. International Publishers.

Mearsheimer, J. J., & Walt, S. M. (2013). Leaving theory behind: Why simplistic hypothesis testing is bad for international relations. *European Journal of International Relations*, 19(3), 427–458.

Mills, W. C. (1959). *The sociological imagination*. Oxford University Press.

Neelsen, J. P., & Malik, D. (2007). South Asia: Social fragmentation and political crisis in the periphery. In J. P. Neelsen & D. Malik (Eds.), *Crisis of state and nation: South Asian states between nation-building and fragmentation*. Manohar.

Pratt, M. L. (1992). *Imperial eyes: Travel writing and transculturation*. Routledge.

Reus-Smit, C. (2013). Beyond metatheory. *European Journal of International Relations*, 19(3), 589–608.

Spivak, G. C. (1985). The Rani of Simur. In F. Barker (Ed.), *Europe and its others: Proceedings of the Essex conference on the sociology of literature* (Vol. 1, pp. 128–151). University of Essex Press.

Spivak, G. C. (1991). Identity and alterity: An interview with Nikos Papastergiadis. *Arena*, 97, 65–76.

Walt, S. M. (1998). International relations: One world many theories. *Foreign Policy*, 110, 29–32, 34–46.

Weidemann, D. (2007). Crisis of the state in Pakistan. In J. P. Neelsen & D. Malik (Eds.), *Crisis of state and nation: South Asian states between nation-building and fragmentation* (pp. 84–117). Manohar.

AFTERWORD

Despite three quarters of a century having passed since their painful colonial creation in 1947, the relationship between India and Pakistan essentially remains gloomy and perhaps poised for a further downward spiral. This can be chiefly owed to Islamabad's persistence with its stale goal of bleeding India with a thousand cuts, especially via its trusted use of state-backed terror. What might concern the average onlooker is that the Indian subcontinent, largely due to Pakistan's sustained hostility towards India and its firm handshake with China, remains a tinderbox on the nuclear front. The Stockholm International Peace Research Institute estimates that Pakistan has built enough nuclear warheads to balance India's over the past two decades (*Economic Times*, 2018). Islamabad's nuclear delivery systems, as per the US-based Arms Control Association, include multiple short-range and medium-range ballistic missiles (SRBMs and MRBMs), with worse, including an intercontinental ballistic missile (ICBM), being under development (Arms Control Association, 2022). Ahead in the race, besides its hefty stock of SRBMs and MRBMs, India already possesses an ICBM that can reach most of China, if needed, and is building a nuclear-capable hypersonic cruise missile, which can well be one of the world's fastest and suited for launch from any stages of its nuclear triad, that is, from land, sea or air. Yet India remains deeply concerned about the safety of Pakistan's nuclear stockpile, given the untamed rise of radical non-state groups bent on waging an internal war against Islamabad.

While India responsibly upholds its no-first-use ethic, Pakistan has hinted its intention of crossing the nuclear Rubicon and using its tactical nuclear weapons should India's numerically superior conventional forces overwhelm it (Subramanyam, 2016). The surgical strike after the Uri attack and the Balakot air strike, which were launched by the Narendra Modi government into Pakistani territory as retaliatory moves against terrorist attacks pushed by Islamabad, did not, however, trigger any such desperate response from Pakistan. Though sticking to its conventional tactics against India, Pakistan has recently been pulling fresh tricks out of its hat, most notably the cross-border ferrying of illicit materials using drones. In June 2021, drones strapped to explosives, evidently flown from Pakistan, crashed into the Indian Air Force Station at Jammu which may qualify as an unmanned aerial terror attack (*Economic Times*, 2021). An old wine in a new bottle, the attack was yet another sorry attempt to disrupt a serious attempt by India to normalize the sociopolitical climate of Jammu and Kashmir. Perhaps with a design to extend this modus operandi, Islamabad was, at the time, in talks with Istanbul to purchase the latter's medium-altitude tactical attack drones, which had proved their lethality in the 2020 Nagorno-Karabakh War.

The accelerating defence, especially nuclear, alliance between Pakistan and China has, nonetheless, only exacerbated the subcontinent's tensions. Since the 1970s, Islamabad has relied heavily on Chinese state suppliers for the critical components required by its nuclear programme, which have ranged from warhead designs to gas centrifuge units, major thanks to the now infamous underground nuclear exchange network cultivated by A. Q. Khan. On the civil front, Pakistan has already operationalized its first Chinese-built pressurized-water nuclear reactor at Karachi, with possibly more on the cards. While being a current beneficiary of Chinese satellite navigation, a recent client of its towed artillery guns, and a priority future recipient of its stealth combat aircrafts, the Pakistani armed forces have well cemented a string of joint military and training exercises with their Chinese counterparts, several of which are held not too far from India's doorsteps (Ranade, 2019). Furthermore, with the collapse of Afghanistan in 2021, Pakistan is likely to resurface as an enabler of a modern-day great game over it, which shall only spark a few smiles in Beijing, as it would not want to see its strategic infrastructural investments on Pakistan's frontier terrains underutilized.

In the light of such developments, most of which only underscore the perpetuation of India's Pakistan problem, this book has made an effort to trace their roots to Pakistan's troubled bilateral history with India, as well as its underlying colonial baggage and strategic culture.

REFERENCES

Arms Control Association. (2022, March). Arms control and proliferation profile: Pakistan.

Ranade, J. (2019, 2 February). China plans to sell Pak an aircraft carrier and integrate it militarily. Sunday Guardian Live.

Subramanyam, P. (2016, 30 October). Pakistan's tactical nuclear weapons and India's response. *Indian Defence Review*.

The Economic Times. (2018, 14 July). Pakistan has more nuclear warheads than India: SIPRI.

The Economic Times. (2021, 27 June). Two explosives-laden drones crash into IAF station at Jammu airport, two people injured.

ABOUT THE AUTHOR

Sanjeev Kumar H. M. is Professor of international relations and global politics at the Department of Political Science, University of Delhi, India. He has previously taught at the South Asian University (SAARC University), New Delhi; the University of Allahabad, Allahabad; and the Karnatak University, Dharwad. His areas of interest include Islamic thought and international relations, international relations theory, the politics of Muslim identity and the question of world order, India–Pakistan relations, democratization of South Asia, South Asian security, and the history of ideas in South Asia. He has published extensively in reputed journals such as the *British Journal of Middle Eastern Studies*, *Third World Quarterly*, *Economic & Political Weekly*, *South Asian Survey* and *Society and Culture in South Asia* on related themes. His publications include the textbook *Modern South Asian Thinkers* (2018), a co-edited encyclopaedic volume. He is currently working on the Indian Council of Social Science Research (ICSSR) project 'Popular Imaginaries and Discourses on Politics in India: Exploring Cultural Narratives as Alternative Sites of Knowledge Construction'. He is also working on a co-authored book titled *Deconstructing Islamophobic Public Culture: Hindu Nationalism and the 'Muslim Other' in India*.

INDEX